24,

*for my de...
whose acquain...
has made my life richer;
a bringer of joy,
always clear on the
concept — yours
Jacobus*

A BANQUET OF CONSEQUENCES

JAKE ROHRER

A
BANQUET
OF
CONSEQUENCES

TRUE LIFE ADVENTURES OF
SEX, DRUGS, ROCK & ROLL,
(NOT TOO MUCH)   (PLENTY)   (OF COURSE)

AND THE FEDS
(WHO INVITED THEM?)

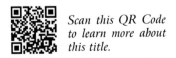
*Scan this QR Code
to learn more about
this title.*

Publisher: Inkwater Press | www.inkwaterpress.com

Paperback
ISBN-13 978-1-62901-138-7 | ISBN-10 1-62901-138-X

Kindle
ISBN-13 978-1-62901-139-4 | ISBN-10 1-62901-139-8

Printed in the U.S.A.
All paper is acid free and meets all ANSI standards for archival quality paper.

1 3 5 7 9 10 8 6 4 2

Your life is the fruit of your own doing.

-Joseph Campbell

CONTENTS

Book 4: Roots · 177

Book 5: Final Course · 239

AUTHOR'S NOTE

LIFE ITSELF IS A BANQUET, A SUMPTUOUS FEAST OF THRILLS, LOVE, AND color; of memory, sound, and creative effort; of smells, tastes, and textures; of perceptions, joys, and sorrows. Everything we do comes with consequence, the fruits of our life. Some are positive and good, some not so much. As such, life is also a learning process. More often than not, our world resembles a carnival filled with barkers, come-ons, false promises, rigged games, hallways of mirrors, and distractions. Once we manage to fight our way through the frenzy of commotion and clutter that's been placed in our paths, we discover who put it there, the man behind the curtain. He divides the world into two kinds of people: tunas and mooches. A tuna is a mark, someone to be exploited. A mooch is someone who seeks something for free. Mooches are discarded and recycled until converted to tuna. There is no middle ground. Once you recognize the carnival midway aspects of the world we live in and the character of those who run the games, you are free to move on.

The baggage of consequence can be a brief snack or a lengthy banquet, and is a result of the life you've lived and the choices you've made. It can be harsh and bitter or easy and sweet, but there is no stopping it. Everything we do has its consequence, and every consequence mirrors the action that produced it. There are no free rides, only the resulting karma we ourselves create. Once you discover that bitter can also be sweet, that harsh can be easy, you begin to understand that much of the difference lies in how you imagined things to begin with. Sometimes it's just a matter of how you choose to see and experience that which is in front of you. Discovering this, you are, again, free to move on.

But don't forget: random shit happens, strictly happenstance, unrelated to your karma. Don't let the pigeons get you down.

In a nutshell: beware the midway and embrace your karma; wear a hat.

-JR

A BANQUET OF CONSEQUENCES

A BANQUET OF CONSEQUENCES

Everybody, sooner or later, sits down
to a banquet of consequences.

—Robert Louis Stevenson

1

ONE IF BY LAND

B IG DOG CAME BY THE HOUSE ON A FRIDAY AFTERNOON, LATE IN THE day and unexpected. Watching his arrival from the front room, I wondered what might have prompted his visit. It wasn't like him to just show up without first calling. He got out of his car and surveyed the street as though looking over his shoulder for some unseen menace. His walk to the porch seemed hurried, and the concern I could read on his face suggested this probably wouldn't be a social call. As I was about to learn, he was a man on a mission, like Paul Revere, sounding the alarm: The feds are coming! The feds are coming!

"I have grim news," said Big Dog making his way into the house, his head bowed as though in distant thought. As usual, he was well groomed and neatly dressed. Of high-caste Mexican heritage, he was six-foot-plus, lean, and good looking, with wide-set dark eyes under a broad forehead. Wire-rimmed eyewear gave him the look of a learned man. His normal carriage was patrician, calm and in control, but today he seemed distracted and a little out of breath.

"The feds just popped John Bump," he announced. "I was there when they came to get him." I could tell he was running on adrenalin. He continued, rapid-fire, "They talked a lot of stink at me too. Obviously, they didn't have a warrant. Scared the hell out of me, though. I came straight here."

I didn't know Bump but I'd heard of him, and I knew he was one of Big Dog's friends. In addition to trafficking in illicit drugs, these were men who also dabbled in Tiffany lamps, Persian carpets, and other fine accoutrements. "They picked off John Viljoen earlier this morning," he continued, building the drama of his message. "My lawyer says they rounded up a couple of Green's friends in San Francisco yesterday."

I knew Viljoen, a friendly and fun-loving South African whose company I enjoyed, and who had been associated with "Mr. Big" Stephen Green. Viljoen and I didn't do business together, but we sometimes met for dinner or drinks. We also shared separate professional histories in the automobile business.

"Green's let it all fly to the feds. I think you're next," said Big Dog, getting my full attention.

"Can't be true," I pleaded. "They couldn't possibly have anything on me, other than hearsay." I assumed they had at least that after being rousted at the border in December coming home from Mexico.

"Wake up, man!" scolded Big Dog, peering at me owl-like over the rim of his glasses. "It wasn't the local sheriff. They were feds. They have Green. They don't need anything else. The charge will be conspiracy." It was the first time I ever heard Big Dog bark, at least at me.

"How come they didn't get you?" I asked, trying to fend off the stark reality he had just presented.

"I don't think they have enough on me through Green," he speculated. "I never did business with him. But there's no doubt he's blabbed all that he knows about me. Everyone's a wild card right now. The feds might try to roll Bump to get at me, but I know he'll stand tall."

For someone involved in a game as serious as this one could be, I was amazingly ignorant of the rules by which it could be played. I hadn't made a study of legal realities as they applied to the drug trade and had only a hazy concept of what a criminal conspiracy might consist of. I was yet to meet the elite of San Francisco's criminal defense bar, a dozen or so of whom were at that very moment scrambling for new clients in the wake of Green's betrayal. With Green as their puppet, the feds had generated a vast web of conspiracy charges now spreading like a wildfire across San Francisco's high-end drug and legal communities. What we viewed as "betrayal" was viewed by the feds as "cooperation."

"Sorry to be the messenger of such news," said Big Dog. "There are a few more people I have to see, right away. Gotta run."

I followed him out to the street. "Make sure you're clean!" he said as he shut the door on his vintage Mercedes coupe. He lowered the window for a final admonition as he pulled away to continue his midnight ride on this Friday afternoon. "Protect yourself!" he called.

I was left standing at the curb with my thoughts and questions. The idea of Stephen Green in bed with the feds was a new concept for me. No one preached the gospel of silence with more fervor than Green. Even so, could they really make a case like that just out of words? Don't they at least have to catch you doing something? How does one protect himself from a federal arrest warrant?

Okay, I thought, I'll humor Big Dog ... just in case. Aided by false hope, I reasoned they must have some hard evidence on the others, unable to accept the idea that they could make a case just on someone's say-so. I moved everything incriminating out of my home, a scale and some accessories, along with a wayward half-kilo of cocaine. I put notes concerning transactions—receivables and payables, weights and dates—into code, burned the notes, then hid the coded document in a single record album sleeve wedged in among many hundreds. Even if found, they'd need a cryptographer with a Rosetta Stone. A specially built container filled with cash remained in an ingenious hiding place built into kitchen cabinets by a clever and talented friend who'd done some remodeling for me. To open it required some requisite mechanical steps, like a Chinese puzzle. Short of demolition, I defied anyone to find it. I was so proud of the clever construction I, of course, showed if off to all my friends and conspirators.

The weekend passed without incident and I relaxed about the impending doom. I was still hopeful that Big Dog was overreacting, wrong about my inclusion as a target for arrest. If he could escape arrest, why not me? It didn't occur to me that even feds will take the weekend off. The knock on my door came at the start of the workweek, 7:00 AM Monday morning, loud and demanding. A bolt of shock and realization shot through me on my way to the door, a lightning stab down my spine and into my gut.

"Who is it?" I called with a musical lilt, knowing full fucking well who stood on the other side. One of the fringe benefits of being a criminal is the ability to sleep in. I didn't know anyone who'd be up at that hour, certainly no one who would come to my door with an insistent, ball-breaker of a knock like that. I was answered with an official-looking federal ID encased in clear plastic slapped up against one of the small, decorative windows across the top of the door.

"Hold on, I'll be right with you." I went back to the bedroom and pulled on my pants, telling the woman who shared my bed, "They're here. Get word to my brother."

SO BEGAN A NEW CHAPTER in my life, the one with the feds in charge. I was living in a Berkeley brown-shingle my brother and I had purchased as an investment a couple of years earlier, a two-story, three-unit conversion near the campus. It was 1981 and November was just getting underway. The feds would stay in charge for a long time.

On Halloween night, just days before my arrest, the sun had been down for about an hour when someone in a convincing gorilla costume came to the door. When opened, the gorilla bounced ape-like into the foyer. He made himself at home, wandering around on all fours into the front and dining rooms, peering into the kitchen, and shuffling around the corridor that led to the bedroom. Half a dozen friends were there at the time, cocktails in hand. Everyone was charmed, thinking the gorilla a perfect component for the occasion. Everyone but me. The gorilla never said a word and I didn't like the way he looked at me. He lacked any note of gaiety. He seemed nosy too, and he wasn't there for treats. After just a minute or two, he lurched across the floor on his knuckles and disappeared out the still-open front door. I thought it an eerie visit and I was unnerved by the gorilla's gall and impertinence.

Later, my ordeal with the feds well underway, I gave some thought to the gorilla incident, looking for reason and logic. What do you think? An advance fed? Wanting to confirm that I lived there, a chance to case the joint for the bust without tipping me off? Nah, probably not. I never met a fed with a sense of humor. But not a gorilla with the demeanor of a fed either. I never learned for certain what the gorilla was all about, if indeed anything at all.

⋯⋯

THEY SEATED ME IN THE back of their nondescript four-door sedan, caged off from the front seat, my arms handcuffed behind me. I told them the cuffs were unnecessary, but they were having none of that. There were two feds in front, one a female. We were on our way to DEA headquarters in San Francisco. They had nothing to say to me, engaging only in boring chitchat between themselves like morning commuters on their way to the office, exactly what they were. Two other feds who'd come into the house with them were in a separate car. I think I actually invited them in, but they could have simply walked in at their own invitation. I was too shell-shocked and scattered to have my wits about me. They took some liberties looking around while I finished dressing and washing up, one of them keeping an eye on me. The lead fed, playing the friendly sort, told me he liked the western-style cabinets in my kitchen, giving me a momentary start. I didn't realize it at the time, but they were likely looking for something that would give them cause for a search warrant.

Four feds to arrest one guy. They could have called, told me they had a warrant for my arrest, and I would have turned myself in. Not much fun for the feds, though, and it would remove the possibility of finding an excuse for a search warrant during the arrest. They looked hard, but didn't have the fortune with me that they had with Bump. During Bump's arrest, a challenging fed said something to him about being a lucky man that they didn't have a search warrant. Bump's cocky response was, "You wouldn't find anything but a little grass," which gave them cause to search for it, coming up with a scale and some sandwich baggies they could parade in front of a jury, obviously the accoutrements of a drug dealer. Laboratory analysis would find minute cocaine residue on the scale.

The crush of morning commute traffic surrounded us as we inched our way to the Bay Bridge toll plaza. My mind was a whirl of thoughts and pictures. I was trying to concentrate on how to be ready for them, their questions or some sort of interrogation. I'd never been arrested before. Would there be any rough stuff? But Oliver Hardy kept popping up in my thoughts, angry and scolding: "Now you've done it! A fine kettle of fish you've gotten us into this time!" He wasn't talking to Stanley. My brother and I, along with Max, used to invoke Ollie, laughingly, whenever something would go awry with whatever it was we might have been doing. Max was a dear friend and a central character in my life for many years.

But I couldn't find anything to laugh about. I took a deep breath and chased Ollie from my mind, only to be replaced by thoughts and images of my former life. I thought about my family and wondered what Dad would have thought about my predicament. I was 38 years old, allegedly an adult, and I'd have to start all over again. And who knows when that would be. Pop would have hidden his disappointment and just shook his head, "At least you didn't kill anyone." An accomplished businessman, I think he would have found a certain intrigue in a business where you carried your money around in a suitcase rather than a bank account. I knew life would have been otherwise if we hadn't lost Dad before I turned twenty. *I wouldn't be here now if Dad was still around.*

I remembered the "Factory," the warehouse headquarters where I'd come to work for Creedence Clearwater Revival as they realized their dreams, climbing with them to the top of the mountain. What a ride! Creedence embodied the spirit of "rock & roll" like few others. They exemplified young musicians who believed in themselves, each throwing all else to the wind in order to make a vision come true. *I'd rather be on the road with the boys right now, all things considered.*

I pictured John Fogerty, for whom I had worked during the years following Creedence, and his music played in my head. I admired John like few others throughout the time we were associated. We'd come to know one another well during those years, but it'd been nearly five years since we parted ways. I didn't know John anymore. A more private individual is difficult to imagine. *I wouldn't be here now if John was still the John who needed me.*

But he wasn't. And there I was, a banquet of consequences descending all around me. *Hors d'oeuvres* had just been served and my lack of appetite was of no concern to the host. As a federal banquet, many courses would follow, the menu stretching out before me like a calendar of many years.

IRREVOCABLE MOMENTUM

NEARLY TWO YEARS FOLLOWING MY ARREST, I WAS FINALLY ON MY WAY to prison. Those intervening months, free on bail, pending trial and appeals, would prove to be the least satisfactory period of my life. Freedom's largely an illusion we manage to sell ourselves. I was anything but free, dangling in a federal "purgatory," awaiting edicts and decrees, the outcome of which I had little doubt. Freedom would seep back into my life one day at a time, starting with the first day of my incarceration.

> Never let your head hang down. Never give up and sit down and grieve. Find another way. And don't pray when it rains if you don't pray when the sun shines.
>
> –Satchel Paige

I was an emotional wreck, grieving with my head hung down. I would have considered prayer if I thought for one moment it would be heard by anyone in a position to improve my immediate prospects. A guard tower and chain-link fence topped with circular rows of razor wire came into view through the windshield of Ed's Cadillac. We crested a rise to see dull concrete buildings without windows, stark and naked against a bleak background. The fierce fence encircled the buildings and nearby landscape: climb me if you dare. The setting had all the flamboyant charm of a third world urban landfill. But I didn't imagine it would be otherwise. This is what a prison looks like, a place of confinement, an utter dungeon.

"Aw shit," groaned Ed, surveying my destination. He was apparently expecting something a little more welcoming.

My friend was delivering me to the Federal Correctional Institution at Terminal Island, located in a gritty industrial section of the Long Beach harbor south of Los Angeles, where I was to begin a 15-year sentence for my role in a drug conspiracy. Self-made, successful, and wealthy, Ed was used to having things only his way. When he was conducting business, we called him "War Horse," at other times, "Uncle Eddie," sometimes just plain "Olson." He blamed my lawyers for my plight.

"Those assholes took your money and didn't deliver," he fumed. He, of course, never had to deal with criminal lawyers. In his world, you paid huge sums to civil practitioners who did the things you told them to do and got the results you expected. Result was the only measure of competency, and heaven help the lawyer who didn't deliver.

My result couldn't have been worse. A maximum sentence and a maximum fine. There were no weapons or violence involved, and heretofore my record was spotless. Ed felt certain his lawyers would have provided a better result than the celebrated J. Tony Serra, my counsel at trial. "How could he have fucked things up so badly?" wondered Ed.

Looking back over the preceding years, I blamed only myself ... and the informant who'd put my circumstance into play.

→•←

ATTORNEYS REPRESENTING FELLOW DEFENDANTS IN companion conspiracy cases, all of them launched by the informancy (a new word:
informancy, n., a period of time during which one acts as an informant) of
Stephen Green, urged that I hire Tony Serra. They hinted it would
indeed be my good fortune should he agree to defend me. I knew
next to nothing about Tony Serra or criminal law. My lessons were
about to begin.

Tony Serra was a fascinating individual and I liked him right
away. He was highly principled and his reputation as a fierce opponent in the courtroom was widely held. He was eager to defend
the underdog and those subject to racial discrimination. I didn't
consider myself qualifying as either, but soon learned that almost
anyone whose opponent happened to be the "United States of
America" qualified as an underdog. All of his skills and admirable
values, however, may have presented an intellectual enigma to the
jury of sheep selected to decide our case. When later polled, many
thought I was guilty because I hired an expensive attorney like
Serra, whose fees were in fact considerably less than other attorneys involved at the trial stage. But he loomed larger than most
in the courtroom, his fiery character perhaps leading the jury to
believe this meant expensive.

If Tony presented an enigma to the jury, he presented something of a different nature to Federal Judge Robert Schnacke.
The elderly though razor-sharp judge didn't like Tony Serra, his
ponytail, his courtroom demeanor, his rapier-like undoing of prosecution witnesses, or the way he dressed—a little too bohemian,
barely meeting bench standards. The required necktie looked out
of place on him. Tony didn't like the judge either, but he respected
his intellect. Everything about Tony that might have offended the
judge, I admired. His best efforts notwithstanding, the jury voted
to convict.

The judge had a gruff exterior, but he was soft-spoken and kind
to witnesses who he seemed to view as innocent and lesser animals
than the other players. His control of the courtroom was complete,

maintaining decorum with a mean-spirited edge, occasionally smoothed over by a highly honed sense of humor. Schnacke was as smart as they come. Even when it looked like he was napping, nothing escaped his notice.

When Tony was eloquently pleading for a probationary sentence, I could sense the tempest building in Schnacke, scowling and incredulous, restless and shifting in his chair while Tony did his best on my behalf. I imagined a low, guttural growl emanating from Schnacke's bowels, a carnivorous beast impatient for his turn at the carcass.

On pronouncing sentence, the rising wind of Schnacke's furious vent and judgment thundered into me, rocking me back on my heels. In my mind, I saw Dorothy and her friends quaking in front of Oz, the Great and Powerful ("Silence, whippersnapper!"). I, too, wanted to dive headfirst through the nearest window, but I was 21 floors up in the San Francisco Federal Building. I vowed then and there I would one day find where he lie and have a good piss on his grave. My need to escape his wrath and judgment was such that I slipped away into a daydream, picturing myself in some graveyard with a full bladder, lurking behind trees while I searched for the headstone with that strange Germanic name engraved on it. It was a vow I was to later recant. Before he was finished, Schnacke also directed his wrath at the numerous people and letters who had come forward on my behalf, attesting to my good character. He accused them all of either being in league with me or turning a blind eye to my activities.

"Bail on appeal is denied," roared Schnacke.

"Could you at least recommend a camp setting?" pleaded Tony. A camp is a low security prison camp reserved for nonviolent offenders who are not viewed as a flight risk. In addition to drug offenders, tax cheats, white-collar criminals, informants, politicians, even judges could be found there, along with others who had earned their way from higher security institutions.

"I prefer to leave that to the Bureau of Prisons," huffed Schnacke, not willing to concede the slightest crumb to Tony or me. The recommendation of a federal judge is not lost on prison administrators.

I sensed I was about to be remanded to custody and trundled off by US Marshals, then struck by total surprise when Schnacke finished up, granting me two weeks of freedom to get my affairs in order before self-surrender to prison authorities. I was not viewed as a flight risk, although I gave it some brief thought. Somewhere, my brother and I had heard the Caribbean island state of Tobago had no extradition treaty with the US. We joked we could become "Toboggons," like fast moving snow sleds! We rejected any such idea as foolhardy.

In the two weeks granted, I replaced Tony with Doron Weinberg, a skilled appellate attorney of lofty intellect, greatly respected throughout the legal community. Doron was more to the judge's liking. Just like magic, he reversed himself and bail on appeal was granted. As a result, I spent nearly two years rather than two weeks getting my affairs in order, recklessly hustling more cocaine to pay legal expenses and put together some cash to see my family through what I knew would be a long, hard winter.

⇻⇺

THE GREAT MAJORITY OF THE evidence presented against me at trial consisted of the testimony of a one-time associate turned informant, Stephen J. Green, engaged in the process of saving his own skin. I hadn't been caught doing anything—I'd been told on. It wasn't a victim providing testimony. It was instead the man said to be at the top of the conspiracy, a major trafficker who was caught red-handed and sentenced to 20 years. The government was giving him his freedom for informing on his associates, prosecuting those farther down the ladder. Imagine Bernard Madoff going free while prosecuting his lieutenants. That, of course, didn't make me any less culpable, but it might anger the jury enough to turn the table on the government's case if we could get them to understand that others would be serving far more time in prison than the informant, rules against such disclosure notwithstanding.

Not a chance. When they were polled, all were aghast at learning my prison time would far exceed that of the informant, who would serve only about 18 months of his 20-year sentence, most of it in tight security helping the government build their case. Nonetheless, the jury got it right. Rather than own up to the feds, I insisted on doing things the hard way.

Stephen Green. In all fairness, what can I say about him? He was smart and had an outgoing, even charismatic, personality. He walked his walk with a lot of bluster, like an aggressive salesman enamored with his product. He was small in physical stature, but we called him "Mr. Big" for his purported successes and connections. When members of our fraternal brotherhood of drug dealers—we "spice merchants" if you will—talked about "holding your mud" (maintaining silence) if you happened to be arrested, Green's voice was the loudest. Among his associates he assumed the strut of a general.

He liked to host lavish parties, once renting facilities at an upscale Napa Valley winery where his guests arrived at the dining room in gondolas, like a ski lift delivering passengers to a chalet. It was supposed to be a classy affair, the sampling of fine wines with a catered dinner, a lot of canapés and tête-à-tête, Green playing the role of an aristocratic and generous host. He was doing his best to establish a legitimate persona at the winery and had asked his guests, "No drugs, please."

But the room was filled with his friends and associates, cocaine merchants, distributors, dealers, smugglers, and users. Once everyone was a little looped on the wine, out came the coke. My brother Robbin got things started by pouring out about half an ounce of high-end cocaine onto a saucer that got passed around the tables. Others followed suit, revelers snorting up line after line of pure cocaine through rolled-up hundred dollar bills, indeed ...

C-notes. Consumption was open and obvious, spiraling out of control by a like-minded gathering of criminals who had no thoughts of hiding their activities among themselves. The dining room staff became anxious and alarmed. Green did his best to calm them and continue his masquerade as the wealthy, legitimate host, but it was too late. Any fool could see that Green's carefully choreographed propriety had been swallowed up by a room filled with swaggering, coke-sniffing pirates.

Green didn't choose his role of informant from love of country, nor did the feds wire his genitals with electric current to force confession. He was a self-serving, braggart of a man, and he used his illegitimate wealth to prove his place in the world—somewhere above the likes of you or me. He had a Ferrari to play with when he tired of his Porsche and a San Francisco penthouse staffed with a butler, there to answer his door, polish his shoes, and dust his wine cellar. Among his associates he would strut and preen while articulating the code of the honorable outlaw, taking your own medicine while maintaining silence in the face of adversity. He pointed derisively at others he claimed would "turn rat" at the drop of a badge. I found him also a racist, particularly anti-black, paranoid of finding himself in the company of colored people. "That place is nigger heaven," he would say of certain clubs and restaurants, refusing to patronize them.

In the press, Green excused his turning informant, claiming he just couldn't leave his newly born daughter without a father. Otherwise, of course, he would have remained silent. It was okay, though, if his friends and associates got separated from their families. More to the point, I would venture that he probably found being jailed among tough, feral, and barbaric criminals, many of them black, his worst nightmare, and would have sold his soul or his daughter to be elsewhere.

Recalling my intention to be fair, now that I've thoroughly gutted and dressed Mr. Green, it must be asked: Who was the half-witted fool who trusted and did business with such a man? Does lack of appetite for toys and showy trappings make me a better person? No, just a different person, who engaged in many of the same crimes as Green did, save the distasteful offense of informing on friends, family, and associates solely for personal benefit.

It did not sit well with me that the feds were proposing to let Green go free, trading him for people who were at least unpretentious and honorable, cocaine merchants nonetheless. It was I, of course, who was on the trading block, coloring somewhat my personal view of events. Giving the feds their due, I have to admit that they exchanged Green, giving him his freedom, in order to lock up ten others. Nothing at all, however, was accomplished that put the slightest dent in their purported purpose, the reining in of the runaway-train drug trade, although the industry that thrives on policing drugs was further fattened with a feast of new fodder.

My anger at Green and the feds, accompanied by a fear of what lie ahead, served as brush and canvas. With such tools at hand, I proceeded to paint myself a victim, able now to wallow in some self-pity about what I looked upon as the unfairness of it all. I chose to ignore what was right in front of me and pushed aside the obvious: My "karma" had arrived, its momentum irrevocable.

How was I supposed to know prison would be for me a salvation, a cleansing episode that would provide valuable personal growth and life experience? That I would look back on the incarceration I had once feared with a weird sort of fondness?

❧

THE MOST SATISFYING MOMENT DURING my entire ordeal with the feds came when I learned that the priggish Judge Schnacke had been rounded up in a vice-squad raid on a Mitchell Brothers porn theater in San Francisco, creating scandalous headlines. Both the district attorney and the defense attorneys wanted the judge as a witness for their cases, and he hired my lawyer, Doron Weinberg, to get him out of this damning public spectacle. My delight at the judge's public shaming was immeasurable. He was exceedingly bright, but I saw him as a bully, drunk on the power of his robes. There you go, Judge, what goes around comes around.

Some years later, another unexpected and equally mindboggling twist of fate occurred: the Assistant US Attorney who prosecuted me, Eric Swenson, was caught criminally tainting evidence against some Chinese heroin smugglers and drummed out of office. Most thought he should have been jailed, but I felt no glee at his censure. He had spared me the piety of his office, an acknowledgment that it wasn't a vicious animal he was prosecuting, suggesting only that a maximum sentence would send a message to the criminal element. That, of course, was bullshit. The real message, aimed at those awaiting trial in the same conspiracy, was this: You'd better not waste our time with a trial unless you, too, would like a maximum sentence. My role as first to come to trial had been that of sacrificial cow.

⋙⋘

I GREW UP BELIEVING THAT the feds were the "good guys," people of strong moral character who always played hard but played fair. Then I learned firsthand to expect federal authorities to always play by the rules is to be naïve. No different than most, the feds will break the rules any time they think they can get away with it, no penalty if the ref doesn't see it.

While I was washing up and getting dressed on the morning of my arrest, the arresting feds had a go at my personal documents and desk drawers. I came from the bedroom to find DEA agents frantically riffling the contents of my desk, thinking they would be unobserved. They quit, red-faced, when I asked if they had a search warrant. Thanks in large part to Big Dog, they wouldn't have found diddly-squat, but the attempt was an affront. They were given free rein in my home and they behaved shabbily. Imagine that, the dope dealer calling "bad manners" on the feds who were in the act of arresting him. But I was too fucking scared to strut about it ... until just now.

The DEA was also skilled at making itself look good in the media, usually at the expense of the accused. Stephen Green's cocaine was put on display as though it belonged to other defendants. They wailed in the press about nebulous "street values" that tallied seven figures and about the significant dent they had just put in the drug trade .... blah, blah, blah. The tricky bastards also managed to get a booking photo that made me look like Jack the Ripper, handing it out to the press. When I saw it in the paper I couldn't even recognize myself. I was reminded of Hoover and the importance he placed on our country's great con game: image and public manipulation. As in the pastures of everyday life, the pastures of justice are strewn with backroom agenda and bullshit, and you'd better watch where you're stepping ... that's not second base, you know.

Later, during my trial, FBI agents harassed and threatened a witness who was to appear on my behalf, afraid she would destroy the credibility of her brother, who was scheduled to testify for the prosecution. I thought it thug behavior. Her presence had been unearthed in another state by private investigators from my team, billing me $175 hourly for their services. She represented an unhappy surprise for the prosecution.

A criminal trial often takes on the fervor of a heated chess match. Each side postured and moved their pieces warily within the ever-changing landscape of the game. Insults were traded, like in a nasty election campaign. The jury looked on, unaware they were the pawns. The judge ruled over both sides like the all-powerful queen, able to move in any direction he saw fit. Justice and our constitution were represented by the slow-moving king, the ultimate object of capture. Prosecutors and defense lawyers were themselves the knights, bishops, and rooks who battle it out in the trenches, aided by their minions and seconds, the investigators and expert witnesses. Watching from the gallery, I was the accused, a eunuch of the court, flaccid and speechless, powerless save for my pocketbook used to purchase the services of my champions. The informant, a knave, seeking to better his circumstance at any cost.

"Buffalo," the fellow whose sister was harassed, was at one time a distant friend, closer to my brother and some of his associates, but who nonetheless could provide some damaging testimony about me. Attempting to establish himself in the drug trade, Buffalo found himself on the wrong side of some bad hombres in a drug deal turned sour. He had reason to believe they were out to kill him. Broke and with nowhere left to turn, he went to the DEA and made his deal with the devil: He sold himself as an informant. Trying to impress them with the magnitude of the secrets he possessed, he went beyond the bad hombres and told them a lot of grossly exaggerated bullshit about me and my brother (we were supplied with copies of his debriefing in discovery). It was laughable until you thought about who he was telling it to.

Late in the trial, the prosecution maneuvered one move ahead of my team, who failed to see it coming. After Buffalo testified, Tony thought he had "stiffed" the prosecution, testifying only that I had at one time given him a him a small, unspecified amount of cocaine I had called "Baked Alaska." Not a word was said about any real transactions. Tony was pleased, fearing Buffalo might do our side some damage. But it proved to be the opening the prosecution needed. They were then able to establish as fact that Buffalo and Stephen Green didn't know one another, had never met or spoken to one another. Buffalo had unknowingly corroborated Stephen Green's testimony, confirming for the jury that I had christened a particular load of Green's cocaine "Baked Alaska." Checkmate. It was a key point for the jury when they voted for my conviction. They didn't like Stephen Green. No one did. But now they had something to hang their hats on. Buffalo obviously didn't want to testify against me, but had unwittingly given the jury reason to believe Green's testimony. Hats off to the prosecution.

When he was done, Buffalo sauntered by the table where I was seated and gave me a knowing glance, as though to say, "See, brother? I wouldn't do you no harm."

→-←

MY ANGER AND SENSE OF unfairness would gradually soften and melt away, replaced by a better understanding of my own nature and an acceptance of responsibility for my lot in life, the good and the not so good. I became embarrassed by what had been my mindset as a victim. Mine were just desserts, "Baked Alaska" at the top of the menu. I had learned, yet again, the hard way; the only person on whom I could place blame for my circumstance, or from whom I might seek vengeance, was standing in my own shoes. In the long run, we mostly get what we have coming. No one outdistances their own karma. Sooner or later everybody sits down to a banquet of consequences. Green is forgiven, free to deal with his own banquet, this one not so lavish.

→-←

STILL SEATED IN ED'S CADILLAC, I looked once again at the prison setting that would become my residence for an indeterminate period, and an involuntary tremor passed through me. The enormity of what I'd lost and the impact on those I loved all hit home at once.

"Thanks for the lift, Ed. You're a pal," I told him, trying to sound like he'd just delivered me to the grocery store, but there was a huge lump in my throat, a result of holding back the tears. I no longer harbored a fear of what I was about to walk into. Sorrow and regret had eclipsed dread and anxiety.

"Keep your eyes open," advised Ed. "And watch your back. If there's anything I can do for you, let me know." He gave me a wink and a weak smile as we said our farewells.

The hollow feeling inside seemed to expand as he drove off. I hadn't felt so all alone since Mom dropped me off for my first day at kindergarten. One last deep breath of free, fresh air …

MR. HOLMES, I PRESUME?

What will happen can't be stopped.
Aim for grace.

-Ann Beattie, *Learning to Fall*

A S THE TAILLIGHTS OF ED'S CADILLAC ROLLED OUT OF SIGHT, I WALKED a few paces to a kiosk in the fence line and handed my surrender papers to a big, barrel-chested guard who looked like he may have one day played for the Raiders. Beads of sweat added to the glossy sheen of his shaved head, smooth and chocolate-colored, a mouth full of pearly teeth the size of Chiclets. He gestured for me to follow him, producing a ring of keys that looked heavy enough to make a smaller man lean to one side. He opened a gate in the fence and spoke into a two-way radio carried on his belt.

"West gate to R & D."

"Go ahead, west gate," crackled the radio.

"I got one in the chute for ya." With an enormous brass key, he opened a large, solid door almost hidden in the wall of the nearby building.

"In ya go, son. Hope you enjoy your stay with us." His humor was lost on me, but there was no venom in his delivery or manner.

I took one last look around and strolled through the open door into the "chute," feeling not unlike a stockyard steer being ushered onto the killing floor. The bolt slammed home with a hollow report that echoed off the walls of the dingy, narrow passageway I now found myself in. My surroundings melted into shades of gray, and the place had a bitter odor of acrid dirt. Dim illumination was provided by a bare, low-wattage bulb in the ceiling. I walked to a door with a small, eye-level window etched with wire at the end of the passageway, found it locked, and placed a cardboard box containing personal possessions I hoped to bring in with me on the floor.

Together with my last hangover for a good while, I leaned my back against the concrete bulwark and waited in airless, oppressive heat, sweat forming on my brow, my shirt sticking to my body. I was surrounded by concrete and I could hear the echoes of closing doors and voices reverberating up and down the narrow stairwell on the other side of the windowed door. I pushed all thoughts of the outside world from my mind and concentrated on steeling myself for the coming debut into a world foreign to my experience.

The sound of the bolt to the outer door yanked me from my thoughts, and I walked back a few steps to see what was going on. A man in bright blue coveralls and a cap led a string of about 10 prisoners into the corridor, followed by another identically dressed man bringing up the rear. Bright monogrammed insignias featuring eagles, flags, lightning bolts, and the like were sewn to their clothing. These were US Marshals bringing in a string of new recruits. The line of prisoners looked hot, unkempt, and scruffy. Their hands were bound in front of them with steel bracelets. A chain rope attaching each to the other circled their midsections. They were dirty and silent, eyes cast downward, and for a moment, I wondered if this could be a chain gang returning from road duty. The Marshals ignored me as though I wasn't even there and marched their string of prisoners by me to the rear door.

"Hey!" yelled the first Marshal. "What's this box on the floor?"

"It's mine," I said.

"Well, keep it out of the fucking passageway, for chrissake!" He opened the door and the parade clomped through the passageway in perfect step and up the outer stairs, easily passing by the box, which didn't amount to an obstruction. The door closed with a cavernous slam.

I wanted to point out to the dickhead barking Marshal that there was nothing other than passageway available, but said nothing. I was alone again with my thoughts, sweat, and stale air. After what seemed a long time, but was probably only 15 or 20 minutes, the door opened from the inside and a mousey little man wearing spectacles, gray slacks, and a blue shirt appeared in the opening.

"Rohrer?"

I nodded.

"God, I thought we lost you. I've been looking for you in all the wrong places. It's uncommon that we have someone self-surrender here."

That's wonderful news, I thought. Does that make me some sort of patsy? I would later learn that the act of turning one's self in while facing a 15-year sentence was an enigma to the great majority of inmates here, "No fuckin' way! You gotta be shittin' me!" said most.

A foreboding image of what awaited inside ran through my mind. That they didn't know where to find me was my first hint of how things operated there.

"Follow me," said the mouse-man, and I picked up my box, anxious to leave the confines of the passageway. We climbed the stairs and entered R & D (receiving and discharge), where I was shown into a barred cell containing the chain gang, now unchained. I was instructed to leave my boxed possessions by an office door. One of the prisoners, a Mexican with high Indian cheekbones and thick, dark hair, had the receiver from a wall phone to his ear.

"I thought I told you to stay off the phone!" roared the mouse.

With deliberate calm, the Mexican replaced the receiver and

assumed a posture of hurt innocence. "Me?" he asked, the fingers of one hand against his chest.

A look of frustration came over the mouse-man. Summoning every ounce of authority and menace he could muster, he cried, "I'm not going to tell you again!" and his voice cracked, contradicting his feigned potency. He locked the cell door and walked off.

The Mexican immediately picked up the phone and started dialing. This was my first experience of Chris Saldivar, with whom I would soon become fast friends and share my living quarters. I don't think he ever found the "line out" he was seeking on the phone.

The other prisoners sat around trading tough talk, everyone agreeing on what shitheads the Marshals were. I learned that some were "stopovers" headed for US prisons in the East, others designated here. My anxiety to see what this place looked like was relieved by a broken pane in a bank of frosted windows in the cell. From the outside it looked like a prison, a shithole similar to others I had seen, a place to be avoided. Inside, however, from my second story vantage, I could see a large brick-lined courtyard neatly laid out with lawns, some trees, and landscaping. Casually dressed inmates sat on benches with tables; two of them were playing guitars. Whew! Not so dreary at all, considering the outer appearance.

A guard entered the cell and offered everyone a bag lunch, which I declined, my appetite squeezed by the day's events. I wasn't savvy enough to realize that others might have wanted more. They also neglected to mention that dinner was already being served and nothing more would be offered until breakfast the following morning. It was then sometime in the late afternoon.

After everyone had finished their bologna sandwiches on Wonder Bread, one of the stopovers, a brash, boastful, snot-nosed little punk, was peering through the broken window pane. "Hey, lookit this ... they got a cunt-guard here. What a ugly bitch!" He cupped his hands around his mouth and rained down an avalanche of foul insults on the blameless woman, then quickly ducked back to his seat on the benches where we sat.

How quaint ... absolutely brilliant, I thought to myself. That should improve matters around here. The woman guard was at the cell bars in short order, fuming. Not a cover girl, but not exactly homely either. No one said a word, but if looks could kill, we'd all be dead.

The stopovers were moved to an adjacent cell and we who remained were called, one by one, to the receiving line. I was photographed, fingerprinted, and issued a registration number. Scars and tattoos were cataloged, medical forms completed, and a blood sample was taken. I was given a receipt for the money I brought for my commissary account, and then, strangely enough, I was given another receipt for having voluntarily handed over to them my own self and body. I guess if I didn't have a receipt it could be claimed I wasn't here.

Now the fun would begin. I was subjected to a strip search. Standing naked as a peeled orange, they started at the top:

"Okay. Head back, open your mouth. Lift the tongue. Brush behind your ears. Good. Now the hair. Do the beard. Good. Okay. Arms up. Fine. Turn around, legs apart. Bend over and spread 'em. Thank you. Now, face me. Lift 'em."

At this last command, I dutifully lifted my right foot, then my left.

"No, no! Your balls, man! Haven't you ever been strip-searched before?"

I admitted I hadn't. A totally green rookie. There were many protocols I had yet to learn. The R & D staff accepted everything I brought with me, noting that I had called ahead to inquire about regulations, another rare occurrence at Terminal Island. In the days to come, I would find I didn't exactly fit the profile of the average inmate there.

I was issued bedding, which I balanced on top of my box, and told to report to B-unit. The Mexican with the predilection for telephones was released with me and we walked across the yard together in the warm evening twilight. The hum of life on the yard buzzed around my head like a swarm of insects, a low murmur of voices sounding as if from a movie soundtrack. Inmates clustered in tight groups engaged in prison yard conversation, joshing and jiving. I wanted to take in everything that was going on around me, but I had to concentrate on balancing my load. The Mexican, of medium stature and a cheerful chubbiness, seemed calm and sure of himself. He asked my name.

"My fren' Jake ... you been down before?" He sensed that I had not. I told him no, this was a first for me.

"Don' you worry. I will show you what to do."

I was drawn to his friendly manner and warm smile, but wary nonetheless. I had just walked through the door and he was the first person I had met. He had a sly, knowing twinkle in his eyes and a confident manner that seemed to say, *These Federales got nothin' on me.*

He introduced himself as "Chris," which I would later learn was short for Cristobal. Streetwise and prison-smart, Chris had spent half of his then 38 years in jails and prisons. He would become my teacher and confidant, a reliable friend and provider of good humor. I arrived at B-unit, where I was told there was no vacancy and to report to C-unit, where I was reunited with the Mexican.

FCI (Federal Correctional Institute) Terminal Island was a level 3-4, medium security prison. There were cell blocks or jail units for trouble makers, holdovers, and temporary assignments, but once "designated" by the Bureau of Prisons, most were housed in dormitory-like "units," each containing about 90 inmates. There was also a hospital unit, TI being the inmate medical center for those federal prisons in the western states. C-unit was the drug unit, where they housed prisoners with addictions in their background. Most had been heroin addicts. Many still were, would always be. I was there on temporary assignment due to a space available circumstance.

I was never considered an addict, by myself or by federal

authorities. Though I recognized its habit-forming tendencies, I never thought of cocaine as a physically addicting substance, at least in its powder form. I never admitted to authorities that I had been a habitual user, not that they had asked, and I looked askance at those who blamed their substance of abuse for their behavior. I thought of cocaine as mostly a social drug, a focal point in certain social groups until it either destroyed the relationships within the group or people just walked away from it. Its use pushed you to drink alcohol (or ingest sedatives, if you had them) to help smooth the jagged edge created by the cocaine, and then to do more cocaine to overcome the stupefying effects of the alcohol, making you the loser on both ends. It did, though, seem to have two medical benefits: It served to block nasal allergens and constipation was never a problem. A lifetime of hay fever and pollen allergies disappeared when I used cocaine, and that first hit always sent me straight to the toilet. Used in its other form (freebase or crack cocaine, the smokable variant) it seemed to become something different, quickly dragging users into the deepest of holes and rendering them unable to climb out or cope with life, hiding from the world with only their pipe to befriend and protect them. I was never attracted to freebase cocaine.

The first thing you learn in a prison setting is the count, the lifeblood a prison runs on. Several times daily at appointed hours they count heads, and you'd better be either at your job or at your bunk. There were also surprise counts that could happen anytime, just to remind you who was in charge. The unit and cell counts were tallied at prison count central, and no one was released from holding their count position until every head in the prison was accounted for.

The 4:00 PM count set the stage for the evening meal. Following the count, the units would be released to the dining hall, one by one. Weekly inspection results determined the order of release, a dangled carrot that created a competitive camaraderie in some units and indifference in others. In C-unit the orderlies were led by Big John, a heavily tattooed biker-sort, who spurred the others on to work hard and win the inspections. C-unit usually ended up at or near the top. Whenever another unit would win, John complained bitterly about the inspectors and the winning unit, "That place looked like a holding tank at the county jail," or, "I've seen a cleaner shithouse in a back-country Mexican slam," and so forth.

The 10:00 PM count was the "bedtime" count. You weren't required to stay in your bunk, but the unit doors were locked and the yard became off limits. I became convinced that the early morning count, around 2:00 AM, was in place just to make sure no one got a full night's sleep. Night-duty guards, keys clanging, would bang their batons against metal stairwell railings, the report echoing in concrete stairwells, announcing their approach. Some guards were gleeful over fucking with their wards, others just did their job without being assholes about it.

Sometimes the inmates would ask for it. This was a time just before a urine test for marijuana use was perfected and some thought it would be fun, an intentional "fuck you," to have the guards walk through a cloud of marijuana smoke during the count. The cops would have to find the substance in someone's possession in order to make a bust.

Inmate quarters consisted of cubicles, most with two inmates sharing a space about 8x10, with a single chair, a writing desk, a bunk bed, and locker space. There were a lesser number of single inmate cubicles, awarded to well-behaved, long-time residents. The unit prized above all others was the "South Yard," where inmates were housed in condo-like individual studios, with three or four inmates sharing their own little apartment. There was a peaceful demeanor there, and it created a social class of inmate by providing the tracks from which side you might happen to be from. The best pool tables were in the South Yard.

My first day was spent in wide-eyed exploration of my new surroundings. I strolled everywhere I could go, taking it all in. The east side of the facility bordered a wide canal that gave way to the harbor and all the commerce that took place there. A long corridor with a high fence connected the south and main yards along the harbor. There was a ball field and a running track in the south yard, along with a weight room, a billiards room, and other amenities for crafts. The grass was kept green and the landscaping attractive.

My best discovery on that first day was the library with a bank of crappy but serviceable typewriters. I started to write about my experiences and emotions, pouring out all I did and saw, mostly wanting loved ones to know I was okay. I found writing created a cerebral world apart from the world I was in and could provide a sense of joy and accomplishment, something to look forward to each day. The challenge and pleasure of writing kept the blues mostly away from my door at Terminal Island.

⇝⇜

CHRIS AND I SHARED A cubicle in C-unit. We spent our time together those first few days, walking around the yard, slowly introducing ourselves to one another. Neither of us had yet been assigned a job. Chris said he was going to apply to "Prison Industries," where they made furniture and other hard goods, and inmates could make something like $1.15 hourly. Regular prison jobs, orderlies, clerks, custodians, and such, paid about twelve cents an hour.

"You know, Chris," I remarked on my second or third day in residence, "there must be someone here who looks exactly like me and whose name is 'Holmes.' Everywhere I go someone thinks I'm this Holmes person."

"No, no, my fren'," laughed Chris. "'Holmes' means 'homeboy' or 'homie,' you know, like someone from where you are from."

"I didn't recognize any of them."

"You don' recognize them from there. You recognize them from here. Now we're all from here. You know what I mean?"

"I think so. It's a friendly term, isn't it?"

"Not all the time. A dude could say, 'I'm gonna fuck you up, Holmes!'"

"Hmmm, I see. Thank you, amigo. This stuff is all new to me."

Everything there was new to me, including the Southern California climate. Many nights were hot, humid, and still, sometimes making sleep elusive. I awoke my first morning to the barking of a seagull out on the yard and was later charmed to find that an inmate, a large, quiet Indian fellow, had tamed a seagull ("Jake") that would come every morning to eat a hardboiled egg, smuggled from the kitchen, from his hand.

Many of the inmates transported me back to junior high school, where some students had reminded me of dangerous animals to be approached with caution or avoided entirely. Here, large black men, brimming with muscles, sauntered around the yard in groups. A system of self-segregation kept them apart from the tattooed Chicanos, many of whom seemed to ascribe to a gang-like dress code. Bearded biker-types, often adorned with tattoos of swastikas, confederate flags, and the like, also seemed to keep to themselves. There was a lesser assortment of Asians, most unencumbered by muscles or tattoos. There were no females, but there was a curious group of transvestites, some with hormone-induced breasts. They wore makeup and headscarves and other feminine attire. They looked out of place and also seemed to hang together in a group. White people of my social background were a definite minority.

I found mysteries everywhere I looked. It didn't feel to me like anyone of authority was even aware I existed. I imagined I would be assigned duties at some point, but so far, for the first several days, no one of higher office had said a word to me other than the initial indoctrination at R & D. I was just 737064-011, hardly worthy of notice. It would take some time for me to adjust to my new universe.

4

YARDBIRDS

WHAT A NASTY RING "TERMINAL ISLAND" HAS TO IT, AS THOUGH A place where people are deposited to die, like Kalaupapa, the famous leper colony on Moloka'i. The "terminal" designation, however, refers to the area as a central depot for commerce. When I looked around me in my new surroundings with no idea how long I'd be there, a dark foreboding would sometimes creep up on me, enveloping my mind and causing a shudder in my spine. I knew it was time to buck up and hunker down, to put my mind to work at bettering my circumstance, one day at a time.

⇥⇤

I HAD GONE TO BED secure in the knowledge that tomorrow would be Saturday and the prison would run on its free and easy weekend schedule. A light breakfast wouldn't be served until 7:00 AM, and if you wanted to sleep in, there would be a brunch at 10:30. I was rudely awakened at 3:30 AM with a firm shake of my foot by a black, female duty guard.

"C'mon now. You got to be in the kitchen in 20 minutes."

"What for?" I wanted to know.

"'Cause that's where you be woikin' now. Let's get movin'."

"Damn, ma'am, they could have let me know."

"It was posted on the duty roster," she said. It was the first time I ever heard of the duty roster. "But if you'd rather not go to the kitchen, they's room in the hole for you."

Holy shit. I considered my options, got dressed, and headed for the kitchen, where I just stood around until one of the supervisors noticed my presence. I was told I was going to be the new "diet cook," and it would be my job to make up bland, low-sodium, and vegetarian food plates for the jail and hospital units, after which I would serve up the same sort of plates to those inmates with diet cards during the regular meals. Imagine the thrill of it! I would have to wait until after the morning meal for my training to begin. In the meantime, I was told to assist "Too Sweet" in cracking open 13 cases of eggs into two giant vats for the morning egg dish, some sort of an omelet. Each case had 144 eggs in it.

"Too Sweet" was a tall black man in his late twenties, well groomed, handsome, and calm in manner. He had come to California from Miami to make it in the record business as a singer-songwriter, but his career was temporarily sidelined by a parole violation. He forgot to get permission to leave Miami. Soon we were talking music and Too Sweet sang one of his compositions for me, "Don't Blame It On the White Man," an ode to his fellow brothers to take personal responsibility for their lot in life, even in the face of discrimination and the historic atrocity of slavery. I discovered he really did have a fine voice, mellow and melodic, along with that built-in sense of rhythm I never had but is common to a lot of black people. Soon he was snapping his fingers and creating a counter rhythm with the crack of the eggs. I joined in as best I could, pleased to have found such pleasant company in my first kitchen endeavor.

The first month at Terminal Island was a hard one. I struggled with my 3:30 AM wake-ups, and though I became competent as the diet cook, it was tedious and boring. After three weeks in C-unit, sharing my quarters with Chris, I was moved out of the drug unit and into D-unit, where I missed Chris, my second floor view of the harbor, and the warm camaraderie of the addicts. I seemed to have some sort of bond with many of the druggies, even though one of them had boosted a pair of my sunglasses. My Cuban bunkmate in D-unit listened to Spanish language radio broadcasts throughout the night but was cool about turning it down when I asked him to. Across from my bunk was a sullen and quiet George Manuel Bosque, the famous Brinks robber. Known as the "Dog" unit, D-unit was recurrently called last for the evening meal. No one gave a damn about winning the inspections.

Over in the kitchen was a harmless but delta-brained cop whose name was Metz. He was always coming into the diet kitchen to strike up a conversation with me, generally centering on his love of firearms, manly endeavors, and his favorite TV programs. One day he was wearing a brass belt buckle with a pistol on it, and he told me he was going to the range to practice. Even kitchen cops have to be checked out with weapons. I was willing to bet money he owned a .44 magnum. I lost. "Thirty-eight police special," he said. Then he went on to tell me about a new TV drama series, *Trauma Center*, starring the guy who used to be the Hulk. Now he's an ambulance driver who gets people out of their wrecked cars by tearing the doors off with his bare hands and so forth. Metz got very excited about this stuff.

Within a week of moving to D-unit, I learned that C-unit was looking for a new inmate clerk, right up my alley, and the competition was slim to none. The unit manager, Cad Owens, was a reasonably cool guy. He was able to talk with inmates, one on one, without the stiff appearance of being your overlord. He was anxious to have my typing and clerical skills, and was happy to make the transfer arrangements. To qualify for residence in C-unit, I was supposed to be an addict—which we all are anyway, of one substance or another—and I would be required to enroll in the drug program.

I stayed in the kitchen for another week or so while the transfer went through. The diet kitchen was apart from the main kitchen activities and provided a hideout of sorts for those wanting a little privacy. Some mornings I found other kitchen workers in there smoking a 5:00 AM joint, and at other times, Chicano "burrito bandits" stuffing, folding, and wrapping burritos at a frantic pace, producing an edible black market currency.

A drama played out one morning in the bakery when a kitchen worker opened a large can of sliced apples and left the top hinged to the can, sticking straight up, its jagged edges razor sharp. In a quirk of fate, the can was bumped from the counter and he attempted a mid-air catch. He missed the body of the falling can, and the lethal top, still upright, sliced effortlessly into an inward-turned wrist. A geyser of blood from a severed artery shot from the man's arm, spurting into the air.

Metz was there and his eyes momentarily glazed over. He was no longer at FCI Terminal Island. This was *Trauma Center*. Assuming command, Metz dashed into action. Filthy rags were applied to the wound and held in place by other kitchen workers while the would-be can catcher lay on the floor in shock. Metz raced for the outside door at top speed, and like one of the Stooges, he bounced off the locked exit. I was waiting to see if he would attempt to rip the door from its hinges, but after some fumbling, he produced a key and headed full-speed to the hospital unit. In a few moments, cops and officials poured into the scene and the stricken man was hurried out on a stretcher, Metz bringing up the rear and barking orders, admonishing that someone had better "open that fucking door!" I understand the worker made a satisfactory recovery.

⟫•⟪

BACK HOME IN C-UNIT, CHRIS and I were lazing around after the evening meal. I was reading a book and Chris was writing to his sweetheart. Pretty soon he turned from his writing and asked, "Jake, my fren'. How you spell 'shane'?"

"What's it mean?" I asked.

"You know what a shane is ... like that song, 'Take these shanes from my heart.'" Talking with Chris was sometimes like learning a new language.

Finished with his letter, Chris started thumbing through a book on world civilizations and came across a picture of da Vinci's Mona Lisa. "You know, my fren' Jake," he says, a puzzled look on his face, "I don't see anything pretty in this Mona Lisa bitch. She looks like a dude, George Washington or somebody like that."

"I guess she was considered pretty for her time," I ventured, remembering an old R&B love song that included the lyric, "And Mona Lisa was a man."

"I could never love a bitch look like that," says Chris, turning up his nose at classical beauty. "Let me tell you about love and bitches, my fren' Jake. The first rule is never give a bitch all your love or all your money." More rules would follow.

I was amazed by Chris' ability to maintain his charismatic joyfulness and grinning humor in the face of 19 years of imprisonment. Woman as bitch was ingrained in him, a part of his everyday vocabulary and mindset, never considered for its inherent revilement. To Chris, and a lot of others, woman was a lesser creature to be dominated by man, a credo I never adhered to. Chis went on to tell me how he harnessed his Patti:

"I had plenny bitches, my fren' Jake, all aroun' me. But I wanted this one."

But Patti held back and told Chris she couldn't give herself to a heroin addict. Chris was running heroin across the border from Tijuana and had a runaway locomotive habit roaring through his veins. Nonetheless, Chris spent months courting Patti with a courteous display of his best manners.

"I even take baths for her before each time I see her." More weeks rolled by, but Patti remained steadfast in her denial and Chris was beside himself with desire.

"I am making love to all these other bitches, but it is no fun anymore."

Chris was determined to show Patti how great his love for her was. In a supreme show of sacrifice, he decided to rid himself of his habit, and he steeled himself to this goal. Patti stood by his side and helped him through the awful sickness of withdrawal. Together they spent weeks going to a doctor and fighting the addiction. In about eight weeks, Chris was pronounced clean, free of his habit, and the honeymoon suite was chosen.

And it rained down love. The heavens opened and bluebirds sang among the branches of the trees in paradise. The infinite universe momentarily halted its expansion for the entwined lovers, lost in the sanctity of their love making. Rapture and joy enfolded them, their spent energies finally giving way to the relaxed warmth and security of afterglow, the sweet convergence of loving souls, giving and receiving.

Interrupting the afterglow for a moment, Chris got up from the bed and, with a spoon and lighter, cooked up a slam of heroin on the bedroom dresser. He loaded a syringe from the spoon, tied off his arm with surgical rubber tubing, and "mainlined" the heroin, injecting it into his bloodstream. Patti was left in tears.

"Never let a bitch think she can tell you what to do, my fren' Jake," counseled Chris, completing my lesson for the day.

◆—◆

THE LOW RUMBLE OF THE Port Police boat grew louder as it cruised up the canal outside our window, shadowing the prison fence line and east-facing dormitories. A series of catcalls followed its progress, "Fuck your mother, punk!" shouted out Big John and others joined in. Taking opportunity to insult authority that can't get back at you was the norm.

A drug program graduate, Big John said, "There's no problem too big that a good slam of heroin can't fix." I wondered if that was a part of the curriculum. His release was imminent. Among inmates he was thus considered "short," meaning not much time left to serve. "Shorter'n a fat man's dick," said John. A couple of nights later, he had scored some heroin and came over to visit Chris and me, giddy and intoxicated, unconsciously scratching at his arms and torso with a hairbrush as though tiny bugs were crawling all over him.

Life with Chris in C-unit was a daily series of eye-opening events into a culture as foreign to me as it was commonplace for him. He came into our cubicle—our "house"—one day, excited and proud. He had traded our vending machine money, five dollars in quarters, for a ten-dollar bill. Paper currency was forbidden and five dollars in quarters was the limit you were allowed to possess.

"That's just wonderful, Chris. What are we supposed to do with a ten-dollar bill?"

"You will see, my fren', you will see." Prison-wise and savvy, he found the right man on the yard, and we ended up with cigarettes, coffee, and goodies worth over fourteen dollars at the commissary.

"Not bad, eh, my fren' Jake?"

"Not bad," I agreed. Commissary goods were purchased with an inmate account that was funded from the inmate's work at the prison or money sent in from the outside. Among inmates, the commissary was also known as "canteen." Not long afterward, Chris again confiscated our vending machine money.

"What are you up to, Chris?"

"I'm going to get us a joint, my fren'."

"I don't want a joint, Chris, especially if it costs us all our quarters."

"No, no. It is free! You will see."

Chris ventured out onto the yard with our quarters and came back with two joints. He asked a friend nearby to go "on point" for him, watching for any patrolling guards. He disassembled both joints and divided the contents into three piles. With cigarette paper, he expertly rolled up three joints, and with two of them, he headed back out onto the yard, returning with all our quarters.

"See, what I say?" said Chris, holding up the single, if thinner, joint. We went out onto the yard, and in the privacy of a sally port, we shared the joint. The penalty for being caught was not lost on me, and any would-be pleasure was erased by concern that soon bordered on paranoia.

Chris was keen on doing things for me. One day he came into to the "house," beaming and worked up. "Lookit this, my fren' Jake! I have scored two acids for us!"

I considered the potential quality of LSD acquired in a prison black market and the environment in which we would have to experience it, and I declined. Chris was crestfallen.

"I don't think it is a good idea, Chris," and I explained to him what I considered the downside, starting with the probability of a poorly manufactured drug that could easily backfire on us, and stressing the need for a suitable environment in which to experience such a potentially powerful drug.

"I think maybe you are right, my fren'," he said and went back onto the yard and traded the acids for some other form of contraband.

Among the many things Chris taught me, how to do laundry and operate the prison washing machines was one of the first. It never occurred to me before I got to prison that, for my entire life, I'd never had to do my own laundry. From mother to wife to girlfriend, there was always a woman around who handled the laundry chores. On other occasions, I would simply drop things off with a launderer. Chris must have thought I was from some other planet, stymied when I had to use a washing machine.

⇥-⇤

OUT ON THE YARD I met a lot of people, one by one. Each had a personality new to me and was interesting in his own way, each with an exclusive history. One day I sat and had a cigarette with J.T., an older, slender black man with thinning hair, glasses, and a soft, warm voice. Today when I see Ron Washington, manager of the Texas Rangers, I am reminded of J.T. He worked the Mardi Gras train from New Orleans to St. Louis, then to El Paso and Fort Worth, an eight-day run in 1953.

"Was the fust time I evah see womens woikin'," said J.T. "I don' mean natch'll womens' woik, you unnerstan' … I means shov'lin coal 'n washin' down th' railway cars 'n such. Dey was big ol' womens, too, wif great big butts 'n chewin' t'bacca 'n smokin' cigars. One of 'em patted me ona ass 'n said, 'Well bless my soul, looky whas we gots heah … a nice young man.' 'Bout knocked th' wind outta me, 'n scared me half to def!"

J.T. described justice Texas style: "Don' nevah go down in Texas 'n pick up no beef if'n you be black and it be 1953. Dey gots only two sen'nances fo' th' black man in Texas … th' big bitch 'n th' little bitch. Th' little bitch be fifty yeahrs …" his voice getting softer. He looked off at the horizon, as if sorting some old memories floating around in his mind. I didn't ask him about the big bitch.

The social aspects of the yard always fascinated me. It seemed like everyone out there was connected to communications central; nothing happened that wasn't community knowledge in very short order. Gossip thrived. When Joe Bonanno, the notorious Sicilian-born mafia lord, was sent to TI for medical reasons, it was as though the very pinnacle of gangster royalty had arrived. The buzz about Joe reached the prison population in the drop of a hat, as though texted. Out on the yard in his wheelchair, he was visited by groups of inmates who approached him like political emissaries wanting to pay their respects, Joe offering his hand like the godfather that he was.

One of the night duty guards, as though befriending me, once counseled, "You belong over in A-unit. They have the older, more mature people over there. None of these punks and all their noise." I thanked him for the tip, but I knew I wasn't going anywhere. A few days later, three inmates in A-unit attempted to rape a female night duty cop who was making late evening rounds. So much for maturity and lack of punks. They threw a blanket over her head as she entered a bathroom, but she managed to get to her radio panic button, which brings help on the hoof, damn quick.

As you might imagine, prison authorities take a dim view of this sort of behavior. She was also the wife of another prison cop at TI and the prison cops were especially upset. This sort of shit wasn't supposed to happen at a medium security joint. One unfortunate soul innocently walked into the middle of the melee to pee and was locked up in the hole for almost a week before they cut him loose. Word on the yard had it that the supposed ringleader was found dead a day later, hanging in his cell, a circumstance that fueled frenzied speculation. The other two would get an extra twenty years each added to their current sentences before being sent off to maximum security penitentiaries like Leavenworth or Marion.

※

THE JAILHOUSE TATTOO INDUSTRY WAS way ahead of the current tattoo craze, body ink a popular fashion. Some guys wore extraordinary works of art done by skilled artisans. All were done in black ink. I never saw a jailhouse tattoo with color. One man had a panoramic tapestry of an in-process stagecoach robbery tattooed across his back, outlaws firing their guns from behind trees and boulders, the guard riding shotgun in mid-fall from the top of the stagecoach, one hand holding the wound on his torso, his shotgun in the other, the horses rearing, the driver holding on to the reins. The detail was impeccable.

Among his dozens of tattoos, Chris had a graveyard tattooed on his chest with multiple gravestones arranged around a hooded angel of death carrying a lantern and scythe. Below the tattoo was a jagged scar from a surgery to get at internal organs after he had been "shanked" (stabbed) in the stomach with a homemade prison knife ("shank"). I've seen losers and lifers with the name of a prison tattooed across their foreheads in bold, block letters, there just to piss off paroling authorities who would consider releasing them back into society so that they could ostensibly rejoin the workforce. They might as well have tattooed "fuck you" across their foreheads.

Prison authorities consider tattooing "bodily mutilation" and have rules against it, though it's not as serious an infraction as drugs, assault, weapons, extortion, and such. I had occasion to observe some of these artists at work, one tattooing another and sometimes tattooing themselves. The process of tattooing is known as "tacking" by inmates. When engaged in self-mutilation, the tacker (who is also the tackee) would use a mirror to assist himself in hard to see areas, a unique procedure to behold.

The prison-made tattoo gun was a marvel of inmate ingenuity. In the months I had been there, I began to notice that hardly a wall clock anywhere in the prison seemed to be working. I discovered that it wasn't a matter of battery replacement. The clocks' DC drive motors had been stolen by tattoo artists as the direct-current power source for their tattoo guns. The guns themselves were made from the clock motor, a toothbrush handle, a BIC pen barrel, the pen's ink reservoir, a battery, a section of a guitar string, its tip polished to a fine point, and a Q-tip stem. From these innocent scraps, the artist assembled a functioning tattoo gun, capable of fine art. The low, quiet hum of bodily mutilation in progress could often be heard in the dormitory after the 10:00 PM count. From what I gathered, this level of thought and ingenuity among inmates was reserved for tattooing and acquiring heroin, or possibly escape.

❦

THE LEVEL OF HEROIN USE in C-unit was astounding, and I began to wonder if *that's* why they called it the drug unit. Inmates were practiced at hiding a syringe with inventive cleverness. They were also shared among the inmates, sometimes disinfected with Clorox, sometimes not. I never learned where they got them in the first place, although Terminal Island was also an inmate medical center, giving rise to possibilities.

I once accompanied a counselor on an inspection tour of the unit. At one point, he nonchalantly pulled back a decorative edging strip on a vertical panel of a plywood locker, finding underneath a perfectly drilled horizontal hole with a syringe sitting in it. He immediately put the strip back, feigning lack of knowledge like the Nazi prison guard in the TV comedy *Hogan's Heroes*, "I see nothing!" We continued the tour as though it didn't exist.

The heroin itself came into the prison from the visiting room, packed in a plastic baggie that was stuffed into someone's anus. Occasionally, someone was caught in a strip search because they were careless about cramming it all the way in. Cavity searches didn't seem to be the norm, although there were occasions when a suspect would be put into a "dry" cell with no toilet or sink and kept there until bodily function cleared his bowels.

I could always tell when a new load of heroin arrived. A half-dozen or so of the regulars would be walking around the unit euphoric and scratching. Dangers weren't only presented by the cops. There was always a cadre of tough-thug predators around, and if they found out someone was holding, the holder risked being beaten, stabbed, or worse if he didn't hand it over. One Sunday a fellow in C-unit was found dead of a heroin overdose, still seated on a toilet where he had injected himself. I didn't know him personally, but he seemed a calm, intelligent sort, well groomed and quiet, hardly seeming an addict.

❖

THE PRISON HAD AN AUDITORIUM and, from time to time, brought in outside entertainment. One night we were presented with an all-black fashion review, "Originals in the Essence of Elegance." Black inmates filled the first 20 or so rows in the auditorium. When the curtains parted, two pretty black ladies in wigs and skimpy whores' negligees performed vulgar dance-step gyrations to the slap of a disco record while framed in a gaudy backdrop of tinsel and sequins. The brothers went wild, hooting and clapping. A year or so before I arrived, The Police, featuring, of course, Sting, played a concert at TI, leaving behind some of their equipment and instruments for the inmates. The "Hammer," a former member of our brotherhood of spice merchants, also a drummer, once played a gig at TI with his band. He has since acquired FBI and DEA files that would no longer allow him to set foot in a federal prison, at least as an entertainer.

Another evening featured comedy. A black frontman calling himself "Shoo-fly" told jokes and clever stories. Benny the Ferret started to heckle him, Shoo-fly responding, "Look, man, if I want any shit out of you, I'll come down there and squeeze your head." Benny didn't say much after that. Another night featured San Francisco 49er running back Wendell Tyler, along with a musical revue. A couple of songs were sung, and then they came on with the old Jesus sell. An ex-con came out to tell us about how tough he used to be and all the rat-holes he'd been in. Then he met Art Linkletter and Jesus. I was put off by the ruse and didn't stick around very long.

When otherwise not in use, the auditorium could be used for inmate rehearsal of music or drama programs. I fell in with a couple of guys who invited me to join their band. David, a hyper but pleasant black fellow, was the leader and played bass. He was joined by a drummer we called "Sticks" and a singer who had the implausible name Cashmere LeBlanc. Cashmere also played rhythm guitar. I came on board as the piano player, and we soon added a diminutive Thai who played flute and went by the name "Choo-Choo."

We were a ragtag musical bunch. Cashmere could actually sing a bit, and David was a practiced soul-funk bass player who was serious about his music. Anything he might lack in talent was made up for by his tremendous confidence and the stars in his eyes. Cashmere looked like his name sounded: slender and handsome with a warm voice and gleaming eyes, cool and confident, smooth as ... well, cashmere. He slicked back his hair with pomade and sported a Boston Blackie mustache. I wanted to use his name in the band's name and I christened us "Cashmere LeBlanc and the Champagne Brothers of Righteous Ecstasy," or CLB & CBRE.

Cashmere could barely tune his guitar and I had to help him most of the time. The raggedy old piano had several keys permanently taped down and others were grossly out of tune. Sticks had two cymbals, a kick drum, and a snare, but he could count to four and keep time. Choo-Choo played his flute with all the enthusiasm of Pan, prancing around the stage pixie-like on the toes of a ballerina. His broken English was a kick: "We jam down tonight, yes boys? I am too many strengths down for this work all time. Is not in my body working plus four hours of the day on this night." And so forth. When he blew a solo he said, "Lats!" A Thai rodent, I suppose.

David's funky bass playing sounded something like the musical accompaniment to the Jerry Seinfeld show on TV. We played songs by Michael Jackson, Stevie Wonder, and James Brown, but we never made anything really fly. Then Cashmere got rolled up and stuck in the hole, "under investigation," for what I never learned. I never saw him again. He was replaced by a transvestite whose name was Chantay. David came up with a new piano player and I moved to electric guitar, but the piano player proved clumsy at best. Then David found "Two-Step," a pretty good guitar player, and I moved back to piano. All of a sudden, we started to sound at least as good as a second-rate bar band in a skid-row dive. I managed to teach the band *Proud Mary*, and Choo-Choo took the vocal: "Low'lin, low'lin, low'lin ona livah."

We played mostly contemporary black music in what were to me a lot of strange keys, and I always had to figure out a bunch of new chords. David insisted that this was where the soul came from.

I once asked him if we could do something in plain old C major or G major, keys where I could get in some of my better hot licks on the piano. "Naw, man. Them's hillbilly keys. We gonna get down, brothuh!" Right you are, David.

5

GRADUATION

**Carpet creeper, sizzly-juicy, cal-
liope, asshole tear, blockbuster,
and atomic bomb.**

–Grade school fart classifications

CHRIS WAS WORKING OVERTIME AT HIS JOB IN PRISON INDUSTRIES AND I was lying back on my bunk reading a book, passing not only the time but some noxious gas as well. Whatever they had served for the evening meal was at war in my stomach. I spied old Lame Dave, the chaplain's assistant, wandering around the unit with his broom, an accessory that sticks to him like his shadow. He's a quiet, unassuming fellow, friendly but sort of strange looking, with bad posture and a crooked smile, as though pasted on his face lopsided. There was also a mild vacuous presence about him that sometimes made me wonder if he was really all there. I'd heard it said that they kept him drugged with Thorazine, a powerful sedative.

Across the canal from our side of the dormitory was a cannery where tuna and other fish products were processed. Sometimes, especially when the wind was right, a rank and horrid smell snaked across the water and permeated the air at TI. Pretty soon, Dave sauntered into my cubical to bum some coffee and walked smack into the invisible cloud of my most recent fart, if not an atomic bomb, maybe a blockbuster.

"Man, that smell from the fish factory really comes in on this side of the dorm," said Dave. The fish factory was benign this night, but I thought I'd play along.

"Yes, Dave, it certainly does. Sometimes it can be downright dreadful."

"Whew! It's really strong tonight!" he said, scrunching up his nose like a rabbit.

I mimic HAL, the mad computer from the *Space Odyssey*. "I've noticed it myself, Dave. It really is. I've found myself wondering just how titanically awful it might get."

"Jesus! I didn't know tuna fish could smell that bad!"

"Just a moment... just a moment," I said, deciding it was time to change the subject. "I'm picking up on a change in atmosphere. I think an offshore breeze is taming the situation. It seems to be diminishing now. Yes, I'm sure of it. Living on this side of the dorm, you know, one gets used to it."

"I don't think I could ever get used to that," says Dave.

Poor old Lame Dave. I was a little ashamed of myself for toying with him and not stepping up to claim the fart. He thanked me for the coffee, turned, and with his broom, ambled off about his business. I picked up my book and continued where I left off, thinking an antacid might be in order before Chris got home.

❧⋅❦

CHRISTMAS CAME TO PRISON AS only the government could bring it. The warmth and cheer of Nancy Reagan presenting Cabbage Patch dolls to Korean orphans under the perfect symmetry of the White House Christmas tree pervaded the air. We were provided with a scrawny, wire-and-bristle, fake Christmas tree and tinsel strips, along with pretend wreaths, ornaments, and other deco-rations. Inmates seemed divided between Scrooge and delight. A couple of the more delighted cons masqueraded as elves and helped me with the preparations. DeLafayette Washington and Leon Swackhammer assisted me with decorating the tree and the C-unit lobby with cheery enthusiasm. DeLafayette was about six-foot eight and had to bend over to put on the crowning ornament.

"Tha's ... ah ... one ... fine ... uh ... muthafucka!" he said in his heavy, slow motion drawl, his words reaching me with the velocity of a pearl dropped in honey.

The dope addicts are generally ecstatic about Christmas because with Christmas comes dope. Tiny sleighs bearing the devil's own fruit make their way into C-unit, sealed in plastic wrap, then con-cealed in someone's colon while visiting with a connection.

Another crew of enthusiasts was trying to fix a string of flashing lights, but someone crossed some wires and plugged them in back-ward and blew out the power in all the wall circuits. We called maintenance and they sent over their top-gun inmate repair ace, "Arky Malarky," who announced his arrival with his trademark, "Howze it goin'?"

He was his own self-opening bundle of addled humor, pouring out the corniest jokes imaginable, most dealing with the purported enormity of his reproductive apparatus ("Do yew know what a man with a 12-inch penis has for breakfast? Well, this mornin' I had tomato juice, toast, an' eggs ..."). Tools and rolls of electrical tape hung from his midsection.

"Yew fellers got a little problem here?" he asked. Arky reset the breaker and all was well. Subjected to a pat-down coming out of the kitchen, Arky told the cops, "Watch out when yew come to that 40 pounds of swingin' meat there, boys. That's how I got my hernia, yew know, liftin' that thing all the time," guffaw, chortle, snicker.

❧—❦

PHYSICAL CONDITIONING WORKED ITS WAY into my weekly schedule, and I began to run on the South Yard track and started to mess around with some weight training as well. I read a few books on the subject and began to understand the benefits of aerobic training, something I'd ignored while dealing dope. In the nine months I spent at Terminal Island, I lost the extra 30 pounds of unhappiness I had brought in with me. By the time of my final release, I left over 50 pounds behind me and was in the best physical condition of my life, at least since high school. I later met a fellow at camp who was over 300 pounds on arrival and went out the gate at 160, essentially leaving a whole person behind him.

Running on the track, I found an opportunity to meet Charlie Harris, also a runner. Charlie lived in C-unit too, but his house was at the opposite end of the dorm from me, and it took some time before we sought each other out. Charlie was quiet, bright, and educated, and his social background was similar to my own. He and I stood out from the norm in C-unit like a couple of chunks of coal in a snowbank. Charlie, too, would get transferred to the camp at Lompoc and there eventually become a roommate. We remain in touch to this day.

Shy, a sleepy-looking black man who lived near Charlie in the unit, had just been "rolled up" and put in the "hole" by the prison cops. Charlie filled me in on what had happened:

"He'd been down *eight years*," said Charlie, unbelieving, "and was a week away from release. I think Horace put him up to it."

Horace was a good-looking and smart black man, a smooth operator who also made it habit to run on the track. Someone on the yard owed Shy five dollars, the debt long overdue. "Dat man disrespectin' you, Shy," said Horace, the devil in Shy's ear. "Makin' you look a fool!"

Worked up by Horace, Shy found a makeshift weapon and went looking for the debtor. Upon finding him, he whacked him over the head with a two-by-four, damn near killing him. Shy was charged with felony assault, likely to add several years to his stay.

"A week away after *eight years*," said Charlie, shaking his head in disbelief, "For five lousy dollars ... *eight years!*"

➤-◄

ONCE WEEKLY FOR 12 WEEKS I attended the prison drug rehabilitation program, mandatory for every C-unit inmate. The program leader was Gurucharan ("Feet of Wisdom") Singh, a pleasant and well-meaning Sikh who wore a turban that earned him the inmate designation "Diaperhead." I assume he had some sort of professional degree in psychology. It's hard to imagine a more hapless, unappreciated task than trying to rehabilitate the C-unit addicts. Cooperation from the inmates was nil to nonexistent. The idea of participating in a meditation or yoga exercise was beyond most.

"Can't get into it, man. Ain't my trip."

"Wasn't me robbed that bank, man. Was cocaine robbed that bank! I don't even belong here."

One biker-type started bragging about how tough his chapter of the Gypsy Jokers motorcycle club was, when a black inmate interrupted him: "Dey ain't shit, man. My uncle whupped a buncha dere asses in Portland las' year." And they bristled and foamed at one another, almost coming to blows before Gurucharan could settle them down.

Then we started into a meditation exercise that attempted dialogue with that part of your inner-self that feels drugs are necessary in order for life to function at a satisfactory level. More than half the class rejected the idea of closing their eyes and trying to relax. A discussion on the merits of injecting methamphetamine into a vein while participating in sexual intercourse ensued, and poor Gurucharan's control of the class was tenuous at best.

There was a one-way, see-through mirror in the classroom, and on this day, apparently, an observer behind the mirror. Someone spotted a shadow moving in the mirror and shouted out, "Dere's a dude in dere!" and the class again came to a halt, demanding explanations from Gurucharan, who seemed lost for words. The only time I recall an interest from the class at large involved a meditation during which you were hooked up to a meter that measured your pulse. Some found this a challenging game, trying to control their pulse rate. Otherwise, most found the rehabilitation classes a convenient naptime.

⋗-⋖

BACK IN C-UNIT I ENGAGED in the paperwork required when new inmates arrived. In prison vernacular, inmates don't arrive, they "drive up." The duty officer usually assigned the bunks, but sometimes that, too, would fall to me. Eight new arrivals had driven up one day, and the duty officer, Morales, was assigning them their bunks. One white boy, "Gator Red," tattooed with Confederate flags, swastikas, and "White Power" down the back of his arms, wanted to make sure he didn't get bunked with a "Nigra" person. He was at least polite about it, just wanting Morales to understand such an arrangement would be untenable. Morales looked to me and I pointed to an open bunk above Slammin' Sam, the tattoo artist. Sam was so laid back and gregarious he seemed to get along with everybody in the unit. Then I came across a new recruit who would go through life with no balls and one strike: Owen Juan. From the back of the unit, Clearthur Sims stormed up to Morales, demanding, "Whuffo you put that big, nasty white boy in mah house, Morales? Whuffo?" He was referring to a new inmate called "Moose." It was hard to keep everyone happy.

Morales threw up his hands and told me to make the rest of the assignments. I made Clearthur happy by moving Moose out of his cubical and put him with Owen Juan in an empty spot. Next, a rat-faced little man with scraggly, pageboy hair followed on my heels as I set out to find an empty bunk for him. "Make sure it's with a white man," he said. I headed for "Pig Iron" Biggs' house, but found he already has a bunkmate. Just across the aisle, there was an empty top bunk over a Mexican fellow. Rat-boy flinched at living with a Mexican, but that was the space available unless I moved him in with Clearthur. I don't think the Mexican was thrilled at the prospect of living with rat-boy either.

➤-◄

STARTING WITH THE UNIT MANAGER, then up through the prison bureaucracy, I had been recommended for transfer to a low-security camp setting. The only thing remaining before transfer was my parole hearing. The paroling authority would examine me and my case and history and decide how much of the fifteen years of my sentence I would actually serve before being eligible for parole. The minimum time possible under my sentence was 60 months, about eight of which had been served at this point.

I asked a friend what a parole hearing was like and what I might expect. "Expect to be cross-examined by four or five eggheads in business suits who have the demeanor and attitude of prosecuting attorneys." Four against one didn't seem like a fair contest. I asked my lawyer, Doron Weinberg, to come down and represent me at the hearing, which I thought important. If they were to decide I should do more than the minimum, it could prevent my transfer, and I was very much looking forward to being with my brother. Parole examiners were often the subject of inmate horror stories.

The hearing itself was conducted in a dark and cheerless room without windows or fresh air. Doron warned, "They'll correct you from the record if anything you say disagrees with what they have written in front of them." We were ushered into the dim surroundings, which looked very much like an interrogation room in some TV cop drama. There were only three of them across the table from us, looking exactly as my friend had described.

"You understand that we'll hear from you later, Mr. Weinberg. We want to hear from Mr. Rohrer at this juncture."

"Yes, of course," said Doron.

"Now, Mr. Rohrer, would you care to expand on the causes of your, ah, spurious activities?"

"Yes, sir. Where would you like me to start?"

"Harrumph," he snorted. "It says here that you imported and distributed two hundred, five pounds of cocaine. Would you care to elaborate on that?"

"Begging your pardon, sir, but I think you are confusing the crimes of Mr. Green, the informant, with what is alleged against me."

"Harrumph," again, "... oh yes, I see it here." This harrumph lacked the righteous indignity of the first. He shifted his weight on his chair and rattled the papers in front of him. "Yes, here we are. Now as I understand it, Mr. Green is currently serving a twenty-year sentence, is that correct?"

"No, sir. Mr. Green was released after serving eighteen months, a reward for his cooperation and testimony against me and others." The questioner again retreated into his papers, his ears turning a noticeable crimson. The interrogator to his left took over.

"Can you tell us, Mr. Rohrer, how a man of your background ever got caught up in this sordid business?"

"Yes, sir. A weakness at the time, born of financial need and, I guess, the ease of opportunity. I was without a job and needed to support my family." I looked him right in the eye, buoyed by the simple truth of the statement. "It was a very stupid thing to do," I added for effect.

"Let's go over this, shall we? I see that there are two other defendants in a related case, your brother, who it says here introduced you to this business, and a Mr. Sinclair. Do you know what their sentences are?"

"Yes. My brother was sentenced to six years and Mr. Sinclair, who was Mr. Green's best friend, was sentenced to just one year and a day. With all due respect (a term Doron used at my appeal hearing whenever he wanted to tell the justices they were full of shit), and hoping it doesn't seem presumptuous of me, I would like to suggest that Mr. Green soft-sold Sinclair's role in all of this at my expense." This seemed to get their attention.

"I am not denying my guilt, but I do take issue with the extent of my involvement as alleged by Mr. Green. Mr. Sinclair was sentenced as a minor league participant, even though the only 'hard' evidence in the entire conspiracy was one hundred thousand dollars in cash, a confiscated payment from Mr. Sinclair to Mr. Green, which clearly suggests that Sinclair was something more than a minor league player. What I am alluding to is that Green, in accounting for all of his claims, protected his good friend Sinclair by trivializing his participation, while overloading the claims against me, a more recent acquaintance. As you know, the allegations against me were solely the word of Mr. Green."

"Judging from the outcome, I can sympathize with your feelings," said the suit. "Can you tell us the extent of your involvement?"

And on it went. The hearing ended with Doron defending my character, pointing to mitigating circumstance, and blaming it all on my brother. "A fancy courier," is how Doron put my involvement, "who simply stepped into a going concern in which he had no hand in building. Nor, gentlemen, is it alleged that Mr. Rohrer ever had a hand in importation, as is admitted by other defendants who received far more lenient sentences." I almost broke out laughing at the "fancy courier" remark. But I was certainly willing to wear that jacket for the parole examiners. Doron's ability to bullshit with such credible authority amazed me. A very skilled and competent lawyer, it was a trait he excelled at.

After a brief conference of only two or three minutes, they gave us their decision: 60 months, the minimum allowed. They seemed apologetic it couldn't be less. "The judge saw to that," they said. Doron and I would now set our sights on Judge Schnacke, who we would ask to modify my sentence to a level that would at least approximate my comparative involvement, a process that would take another two years.

At first they wanted to send me to Boron, a federal prison camp in the Mojave Desert, because it was learned that I had a "separatee" at Lompoc. A separatee is an inmate from whom I was to be kept separate, someone upon whom prison authorities feared I might take revenge. It turned out to be the "bicycle bandit," a bank robber who garnered headlines because he used a bicycle as his getaway vehicle and who happened to be in the same jail cell with me for a day or two in San Francisco following my arrest. I actually remembered him, a tall, skinny black kid with a lower lip that looked like a torn pocket. The lawyers called him a "jailhouse yodeler," an informant whose information about someone comes from time together in a jail cell. After I was released on bail, the feds came in and promised him sentencing considerations if he could testify to confessions I had made to him. He was only too happy to give them a statement that essentially said not only did I confess my crimes to him, but those of my brother as well. It goes without saying that I never had a conversation with him. The feds were likely too embarrassed by the patent underhandedness of the scheme and blatant bullshit of his story to consider using it at trial. Tony Serra would have reduced him to roach fodder on the stand.

But here was the same sonofabitch now in the way of me uniting with my brother. We somehow managed to convince prison authorities that, under the circumstances, he should have been separated from my brother as well as me, and they shipped him off to the desert instead of me.

❧❧

I GATHERED UP MY BELONGINGS and said my goodbyes to those I had come to know. Chris was working and I left him a note with a mailing address. I crossed the yard for the last time and had started up the stairs to R & D when Chris came running up behind me. "Amigo! Amigo! I will miss you, my fren'. You are the smartest and best dude I ever bunk with."

I would miss Chris too. As disparate as our backgrounds were, no one ever had a more loyal or fun-loving homeboy as I did with Chris. He wrote me at the camp from a halfway house somewhere, and I sent back a letter that was returned, marked "unable to forward." For years I put off locating him, probably afraid of what I might find. When I did try to locate him, I couldn't find him. I recently engaged the services of someone with experience in locating missing persons. We're still looking.

And off I went, feeling like I had graduated from FCI Terminal Island. My next campus would be the federal prison camp at Lompoc. I never dreamed they would let me out so soon, even if just for a day. I was given ten hours of freedom, a furlough, and it was up to me to arrive at the camp on my own. I got laid on the way, an unsatisfying roll in the hay from a relationship that was mostly dead before I checked in.

BOOK 2

THE BOYS WHO MADE THE NOISE*

* Thanks to Thom Schuyler (writer) and Lacy J. Dalton (artist) for title inspiration from their rock & roll odyssey, "16th Avenue."

1

THE BLUE VELVETS

IT WAS THE FALL OF 1960 AND MY SENIOR YEAR IN HIGH SCHOOL WAS just underway. After a rocky start as a freshman, high school had become a palatable endeavor and social platform. What a glorious time it was, proud and innocent, free from adult responsibility, and still riding the wave of the great music that came out of the fifties—music made by Chuck Berry, Elvis Presley, Jerry Lee Lewis, Fats Domino, the Everly Brothers, Ray Charles, Buddy Holly, Little Richard, and countless others. It would be a few more years before the Beatles arrived, along with the Rolling Stones and other notable British bands, creating a new tsunami of sound that would again change the world. It wasn't long after the school year had started that I began to hear about three sophomores who'd just arrived on campus and who had a band, a rock & roll band. They called themselves "The Blue Velvets," and from what I was hearing, they were damn good, too. I was keenly interested.

My first glimpse of The Blue Velvets came at a school assembly held in the gymnasium. John Fogerty, Stu Cook, and Doug Clifford introducing themselves to the student body with some rock & roll. John played a cheap Silvertone electric guitar from Sears, Doug handled the drums on a limited set, and Stu played acoustic piano, a time before becoming the bassist. They were an all-instrumental trio, no one yet a singer. I was smitten by both their music and their ability to play together as a band. There weren't many real bands among the high schools of the time. The Blue Velvets were the first rock & roll band to come along at El Cerrito High School, wholly contained within the school. There were talented individuals here and there, and maybe what was called a "dance band," but a rock & roll band seemed almost a new idea. On later occasions, John's older brother, Tom, would join them as the vocalist. "Tommy Fogerty & The Blue Velvets" could make the girls squirm and scream. Bobby Freeman's "Do You Wanna Dance" and its B-side, "Big Fat Woman," were anthems that seemed to fit Tom's voice perfectly.

At the assembly, The Blue Velvets came out with a bicycle tire pump and pretended to shoot themselves up with it, as though obligatory to performing, facetiously playing on the widely-held, white adult theme that all musicians who played jazz, blues, or rock & roll were drug addicts. I thought it a stretch and a little corny, but what the hell, I'd forgive them that ... they were just sophomores. Their program set started with an original song they called "Train Time," John bending a treble chord high on the neck of his guitar for a train whistle effect over the lower registers that emulated driving wheels. Their music didn't rely on electronic gadgetry or effects. Simple, pure, and unadorned, it instead came to life through the ability of the musicians to play it, and play it well ... with feeling, of course. They interspersed their original songs with rock & roll standards of the day, and I was swept up by their abilities and the inherent joy in the music they created. John was smooth and fluid on his guitar, even when playing with the urgency required by good rock & roll. Doug's drumming was energetic and reasonably precise, and Stu played the Jerry Lee Lewis and Ray Charles piano numbers that had always captured my ear. I was a piano player too, and I was immediately taken by Stu's grasp and ability on piano. He played a credible version of "Great Balls of Fire," a scorching Jerry Lee Lewis piano classic that has always managed to quicken my pulse. I wanted to meet him, this sophomore who could play circles around me. I wanted to meet all of them.

Over the course of the next couple of months, we gradually became acquainted. Stu, fun-loving and bright, and I formed a bond early on. Doug, not yet known as "Cosmo," was lean, athletic, and outgoing, always with a ready smile and a corny joke. John was the quiet one who seemed to know where he was headed, studying electronics for its applications to what would become his trade. In later years, John would never agree with my praise of The Blue Velvets. He is quoted as saying, "The reason it took us ten years to make it is because when we started out we were terrible." I never heard it that way, my envy and desire to play on their level all-consuming and, I imagine, forgiving. But it would be another ten years before I would actually sit in with them, joining on guitar for rousing and informal off-the-cuff party sessions in bars and hotel rooms when the band was on the road and I was employed as a part of their management team.

One day my dad, an auto dealer, came home and presented me with an authentic early model Fender electric guitar he'd found in the trunk of an automobile. I didn't know how esteemed a guitar it was, or how to play it. When Stu saw it, he let me know it was indeed a treasure. I'd heard that John worked a paper route for months in order to buy the Sears Silvertone, a Fender beyond his means at the time. I'd loan the Fender to John or Stu whenever they wanted it. Stu had already started teaching me songs on the piano, and he and I were about to embark on learning our early guitar chords and licks during a school-sponsored snow trip to the Sierras. We stayed indoors for the most part, eschewing the slopes for a bottle of brandy and a guitar. Later in the spring, we all went to Stinson Beach on the Marin County coast for a beer and beach party, celebrating music and the pristine weather. There on the beach John taught me to play a song he'd written called "Rockin' Devil," an A minor, E7, D minor chord arrangement with a slinky single-note arpeggio sounding like it came from a Latino offshoot of Link Wray's "Rumble." I thought it was way fucking cool. Still do.

Sometime during this year I was asked by the "Commissioner of Entertainment," a student body designation, to play a piano number at an all-student talent assembly. I could play pretty well, as long as I was playing by myself, following only my rules. I figured I would play my standard boogie-woogie stuff, but then one day I heard John, adept on piano as well as guitar, play Fats Domino's "The Fat Man," a powerful and moving piano-featured New Orleans rock & roll number first released in 1949. It was Fats' first big hit, in my book one of the first great rock & roll records ever. John showed me how the song was put together, the licks and trills, and I worked on it for about a week, figuring I was as ready as I'd ever be.

On the eve of the assembly, I was playing in a weeknight basketball league when I caught a hard elbow right in the mouth. The blow shattered a porcelain cap that had been installed on a front tooth after I'd broken it diving into a pool with a shallow bottom. My lip was bloodied and the tooth reactive, but worse, when I looked in the mirror, I saw a gap-toothed hillbilly with a fat lip looking back at me. There was no way I would present myself at school, let alone at an assembly, looking like that. I called John and persuaded him to take my place at the assembly. He could play "The Fat Man" while I sat in the dental chair. He did and I did and all turned out well, although Stu told me that John, unrehearsed, struggled with the song, swearing under his breath during the performance, but laughing his way through it anyway.

Of all the school years, this is the one I remember most fondly. As admired friends, The Blue Velvets opened up a whole new world of music for me. They were underclassmen, several years my junior, but we invited each other into the socially disparate worlds we inhabited. In the not too distant future, the cultural dividing line in the America of the mid-sixties would be defined by those of our generation. The war in Vietnam, racial upheaval, drugs, and social protest were the topics that would fuel the division, the arrival and metamorphosis of the Beatles, Bob Dylan, and a host of other bands playing their parts as well. The cultural division pulled at me from both sides, but it was The Blue Velvets who provided my link to the youthful side of our generation. Even then, I could almost sense something great would happen for these guys.

As graduation neared, a gala celebration party took place at my parents' home, the music of course provided by The Blue Velvets. Mom and Dad were very cool about not being visible that night. Mom, too, was a great music fan. She strolled in at the end of the evening, the band finished for the night, but she asked John to play a song for her. He played her a jazzy solo guitar version of "Up a Lazy River," a hit song from her generation that John probably learned from his mother. Like many who would aspire to greatness, John's musical sophistication and special talents were apparent early on. Even so, who then could have guessed that The Blue Velvets would become Creedence Clearwater Revival, the boys who made the noise heard the wide world over?

❖❖

THE BLUE VELVETS REMAINED TOGETHER as companions and a band throughout high school, and they soon included John's older brother, Tom. Tom had graduated from a Catholic high school in Berkeley and the others were still in high school when they released a record or two as "Tommy Fogerty & The Blue Velvets," as well as providing studio backup for a few others. Following high school, they found themselves contracted to a small, local jazz-oriented label, Fantasy Records, for whom they began to record as "The Golliwogs." The name was essentially pushed on them by the label, a lame attempt, I think, to identify with the British musical invasion of the mid-sixties. Tom and John started writing songs as "Toby Green" and "Rann Wild," stage names, as though getting ready for

Hollywood. Or maybe an attempt to take attentions away from "Golliwogs," a name none favored.

While I was attending college classes, I would steer them into frat and party gigs. My connection to the automobile business allowed me to help them keep their cars running, a used tire here, some mechanical repairs there. Eventually they picked up a weekly gig at the Monkey Inn in Berkeley, a loose and dingy beer joint void of any rules governing decorum. John had come around to the idea that he possessed vocal talent and their music began to take wing. A couple of years later, when they got their first big pay-checks, John, Stu, and Doug each came and bought a new Peugeot from me, an honest vehicle but maybe not what you'd picture a rock & roll star to be driving. It was their way to say thanks for past favors. More thanks were on the way.

2

A NEW NAME

O N CHRISTMAS EVE 1967 JOHN ANNOUNCED TO THE OTHERS, "CREE-
dence Clearwater Revival," a new name for the band. Like
his songs that were to follow, the name was a product of John's
remarkable imagination and ability to recognize idiomatic phrase
and expression that worked. He had actually known someone
who claimed his name was "Creedence," odd spelling and all. He
pointed to a beer commercial as the inspiration for "Clearwater,"
and "Revival" was simply a part of his vocabulary, also used in those
days for describing the rock & roll "revival" tours going around the
country featuring iconic artists from the fifties. "Revival" was a
good fit for the band, too, as their music seemed to revive a more
traditional form of rock & roll in the face of all the psychedelic
sounds coming out of San Francisco. "CCR" and just plain "Creedence," their namesake abbreviations, would stick to them as well.
John had developed his gifts as a musician and a poet, the right
words, musical passage, and cadence called to him like a homing
beacon. Three short years after John's announcement, *Billboard
Magazine*, the bible of the record business, would place them at
the head of the class, 1970's number one album selling group in
the world, ahead of the Beatles, the Stones, and whoever else happened to be around at the time.

The year 1968 was a year of change for the band, and for me as well. Mom was done with the automobile business and decided she would move to Maui. I stayed behind with the business, but I had to move it; the long-held real estate had been sold to finance her new life in the islands. It was the beginning of the end for Howard's Motor Sales, the business Dad had started just before World War II.

As 1968 found me in a new locale and circumstance, it also found the band setting out with their new name and renewed intention. They had spent a great deal of time and energy in prior years trying to promote The Golliwogs, even though they cringed at the name. They'd even had a "regional" hit that broke into the top ten in the Sacramento area, but real reward eluded them. It was hard work, playing to tough barroom crowds up and down California's central valleys and being paid very little money. Following the Monterey Pop Festival and the rise of the psychedelic-era bands, they set their sights on San Francisco, recognizing the emergence of a new epoch in popular music. They knew that initial reward would remain modest, but they also knew they were a good band and getting better.

They made it a habit to study the music business from every angle. They knew first the music had to be worthy, then to look for opportunity to present it to people who could make a difference, often a result of luck and circumstance. They knew, too, that when opportunity knocked, you answered the door, and when it opened, you got your foot in there. None knew this better than John. The circumstance was a smoky little club in San Francisco where they had begun playing regularly for very little money. Luck included the opportunity to play their music for striking disc jockeys just down the street at radio station KMPX.

⇾-⇽

PROGRESSIVE FREE-FORM RADIO ("UNDERGROUND RADIO") was brand new and largely credited to former AM pop-station disc jockey "Big Daddy" Tom Donahue, who set up shop at KMPX, an FM station in San Francisco formerly devoted to foreign language broadcast. I knew this station first as a listener (after Donahue arrived), then as an advertiser while in the auto business. The station's sales representative, Milan Melvin, walked into my office one day, looking like a well-appointed hippie: shoulder length hair, bell-bottom trousers, a leather vest, and an array of hand-wrought silver and jade jewelry. I admired this hip and confident salesman who, in the impassioned and socially divided era of the Vietnam War, made cold sales calls in a conservative business environment, leaving little doubt as to which side of the divide he favored. I bought some advertising from him, and he later repaid the favor, sending Joan Baez and her then husband, David Harris, to buy a new Peugeot from me.

I was invited to sit in on a couple of shows with Donahue and Milan, and I invited my pal Sheldon to come along with me. Donahue got things rolling by rolling then passing a cigar-sized joint around the broadcast booth. Sheldon and I sat transfixed while Donahue ran the show with his extraordinarily cool persona, addressing the audience with his deep, radio-perfect voice. He played the coolest music of the day, venturing into folky-blues with Lightnin' Hopkins and Ramblin' Jack Elliott, the best of current rock & roll with Van Morrison, the Beatles and Stones, the psychedelic rock of Jimi Hendrix, and the emerging San Francisco bands. He played mostly album cuts that often extended well beyond the three-minute hallmark of AM hits, which were rarely played. He never lost his place or lapsed into the role of a clumsy stoner, as though the joint just made him normal. This was unheard of radio at the time, a format that would soon take the country by storm.

❧❦

I LATER RAN INTO MILAN at the San Francisco International Auto Show with a then mostly- unknown Janis Joplin on his arm. I had heard her music from a charming and informal tape played on

KMPX, Janis singing a blues number accompanied by Jorma Kau-
konen on guitar and someone in the background on a typewriter,
pecking away in time with the song. I would next encounter Janis
late in the summer of 1970, backstage at a gala music event at
Shea Stadium in New York where Creedence, near the pinnacle of
their popularity and power, would close the show. Janis presented
a much sadder picture than the vibrant, smiling lady I'd met with
Milan. Obviously troubled, she would be dead a month later, following only by days the death of Jimi Hendrix.

While Creedence was on tour the following summer, a fragile
Jim Morrison spent an evening with the band and a few of us at
our hotel in Miami. Band members were staying in an ostentatious
three-bedroom penthouse suite named for Frank Sinatra, complete
with a spiral staircase, a pool table, and a grand piano. Sitting at
the piano with Jim, he sang and played for me a sloppy version of
a new song he had written, "She Wore Yellow Be-bops in Her Hair."
With each verse the color of the be-bops would change. He was
inebriated and stoned, on what I'm not sure, but even so, I found
him warm and personable, even if requiring some patience. But he,
too, would be dead within a month. These were times of a delicate
mortality in the rock & roll business.

❧❦

MARCH OF 1968 FOUND KMPX under a cloud of dissent and opposing
cultural views between the station owner and station workers and
disc jockeys. Donahue had started programming a station in Los
Angeles, in addition to KMPX, and sometimes missed his show.
The station owner decided he had had enough of this easygoing
"hippie chaos" at his station and ordered a dress code for everyone
working there. Donahue resigned. Most of the remaining workers
and disc jockeys went on strike, supporting Donahue. During this
initial walkout, someone got word to Creedence, playing nearby

at a little club called Dino-Carlo. They set up and played for the strikers in front of the station.

CCR and other San Francisco bands would play support benefits for the strikers in the weeks that followed. The strike came to an end in May, when Donahue and other KMPX stalwarts moved themselves and their progressive free-form format to another San Francisco FM station, KSAN, where the format would blossom and flourish for years to come, the flagship station for underground radio.

Whether or not the band knew it at the time, the KMPX strike, followed by the new KSAN, amounted to their first significant and fortuitous break. In the same week KSAN began broadcasting in its new format, the band finished recording their first album, the self-titled *Creedence Clearwater Revival,* and they took a pre-release copy to the disc jockeys they had met during the strike. KSAN played the entire album for weeks, elevating CCR in the hierarchy of the San Francisco bands. The first single release from the album, "Suzie Q.," a remake of a fifties hit, would catch fire across the country. The proverbial door of success had started to open for them. At a celebration dinner, Fantasy presented the band with a half-gold record when the sales of "Suzie Q." reached the half-million mark. Anticipations were soaring, for the band and for the label, whose modest jazz-oriented market share would soon expand beyond anything they could have seen coming.

Against the band's wishes, Fantasy released a second single, "I Put a Spell on You," another cover song, but it didn't fare nearly as well as the first. The eight-and-a-half minute "Suzie Q." from the album had been edited into parts one and two for single release and worked well as a single with its catchy guitar riff. "I Put a Spell on You" was a powerful song and the band created an imaginative arrangement, but it lacked the hook required of a top 10 single. The band seemed to know this and lived by the credo, "You're only as good as your last record," in this case meaning their last single. To them that meant they had already peaked, in danger of becoming a "one-hit wonder." But with the blossoming of a new era in radio, also came the evolution and blooming of John Fogerty as a songwriter and leader of a potent band that was on the verge of taking the country and the world by storm.

3

THE GOLDEN YEARS, 1969 & 1970

A NY CHANCE OF BECOMING A ONE-HIT BAND WAS PUT TO REST AT THE start of the new year with the single release "Proud Mary" (January) and the album *Bayou Country* (February). The proverbial door would now swing wide open, and the powerful reality of their music encased the proverbial foot in a concrete boot. Their credibility would swell with each new release. In a remarkably short period of time they released new singles "Bad Moon Rising" (April) and "Green River" (July), which became the title track for their third album (September). The single releases all had very strong B-sides, inviting radio to simply turn them over after the A-side had run its course. "Born on the Bayou," "Lodi," and "Commotion" all reached the airways as if A-sides, further identifying the band. They were presented to a national TV audience on shows like *Ed Sullivan* and *Johnny Cash*. By summer's end, the whole country knew of Creedence Clearwater Revival and its energetic leader with the pageboy haircut, plaid shirt, powerful voice, cutting guitar, and who wrote songs with the pen of a bard. Before the year was done, "Down on the Corner" (October), a joyous ode to street corner jug bands, backed by the powerful protest of "Fortunate Son," and the album on which they would appear, *Willy and the Poorboys* (December), would also join 1969's remarkable march of success.

Some thought the habit of single releases with strong B-sides was wasting opportunity for more single releases, but the band prided themselves in not having "throwaway" B-sides. Early releases by Elvis Presley served as the pioneer in two-sided hits and the band liked that idea. New technologies have long since replaced the beloved 45 rpm single, doing away with B-sides and the sometimes cool and personal sleeve, like so much else, gone with the winds of progress. Digital singles are released today, but personally, I cannot abide singles without a B-side.

AT SUMMER'S END 1969, I was having second thoughts about the automobile business, the new town I had located to, and the partners I had taken on in the process. It was during this time, mulling my future in the auto business, that Doug turned a little restless in his Peugeot. I got him a new Porsche from a local dealer, also telling him of my growing disaffection with the automobile business. Two days later, John Fogerty was on the phone with the invitation of a lifetime, the opportunity to work with cherished and respected friends who were making considerable hay in the music business.

The best salesmen at the auto dealership were my brother Robbin and my pal Sheldon. I'd been gone only days when my partners fired both of them. I stormed out to the dealership to address this indignity, only to learn they had been discovered smoking a joint on the job, taking the wind out of my protest. I nonetheless tried to convince the partners that a little pot was a small price to pay for the excellence they offered, but they remained outraged at the affront, insisting they would have nothing to do with drug addicts. I soon arranged a buyout of my interest, and the automobile business I had grown up in was forever gone from my life.

CCR HEADQUARTERS WAS IN THE commercial and light-industrial section of West Berkeley, a warehouse on 5th Street, just off Gilman
Avenue. Ordinary looking and wedged in among others just like it,
it had a large, drive-through, roll-up door, along with a regular entry
door from the sidewalk. Nothing on the outside hinted at what
went on inside. It became known, appropriately, as the "Factory."
Inside there was a carpeted rehearsal space against the back wall,
sectioned off from everything else with heavy, ceiling-length blue
velvet drapery, a wink to the band's former name. It left plenty of
room for inside parking, concert equipment, a four-ton truck, and
a makeshift basketball court. A Ping-Pong table, Coke machine,
and coffee counter were also on the ground floor, under a mezzanine. Road manager Bruce Young had a small office just inside
the sidewalk entrance. A couple of bathrooms stood by themselves
against an opposite wall, looking like an afterthought. The road
crew painted the inside of the bathrooms a bright, "Chinese" red,
and when you went in and shut the door, it was as though you
had just entered a giant artery. When the band wasn't recording or
traveling, they kept to a regular rehearsal schedule. When not otherwise engaged in road duties, all of us worked the usual workweek,
Monday through Friday.

My office was up a wooden stairway on the mezzanine floor.
There was plenty of space up there as a central gathering, storage,
and meeting place. It was an austere environment, void of windows
or color, and I immediately set about trying to create a funky cheer
in the place, with posters on the walls, some rugs on the floor, and
whatever knickknacks seemed like they belonged. There was also
a pool table, a slot machine, and a jukebox that played 78 rpm
records with a needle that looked like a finishing nail. I brought in
an old desk and a filing cabinet I had acquired from my days in the
auto business, and there were a couple of ragged but comfortable
sofas and a central meeting table. I had a vintage IBM electric
typewriter, temperamental but serviceable, on which I'd type press
releases, bios, concert schedules, and band related correspondence.

Bruce Young, Ray Francois, and Bruce Koutz, the hardworking road crew, were on the payroll when I arrived, ready for anything, always aiming to please. John and Tom's youngest brother, Bob, (there were five Fogerty brothers) was just 17 and still growing up. John had assumed a caring, guardian-like relationship with Bob, as though overseeing his welfare and providing him with direction in life. He was learning photography and would function as the staff photographer, also available for odd jobs as they came up. I guess it was fitting that, almost eight years later, Bob would essentially replace me as John's aide and support person, seeing to John's business and personal needs. Everyone got along well with everyone else, and we all had a common purpose: support the band however asked, however possible.

I arrived in my new position feeling the wonderful freedom of casual dress (blue jeans, tennis shoes, etc.) after what felt like a lifetime of neckties, slacks, sport jackets, loafers, and the like. I landed right in the middle of their phenomenal explosion onto the world music scene, just on the heels of their third album, *Green River*. I knew music only as I enjoyed it. I knew next to nothing about the business of music. John's easygoing attitude and apparent confidence in me helped put me at ease, "Just stay loose and relax," he told me. "You'll learn like we have, just by doing." Stu and Doug welcomed me with warm smiles and open arms; Tom too, although I'd never had the personal relationship with Tom that I had with the others. I of course wanted to jump right in with sleeves rolled up, ready to please my new employers, if only I had an inkling of where to start. I was much too nervous to simply start where we all do, at the beginning.

When the band wasn't on the road or recording, an almost constant stream of pure musical joy flowed like a river from the back of the Factory. What a thrilling delight it was, listening to them play together almost daily. Sometimes they'd experiment, learning new songs or trying out a new style, sometimes cramming hard for a recording session, and sometimes they'd just mess around, playing only for themselves. Now and then they'd take one of their songs and play it in a different genre. Hearing "Lodi" turned from its pseudo-country roots into a slow and powerful 12-bar blues/rock number made me think they should record it again.

It was clear John was in charge of this operation and that he had everyone's unqualified support and respect. He beamed with an ease and confidence I'd never before seen in him. There was little doubt that the overwhelming success of the band and his own original compositions provided everything needed to frame his poise. These were magical times for Creedence and everyone around them.

>-<

As a band, they worked together on becoming a unified force as a single entity and, individually, on their musical skills. John poured his energies into their music, continuing his string of hit songs, arguably the best of his career. CCR became champions of the hit single, sending one brilliant song after another to the top of the charts for over two years, all of them products of John's active imagination and songwriting skills. He wrote convincingly of the Southern delta, rivers, and bayous, places he'd never been. Other musicians from Memphis or southern parts of the country were disbelieving and skeptical at learning Creedence was made up of California boys from El Cerrito. "Where the hell's El Cerrito?" said most. Sensitive about being from some small-time town, they adopted Berkeley as their announced home base, as indeed it had become.

They had never played in Lodi, but John liked the sound of the name. The song dissed the town with its "Stuck in Lodi again" refrain, offending Lodi's Chamber of Commerce, which sent us some of their "I Like Lodi" buttons. He imagined the phantasmagorical in "Lookin' Out My Back Door" while remembering a childhood book. Memories of family outings as a young boy produced one of his finest, most image-laden songs, "Green River."

The fierce notes John played on "Green River" still ring to me as some of his finest and most original guitar work.

Songwriting was a solitary undertaking for John, and he worked hard to assemble his songs with integrity and intelligent lyrics. He was also an acute observer of life around him. He kept abreast of world events and had his finger on the country's pulse. In one of his most fun and topical songs, "It Came Out of the Sky," he managed to work in the national news team of Walter Cronkite and Eric Sevareid, the White House, the Vatican, Spiro Agnew, and Ronald Reagan, while at the same time inventing an alter ego, "Jody," a Midwestern farm boy from Moline (Illinois) who would also appear in some of his later work. Like Lodi, Moline was a name that called to John's ear. Towns with names like those might have had famous gunslingers roaming their streets, the Lodi Kid or Moline "Dead-eye" Odom. Many of his songs were politically motivated, some scathing, those in particular inspired by Richard Nixon and the war in Vietnam. His clever use of political symbolism in "Who'll Stop the Rain" makes us wonder if we'll ever rise above the political bullshit that runs our county. Forty years later it's clearly apparent we haven't come close. His ominous "Run Through the Jungle" became anthem-like for many of those fighting in Vietnam.

John was (and is) as American as apple pie or baseball. It came as no surprise to me when he later wrote and performed a new anthem that would be adopted by Major League Baseball, "Centerfield," the song even embraced at the Baseball Hall of Fame. Nor was it any surprise to me that George W. Bush would replace Richard Nixon as a target for his acid pen.

❖❖

CREEDENCE AND THE FACTORY OPERATED like a business, serious about our work, welcoming time to play, but the two were always separate. Drugs and alcohol were never a part of our daily focus on band matters. As a group, we played a lot of sports. Basketball at the Factory and sometimes touch football in Tilden Park with "Clover," a Marin County band that once featured John McFee and Huey Lewis. We also had a softball team that played in an organized Richmond athletic league.

I wasn't with the band when they performed at Woodstock, that event happening before I came to work for them. I knew they had declined invitation to be a part of the first Woodstock film, and I also knew that John, perhaps the others too, wasn't happy with their performance there. According to the stories I heard, the Grateful Dead had played one of its extended, two-hour-plus sets that started about midnight. Then Creedence had to follow them in the wee hours of the morning and try to wake everyone up. A band feeds off and responds to its audience. If half of them are unconscious, much of it likely drug induced, it can take all the fun out of performing. Had they not been booked somewhere else the following evening, their performance would likely have been postponed.

Booker T. & the MG's arrived at the Factory in January of 1970 to be a part of CCR's first big "homecoming" concert at the Oakland Coliseum. It was time for the Bay Area to celebrate the prodigal sons who had landed with such huge impact on the world stage. The concert and events leading up to it were to be filmed for a TV special, and the band had invited Booker T. & the MG's to be their special guests. They hadn't met before, but Creedence, to a man, lauded their musical sophistication and prowess. Like Creedence, they were a quartet, and like The Blue Velvets, they were exclusively an instrumental band. They were also the "house band" for Stax Records in Memphis, backing up a host of legendary R&B performers. The individuals in each band seemed to flow together easily, sharing a respect for each other and the music they produced. MG bassist, "Duck" Dunn, especially, would become a close friend. After initial introductions and putting one another at ease, they joined together in a legendary jam session that went into the early morning hours.

━━❖━━

THE FIRST YEAR I WORKED with Creedence was for me the most glorious ever, and I think it was for the band too. As a musical brotherhood, they just got tighter and more adventurous as success buoyed their confidence. I employed my sister, Mary, as my secretary to help me hold down the office and deal with the fan club. We put out a quarterly newsletter, "The Fifth Street Flash," largely Mary's brainchild, named for the Factory address. John was a cornucopia of great music that seemed to spill out of him at will. He was able to call upon the spark within him, coming up with his timeless, radio-perfect songs, one after another whenever the prior release had run its initial course. Everything the band did was done well, every step felt as though in the right direction, each plateau was scaled with precision, and the rewards poured down like silver. Everywhere they went they were greeted like royalty. The exciting times and sense of accomplishment felt like a dream come true.

Their phenomenal success continued through 1970 with the single releases "Travelin' Band"/"Who'll Stop the Rain" (January), "Up Around the Bend"/"Run Through the Jungle" (April), "Lookin' Out my Backdoor"/"Long as I can See the Light" (August), and the album, *Cosmo's Factory* (July), their biggest ever. Ending the year, their last album as a quartet, *Pendulum*, was released in December. There had also been a very successful tour of Europe in April. Even though a Grammy was never to be bestowed upon them, the music of Creedence Clearwater Revival had found extraordinary acceptance and place throughout the entire world, their walls soon covered with gold and platinum records.

They realized all of this by themselves, maintaining an honest approach to their music and their persona in a business known for its ruthlessness. They did it without lawyers or managers telling them what to do, without the marketing machinery of a major label. Theirs was an unheard of ascent, guided by a shared vision of what they perceived as the right thing to do, supported by John's uncanny grasp of the music and sense of the industry that sold it.

❧

I FUNCTIONED MOSTLY AS THE "front man," representing the band to the press and public. But first I was a pal, a reliable confidant who could be trusted to do what was asked of me. Much of my job consisted of the mechanics of promotion, press relations, and touring duties. Later, when they could own their own songs, I started to administer publishing as well. Up to that point, Fantasy Records, through its publishing arm, Jondora, owned all of John's songs, earning millions in publishing royalties and becoming by itself a tremendous asset value through copyright ownership, while John was paid as a songwriter.

That's the way it was for many in the music business, trusting newcomers strapped to unconscionable contracts for years by greedy labels. John Fogerty would never forgive Fantasy head Saul Zaentz for enforcing their contract and taking the lion's share when the boat came in. Saul was working for Fantasy when he and a group of investors purchased the label, essentially inheriting the band. In the early days there seemed to be an assumption that Saul, too, was a member of the same brotherhood as the band and would "tear up the contract" in the event of financial success. Though certain concessions were offered, some accepted, John became increasingly embittered with Saul and the label. Saul then used his financial fortunes as a springboard to launch his stellar career in the film industry.

For what it's worth, Chuck Berry, Buddy Holly, the Beatles, and countless others didn't (initially) own their songs either, and were signed to similar contracts, penned by lawyers largely concerned with the rights of labels. Publishers once functioned as all important intermediaries for songwriters, placing their songs with artists and labels who would turn them into hits, then collecting and dividing royalties. When the songwriters themselves were the ones responsible for the success and popularity of a song, the publisher then served mostly as a collection agency, but still collected the publisher's traditional share.

Bruce Young was my counterpart with Creedence, a wonderfully warm and selfless man Stu and Doug had befriended at college. Bruce was the road manager, in charge of tour arrangements and overseeing the road and stage crew. He exuded integrity and was working for them from the beginning. For Bruce the band came first. He also served as confidant and go-between for legal and financial matters as well, roles I would come to share with him as my familiarity with band matters increased.

Creedence never had a manager other than themselves. Bruce and I were like "executive assistants." Bruce handled the road and tour duties while I traveled with the band and handled hotels, the press, and diplomacy. John was in charge during their climb to the top of the mountain, supported by the others. Even when courted by the likes of Bill Graham, Tom Donahue, and Allen Klein, they elected to keep their autonomy. Their independent resilience in the face of Bill Graham's magnetic and forceful personality was impressive. Klein, a smart man, initially an accountant, didn't trust the numbers bandied about in the press. He went to the source, the plants that pressed the records, to see for himself how many records Creedence was selling, far more than he had imagined. But the band wasn't interested in his proposals. Though band members would later anguish over their lack of a "real" manager, there wasn't any thought of changing course at this point in their career.

⇥·⇤

BEATLES ENVY MAY HAVE PLAYED a hidden role in the destruction of CCR. The world knew and embraced each Beatle individually, in addition to acknowledging the immense talent of Lennon and McCartney, and if lesser so, George Harrison. Ringo was as lovable as they come, his off-key voice charming and perfect for the songs he'd sing. If any group provided a mold, it was the Beatles. The Monkees also featured four individuals, but were created as a group for a TV show, attempting to establish and cash in on a Beatle-like popularity. The Monkees get more respect today than when they first appeared.

We were in London in April of 1970, largely unaware of the drama surrounding the Apollo 13 mission, but when the Beatles announced their disbandment the news reached us immediately. In terms of record sales, CCR probably was the top group on the planet at the time, but that was a far cry from assuming the Beatles' mantle, even though Tom seemed to think that would be their next step. Creedence, too, had wanted to achieve an individual recognition, and it was part of my job to consciously represent them in that light. In spite of his enormous talent, John Fogerty's personality was not particularly extroverted and the role of media hero wasn't a good fit for him. Instead, he quietly, soberly churned out his great music. It was up to the others to radiate a presence as best they could, but it never seemed to penetrate beyond hardcore Creedence fans, of which there were many.

They were always at their best as a band, the four of them creating a fifth entity, and that's where they really shined, John's overweighted contributions notwithstanding. They were like a hot ball team, graced with one-mindedness and momentum, each supporting the other, wining all their games, even if the statistics favored one player. It never appeared to me that John was out to grab the spotlight, but it couldn't help but be directed at him. Creedence, together, would rise to the top, but they would not become the cultural phenomenon the Beatles were, in spite of their huge audience.

The culture Creedence represented existed before they did and could be found, for example, in John's trademark plaid flannel shirts and the broad demographics of their audience and appeal, grade school to grandparents. It could also be found in the imaginative, barefoot-boy lyrics in many of their songs. Even though their first album purposely contained some audio psychedelia, their image and music was unlike the other San Francisco bands. Lyrically, John's songs bring to my mind American originals like Woody Guthrie and Stephen Foster. In many ways Creedence Clearwater Revival represented America's heartland, and their subtle-but-deep songs and understated-but-powerful productions captured multiple generations. Their music was refreshingly real, all of it produced and performed by only them, void of any overt musical bullshit. It jumped out of a radio speaker with undeniable life and energy.

But other than great songs and music, Creedence didn't really bring anything new to the table, unless maybe it was their own brand of integrity. They didn't attempt to sell themselves with the flashy, dumbed-down imagery seemingly required by many rock bands. What Creedence excelled at was reminding Americans from whence they had come, especially in the face of the revolutionary and psychedelic-tinged music of the era. Their public behavior wasn't nearly shocking enough for the press to pay attention to. I always thought being who and what they were was good enough, one of the best and most honest rock & roll bands ever. Still, there was this push to become something else. Push too hard and you might break it.

4

COMING UNDONE, 1971–1973

A S THEY APPROACHED THE END OF THEIR MOST SUCCESSFUL YEAR, THERE came a shift in philosophy. Suddenly, there seemed to be multiple hands on the tiller when it came to guiding the band. They tried on a bit of Hollywood, retaining the powerhouse public relations firm Rogers & Cowan, who would attempt to make them into something other than what they were. It was among several questionable moves the band adopted at the time to help establish CCR at the top of the heap, somehow overlooking the fact that they had already arrived on their own. There was a crappy book, *Inside Creedence*, written by John Hallowell. He may have been a fine writer for articles in *Life* magazine and the *Los Angeles Times*, but the book was transparent, forced, and just plain silly. This was followed by what the band came to refer to as the "Night of the Generals," a gala press junket conceived by Rogers & Cowan for which we flew in prestigious rock journalists from all over the country. We put them up at Berkeley's Claremont Hotel and wined and dined them at the Factory. We would show them a hell of a good time, along with a mini-concert/performance and the new CCR release, *Pendulum*. It contained several fine songs but was never my favorite Creedence record, lacking the rootsy feel of earlier releases. And the cover portrayed four individuals looking intense and sullen, neither happy nor inviting.

One notable member of the elite press corps, a New York critic and blue-ribbon jerk, took full advantage of all the free perks only to write whiny, self-centered articles that largely ignored the music and bitched about the slightly less than royal treatment received at the hands of these West Coast upstarts. He was an elitist, his nose in the air, somehow blessing himself with self-importance and a snob-like musical knowledge he considered beyond the reach and understanding common folk like you or me. I met him earlier that summer at Shea Stadium in New York, where he was parading around backstage with Paul Simon, clinging to Simon like a groupie. I thought then he could kiss my ass.

Our best friend in the press was Bob Hilburn of the *LA Times*. He enjoyed and respected the band and wrote intelligently about them, but he was first a humble and caring human being who seemed to rise above the hype and bright lights, his company always a pleasure. Also a good friend was John Wasserman of the *San Francisco Chronicle*, an exquisite writer with wit and a keen sense of music. Both Hilburn and Wasserman spent time with Creedence in Europe. Following in Wasserman's footsteps, Joel Selvin was also a reliable friend with whom I enjoyed trading musical stories.

None of the out of character moves by the band amounted to anything that couldn't have been overcome, but sadly, tragically, the weight of all the bullshit that comes with fame in the music business seemed to crush the life out of Creedence Clearwater Revival, the entity that was the fifth member of the band. I think John could have resurrected what had been, but in the end, he chose to do otherwise.

✦-✦

IT WAS ANOTHER NIGHT FILLED with generals, among them Tom Donahue, on hand at the Factory for a screening of a TV special filmed by the National General Corporation. He was actually in the film, the master of ceremonies at the band's big homecoming concert at the Oakland Coliseum. It was an easy night for me and the band, no performance, no press to deal with, and no particular business to be conducted. Even good ol' Sheldon was there, and we had some cocaine. At one point during the evening, I asked Donahue if he'd like to join us for a hit of coke. That wasn't a usual habit or practice, but it was a casual night and I figured Donahue probably a fancier. Cocaine was a relatively new drug on the scene, at least as I knew it, following on the heels of pot and the psychedelic drugs. Sometimes people just gave it to me, an offering and symbol of their hipness and cool. My offer to Donahue of course proclaimed my own cool. Then, for some odd and uncool reason, I felt the need to explain to Donahue that we weren't going to inject the cocaine with a needle, a method I'd only heard about, rather, we would sniff it, as though this might be a new experience for him. He smiled his huge Cheshire Cat smile at me and said, "My man, you are talking to the original Hoover," whereupon he produced from his vest pocket a miniature upright vacuum cleaner cast in metal and used it to snort up several lines of the offered blow. I could sometimes wear my uncool like a badge.

⯈-⯇

AT SOME POINT LEADING UP to the "new" Creedence, there had been a meeting among band members where John's control of the music and direction was challenged by the others. I believe Tom, maybe recalling the days of Tommy Fogerty & The Blue Velvets, had a personal need to establish himself outside of the spotlight occupied by his younger brother and was probably leading the charge. I assume Stu and Doug went along with the idea. In light of the effort to establish individual recognition, Tom, Stu, and Doug certainly had a point: How were they to establish themselves as something other than John's backup band unless they, too, at least now and then, were included as a focal point in the band's music? But it would not be an easy road to introduce other composers and singers into the stellar track record John had established. He apparently said, okay, we'll be a democracy, but I don't believe his heart was ever into it. I think John was bitter about this challenge to his leadership and its remarkable success, the fruits of which were shared with all of them.

In my view, therein lies the tragedy that befell Creedence Clearwater Revival, setting brother against brother, friend against friend. I was not a part of these discussions between band members and comment only on what I saw happening and the result. It had been "all for one" up to that point, but the "one for all" seemed to turn up missing. There didn't appear to be any give and take, no attempt at genuine compromise. John's idea of democracy was that each member would contribute a like amount, regardless of resource or ability. The challenge to his control and leadership may have represented a wound to him, and his response was perhaps juvenile-like, as though to say, "Okay, but I'm taking my toys home with me, you guys bring your own." Instead of a workable compromise, they eventually built brick walls between themselves, becoming Congress-like in their inability to achieve the best workable solution.

After succeeding in the push for new direction, Tom then shortly announced he was leaving the band. His thinking in this regard will always be a mystery to me. When Tom left, everyone had sugarcoated comments and statements for the press, "we're all still friends" and other such bullshit, but there was a lot left unsaid that would fester and come to the surface in later years. I thought at the time the band might invite Duck Dunn to be Tom's replacement. We all knew and liked Duck, and he was one of the best bassists in the business. It would be an easy transition for Stu to move to rhythm guitar. He was, after all, originally the piano player. To my surprise, they elected to go on as a trio, once again becoming The Blue Velvets from their high school years, now disguised as CCR. As good as they were as a trio, tight and together as any band, I felt their live performance suffered from the loss of the rhythm guitar and Tom's vocal support, sounding just a little thinner.

When they again got around to recording, John apparently implemented his "democracy" agenda, requiring Stu and Doug to come up with equal portions of the project. The band members themselves have opposing views on what happened around *Mardi Gras*, the album produced by CCR as a trio. I don't think either Stu or Doug welcomed their roles in this project. John, though, claims it was their choice and that when he would have objections about a track, democracy would be turned against him, two to one. The finger pointing goes on decades later. There were cracks in the facade before *Mardi Gras*, but after extensive touring as a trio, I thought they had mostly mended, and for a while, I again recognized the close personal camaraderie the three of them had shared in earlier years. The democracy agenda caught me by surprise. Stu and Doug would later claim John was intentionally seeking an end to the band.

Mardi Gras became the seminal event resulting in the final demise of CCR. The once proud brotherhood who became the mighty Creedence Clearwater Revival would go down in bitter flames. Even though earning "gold" status and containing some fine tracks (most of those, admittedly, featuring John), and some critics were kind, many of the self-aggrandizing critical swine attacked them mercilessly. "You're only as good as your last record," would haunt their memory. If the *White Album* was a recording of individual Beatles, then *Mardi Gras* certainly represents the individual members of the Creedence trio. But there was no George Martin to turn to, and only John stood musically tall enough as a writer and a vocalist to pull off individual songs. Even in those, the intangible spirit that was CCR seemed missing. The bitterness would get worse as the years rolled by, fueled by business disputes and lawsuits.

John would later spend more than a decade literally at war with Saul Zaentz and Fantasy, engaging in major lawsuits that couldn't help but drain his focus, talent, and energy. One such lawsuit went all the way to the Supreme Court, John prevailing and writing new federal law. Even though he had started as the defendant in that particular feud, it had to be terribly draining on him. Just walking into a federal courtroom is a draining experience, even when it's not you on trial. John had been sued by Saul/Jondora, copyright owner of his original songs, essentially for plagiarizing himself, a mindboggling concept. In my view, it was purely a venomous action, although likely in response to John's short-lived recording "Zanz Kant Danz," a malicious and public attack on Saul. John was further acerbated by Fantasy's repackaged CCR releases, which he viewed as dragging the band's legacy through the mud. How many "Greatest Hits" albums can one band have? But the dragging was just getting underway. All thought the bottom of the barrel was reached when Fantasy released a Golliwog anthology.

The others often sided against John when it came to legal issues involving the band. Tom passed away, tragically, before his 50th birthday, a result of having received blood tainted with the AIDS virus at a time before routine screening was in place. On what has to be the darkest night in the history of Creedence Clearwater Revival, John refused to perform with Stu and Doug at the Rock and Roll Hall of Fame induction, pouring kerosene on the flames and spreading their legacy with a sullied film of blame and discontent. Stu's comment was right on the mark: "It wasn't John Fogerty they were inducting." The unofficial CCR biographer, Hank Bordowitz, was moved to title his well-researched history of the band after one of John's more ominous songs, "Bad Moon Rising."

❧·❦

IT IS THE ANIMOSITY AMONGST once great friends that continues to nag at me. Victimhood makes for an ugly mistress. It should have been otherwise. I remember the bright, fun-loving, and talented young guys who came into my world when I was in high school, bringing with them the wellspring of a pure and genuine musical ability. They were bursting at their seams with the energy and spirit of the music that made me want to stand up and shout out loud. At its center, always, a joyful sound.

No matter how skilled the musicians John later came to surround himself with, they would fall short of the magic that had been created when he played with his best friends from junior high. Leading to yet another bitter lawsuit, Stu and Doug founded "Creedence Clearwater Revisited," an assemblage of fine musicians, playing and emulating with superb finesse the songs of their former band. Likewise, they would never completely achieve the magic created when they played with their old pal, John Fogerty. As John would say years later, "Creedence had style." Lawyers would grow fat feasting on the leftovers.

Theirs was a storybook quest, throwing to the wind their jobs, cars, and security, setting out to capture the great spirit and crown of rock & roll, and they succeeded overwhelmingly. They became masters of the discipline, only to fall from their lofty place among the stars when they strayed from the page that reminds us: rock & roll's first requirement has always been a sense of joy and fun in the making.

➤-◆

PRIOR TO THE BITTER END, having emerged from the trauma of Tom's departure and the events leading up to it, all of a sudden, it was party time! It had been the band's practice in prior years to go out and play on weekends. They'd schedule concerts in, say, Boston and New York for Friday and Saturday, then fly home on Sunday. Then they'd do Chicago and Detroit the same way, Los Angeles and San Diego, Seattle and Vancouver, and so forth, the 1970 European tour excepted. Sometimes band members would bring their wives with them. Then, as a trio, they started putting together tours that played 20 cities in less than a month and no wives came along. They leased their own Learjet so there would be no concerns with airline schedules, meaning we could party harder and sleep later. It was time to kick out the jambs and taste it all, a headlong rush to the waiting abyss.

THE TRAVELIN' BAND

LIFE ON THE ROAD WITH CREEDENCE WAS A THRILL-A-MINUTE CARNIVAL ride. Each new city had its own buzz, and the conquest of live performance provided a constant stream of adrenalin and challenge. Most nights during the extended tours included informal party sessions in our hotel rooms, playing off-the-cuff country, blues, and traditional stuff after the big show. All manner of great players would join in, depending on who we might be on tour with at the time. In this setting I could finally sit in with my guitar and, in a musical sense, feel a part of the whole. It was during these sessions that John developed many of the songs and ideas for his *Blue Ridge Rangers* album of country and traditional songs, whereon he was the only musician, although the cover would have you believe it was a group of five, even if each wore the same hat. We somehow managed to keep our noise levels from having us tossed from the hotels. Doug kept time on a relatively quiet practice drum set, and amplified instruments were kept at a reasonable level, resulting in amazingly few complaints. I used to think other nearby hotel guests must have been fans as well. When we were done for the night, the party room often looked like a scene from some drunken bacchanalia, and we'd leave fifty dollars or so as an apology to the housekeepers.

Musically and culturally it was a different era, long before the punks, rappers, and digital world arrived to remake the musical landscape. The boomers were just coming into their own and "Off the pigs!" was a war cry heard on college campuses around the country. In Memphis the Creedence Learjet taxied alongside the private jets of Elvis Presley and the Jackson Five, the on-tour passengers waving hello and goodbye. There were no cell phones, internet, or handheld communication devices, our attentions occupied with what was going on around us. Erectile dysfunction was something known as "beer weenie." Following are some memories of the "Travelin' Band" on the road from a time fondly remembered.

➳-❦

THERE ARE THOSE RARE OCCASIONS when it seems all of your stars and celestial bodies are in a perfect alignment and heavenly deities look down upon you with favor. Such seemed my circumstance the first time I joined the band on the road. The performance was in Honolulu. The next day we boarded private aircraft and flew to Maui, the island to which my mother had moved to a year or so earlier. We then spent nearly two weeks vacationing at the world-class Hotel Hana Maui, the band picking up the tab. I'd have ample time to visit with Mom and explore her new world. I'd never been to Hawaii before. I thought I must be dreaming.

Hana was (and is) known as "Heavenly Hana" and not without good reason. At the eastern end of Maui, Hana is one of Hawaii's special places and remains that way, partly because of its remoteness and the difficulty of getting there. There is no airport that will accommodate jet aircraft and the road to Hana is a world famous slow-going, winding trek through scenic rainforest and jungle, dotted along the way with crystal pools and waterfalls. The people of Hana are known for keeping alive the cultural traditions of their cherished homeland.

The Hawaiians who worked at the hotel were all natives of Hana, and in the Hawaiian way, they all seemed to be dancers, singers, and musicians and provided the nightly entertainment at the hotel, as authentic as it gets. Some of those who were there in 1969 are today legendary in Hawaiian culture. The bartender was a huge Hawaiian man named "Tiny" Malaikini, who would become Hana's ambassador of aloha and a central figure in the Hawaiian renaissance of the early 1970s. Today there is an annual award in Tiny's name, awarded to that local person whose spirit of aloha best reflects that remembered of Tiny. Some bartenders keep a weapon under the bar, but when Tiny reached down there, he brought out his ukulele, and he played and sang for me the first true traditional Hawaiian music I'd ever heard. Then he mixed up a couple of mean Chi-Chis.

The people greeted us warmly, and everyone was seduced by the rich, enveloping experience of Hana. Tropical jungle and the green slopes of Haleakala climb from a warm, blue ocean. The air you breathe is the cleanest found anywhere, moist and scented with plumeria, and feeling like it has its own body and texture, almost thick like you might imagine liquid oxygen to be. Time is an alternate dimension known as "Hana time," where the hands of the clock seem to stand still as the rest of the world hurries by. It really does occur to you: This is what heaven must be like. It's little wonder that a couple of years later we'd do a *"hana hou,"* meaning in Hawaiian we'd "do it again," coming back for another stay after another concert in Honolulu.

⇥⇤

CREEDENCE USUALLY HANDPICKED THE OPENING acts for their tours and show dates, performers whose music they admired. A favorite was Booker T. & the MGs, who band members looked on as representing ultimate musicianship within a band. Others included Tony Joe White, Wilbert Harrison, Freddie King, Bo Diddley, Tower of Power, and The Ike & Tina Turner Revue. The openers would change from tour to tour, a matter of variety, balance, and scheduling. The opening act kept the band honest and on its toes. They could remember only too well the days when they were second- and third-billed, and it was fair game to blow the headliner off the stage, which they often did. It took confidence, sometimes courage, to follow an act that had just brought the audience to its feet. Heaven forbid you get upstaged at your own concert.

The Ike & Tina Turner Revue opened for Creedence at a performance at the Salt Palace in Salt Lake City. I was standing by at the dressing room door while the band tuned up when I became aware of a shift in music volume and audience response. I went to the back stage area and found Bruce Young.

"Bruce, what's going on?" The house lights were up and the music had stopped.

"Tina did something the hall managers didn't like," said Bruce, half-grinning, half-concerned. "They brought up the house lights and stopped the show to let us know we couldn't do that here. Now the audience is pissed off."

"What did she do?"

"It was a slow, sexy song, and she ... fondled the microphone."

"Is that all?"

"Well, maybe she pretended to give it a blowjob. The overseers here are Mormon. I think that thought is a little over the top for them."

"What about the audience?"

"They loved it, but got super angry when the show was stopped. I promised the hall people that Tina would be a good girl, and they said they'd take the lights back down." The lights started to dim and suddenly the audience began to cheer again.

"C'mon, Tina," said Bruce, grinning again, his fingers crossed, "be a good girl."

The band all had a good laugh learning of the incident and the show went on without further delays. Creedence put on a great show, as did Ike and Tina. Everybody at the Salt Palace got their money's worth and then some. After the show, the Ike-ettes, Tina's pretty female backup singers, joined us in party celebrations at the hotel, while Tina and a sullen Ike kept to their room. Ike seemed moody and standoffish to me, and Tina, too, seemed a little distant and withdrawn. These were days when Ike's notorious temperament ruled that relationship.

➤◄

THE LEARJET WAS A MODEL designated 24B. Cap'n John called it a "baby rocket." It carried only five passengers, maybe six in a squeeze, and regulations required a copilot in addition to the pilot. It looked more like a fighter than a corporate jet. It had a range of only about 1,900 miles, which meant on the longer runs, we had to land about every three hours to refuel—good thing, too, because there was no toilet on board, only an emergency bedpan under one of the seats. Cutting out the commercial airlines and their schedules made touring a lot less stressful. This plane could not cross the Pacific, but via Goose Bay, Labrador, and Reykjavík, Iceland, and then into Manchester, England, we could cross the Atlantic and use it throughout a second European tour we called "Mondo Bizarro II," announced as such on the wing tanks of the Lear. Also stenciled on the wing tanks was "Powered by Gort," together with an image of the robot Gort himself, the adopted CCR mascot from the 1951 anti-war and science fiction film *The Day the Earth Stood Still*.

John W. Chadick, Major (retired) USAF, was our trusted pilot and confidant. Sandy-haired and slender, he always seemed to be smiling and eager to help any way he could. A veteran of B-52 raids over Haiphong and Cambodia, John was anxious to use his flying abilities in nonmilitary endeavors and grabbed his first chance at retirement. Time and again, his skills at flying jet aircraft thrilled and amazed us. The copilot was Don Buchanan, younger with far less experience than Cap'n John, but he was nonetheless part of the team and a capable pilot and navigator.

We did all the unspeakable stunts we weren't supposed to do, barrel rolls, loops, fighter maneuvers, and so forth. Each of us took a turn at the controls, Cap'n John, of course, in the next seat, keeping anything from going haywire. John Fogerty once piloted a takeoff, scaring me half to death as we snaked down the runway. It's definitely not as easy as it may look. Cap'n John landed the plane like a skilled artisan at his work. He would hit the runway with the nose slightly up, the rear wheels hitting the tarmac with the slightest bump. Then he'd keep the nose up all the way down the runway, using the wings and fuselage as an air foil to help slow us down, the nose wheel coming to ground with the lightest touch.

Cap'n John and I established a relationship that far outlasted Creedence. Years later, when he found out I was to be sentenced for my role in the drug trade, he flew to San Francisco and tried to get a private audience with the judge, but had to settle for writing a character reference letter. The judge no doubt looked on him as one of my conspirators, which of course he was, but not in the drug business. He once told me about a young band he had flown some dates for who called themselves "Aerosmith", and he talked about band member Steven Tyler who had caught his attention. "You watch," said John. "That boy'll be a star one day." A resident of Florida, John tried his hand at commercial fishing for a while, but it was backbreaking work for very little reward. Then fortune arrived in the form of a new company that called itself Federal Express. He was among the first half-dozen or so pilots they hired.

❖

THE CREEDENCE TRIO AND I were 40,000 feet over the North Atlantic, the Learjet cruising at about .94 mach. The ghostly atmospheric phenomenon known as the northern lights was all around us, appearing like shimmering phantoms, then melting away to be replaced by another. Cosmo (Doug Clifford) had majestic Strauss waltzes on the stereo system and we were all smoking marijuana, even John Fogerty, who would seldom partake of doobage. We were kicked-back, relaxed, and listening to the music while taking in the majesty and wonderment of the night sky with its curtains of ghostly light. Copilot Don Buchanan was in radio contact with a weather ship on duty in the North Atlantic. He mentioned his passengers and some CCR fans on board wanted to send their wishes and regards, and the headset was passed around so band members could express their hellos and thanks.

On the ground to refuel in Iceland, we headed for the nearest bathroom, anxious to empty our bladders. We were about two hours flying time from Manchester, where we would go through British customs. I gathered the guys around and suggested we inventory what reefer we had left. It amounted to over 20 pre-rolled joints. We were already reasonably stoned and there was only four or us. I suggested we flush it all on the spot, remembering a customs encounter in the Bahamas when I had everyone's stash in my jacket pocket and looked up to see a customs cop going through the pockets of John's jacket. "No way," says Cosmo, "we're smokin' 'em." "Damn right," echoed Stu. Even John was in agreement. Soundly defeated, I could only join the opposition.

On our way into Manchester, the Lear cabin was a thick fog of marijuana smoke, and I noticed Cap'n John was wearing an oxygen mask and thought that a smart move. Pretty soon, it became apparent we couldn't smoke all those joints, so we started tearing them open and sprinkling sandwiches with cannabis, eating what we couldn't smoke. I was stoned to a point of being numb, and I was getting anxious about dealing with customs on arrival. Customs would be the easy part.

A thin cloud of smoke rolled out of the Lear when the hatch was opened. The interior was saturated with the heady smell of pot. I got out onto the tarmac and spotted a throng of British press and photographers awaiting our arrival. Behind them, a covey of fans. No way were we prepared to meet the press. It was early morning and the bitter cold was intensified by our overindulgence. No one had had any sleep at all. I began to shiver, almost uncontrollably, and wondered how in hell I was going to deal with arrival matters in my current state.

Salvation was found in the restroom, where we automatically headed after each landing. I bathed my hands, arms, and face with warm water, bringing the shakes under control. Taking some deep breaths, I forced my mind into a reasonable sobriety as best I could. Then the four of us walked down a corridor together to face British border officials and the press.

After passing through immigration, we were guided into a sterile room off the airport lobby, right into the blinding glare of TV and camera lights. We must have looked like zombies, allergic to daylight. If there was one question from the press that the band had come to loathe, asked and answered too many times, it was the inevitable, "How did you get your name?" That question usually signaled a boring interview by reporters who were out of their element and hadn't done their homework. Too many members of the press weren't musically smart enough to wonder about the band's often brilliant arrangements or John's sometimes unique guitar tunings or song lyric sources or production and studio techniques—things musicians can get their teeth into.

The band sat together on a sofa, weary and a little shell-shocked. A member of the press who could have doubled as a dentist stepped forward and got things rolling: "How'd you lads get your name?" Band members glanced at one another with looks of resigned defeat, wishing only to be elsewhere. We made sure our time with the press was brief, begging off with explanations of travel weariness. Some autographs were signed for the fans and we headed off to Manchester. Customs went through the plane with a fine-toothed comb, but we had been thorough in our consumption.

⇥⇤

I DON'T REMEMBER THE NAME of our hotel in Manchester, only that it resembled something out of a Gothic ghost story, a fitting scene for a séance or maybe Dracula on holiday. A large older building of traditional British architecture lacking modern lighting, the interior was dark and the walls were hung with rugs and tapestries. Hallways changed elevations, connecting with more hallways and hidden rooms. It was hard to remember where everyone was or how to get back to where you had started. It was there we would meet up with the rest of our party and entourage.

Bruce Young preceded us and had everything set up at the hotel. Bruce's steadfast support of the band served as a centerpiece for the rest of us. The equipment guys, now joined by a mellow and competent lighting specialist whose name was John Flores, were all there as well, each a part of the CCR family. Bob Fogerty was along to take photos and assist wherever needed. Performances on this tour were to be recorded for a planned album release, and Russ Gary, the engineer for most of the Creedence albums, was along to supervise the recording. Tony Joe White was the opening act, and he brought with him a fine band consisting of Duck Dunn on bass, "Sundance" on drums, Mike Utley on keyboards, and Tony Joe, of course, playing his trademark swamp guitar. We had toured with this group earlier, and all of them were considered friends and comrades.

Then there was Jim Marshall, a fine and famed photographer, along to capture events with his cameras. No other photographer documented the San Francisco music scene of the sixties as exquisitely and thoroughly as Jim. Usually pleasant and cordial enough, he could also be a pain in the ass. In an instant, he could become a whiny, spoiled rock star, demanding and needy, nothing quite coming up to what he considered his deserved station. Many were the times I had to smooth his feathers, or those of hotel management, when his fervent bitching about his room, service, or meal would come close to having him tossed. This annoying trait aside, he, too, was a valued member of the tour.

With the whole crew on hand in this creepy hotel, our first

night was a wild celebration of arrival, fueled by alcohol and hashish. A little out of control, there is little doubt we became a major annoyance to other guests. Music, laughter, and revelry lasted far into the night. I was awakened, slightly hungover, with a couple of phone calls from the local press, who wondered if I could give them the particulars about the goings-on that had occurred in the night. "No, 'fraid not, ol' chap. Don't know what you are referring to. Thanks for your interest, but I'm going back to sleep." I guess police had been called, but I don't recall encountering them.

After the show in Manchester, we headed to London, where record companies and promoters hosted a press reception. The band and I arrived at the reception on bicycles, band members singing a round of "There's no business like show business." This reception was like most others, an utter bore. It was attended by all of the usual suspects and music business generals, occasionally lifted by those few members of the press who had done their homework and were able to draw band members into a meaningful dialogue. The final concerts would be held at the Albert Hall at the end of the tour.

>-<

THOUGH HE WAS INVITED TO travel with us, Tony Joe wouldn't get near the Learjet. He'd heard about our aerial acrobatic antics from Duck, who'd lost his dinner in the middle of a barrel roll on our way to New Orleans from Memphis during an earlier tour. Duck wasn't anxious to join us again either.

We once picked up popular AM disc jockey Tom Campbell in San Jose en route to Los Angeles, where Creedence was to be the guest on his widely broadcast USO radio show. Tom was a nice enough guy, but he could sometimes be annoying. He once called me at the Factory as if just a personal call, then, without warning or agreement, he suddenly put me on the air, live, wanting me to answer questions about the band and their plans. I felt I owed him one and the boys agreed. He climbed aboard the Lear with some pizzas he'd gotten from one of his sponsors, and readily assumed his role of being our close ally ... have some pizza, pals. As soon as we gained altitude and free air space, Cap'n John executed our plan: Without a word, he turned the Learjet upside-down. Tom screamed for his maker and wedges of pizza scattered about the cabin. We laughed ourselves silly. When the plane was righted, I gave an ashen Tom a grin and a little punch on the shoulder, "Relax, we do this to all our friends."

❯-❮

THE BERLIN WALL WAS STILL standing, and West Berlin was like a country within a country, surrounded by hostility. We had to fly a restricted corridor and maintain a precise elevation in order to get there without being shot out of the sky by military fighters. Cap'n John was concerned about the Lear showing up on radar as a fighter plane, which it originally was. He spent a great deal of time making sure the Soviet and GDR MiGs that patrolled the corridor understood that we were rock & roll stars, not military opposition, even though our plane would show up on their radar with a fighter profile. Cap'n John said we may have been the first such private aircraft ever to fly the Berlin corridor. We had been through Check Point Charlie and East Berlin on the prior tour. This year we stayed in the West and visited the music and club scene. CCR's popularity in West Germany actually mirrored that of the Beatles.

We cut out a whole week to spend in Copenhagen, both because we enjoyed the city and because John had a romantic interest there. The rest of us were loose on the town. Russ Gary joined us in Copenhagen, while Tony Joe, his band, and the road crew would meet us at the next venue. We were tickled to discover certain bars and clubs where we could get a hit of hashish as well as a beer.

While in Copenhagen our European tour manager took us to a live sex show, a new experience. John was otherwise occupied, but I don't think anyone knew quite what to expect. We were seated in a small, theater-like room that might accommodate an audience of about twenty-five people. There was a bed in there, center stage, under intimate lighting, and not much else. We filed in and took our seats behind a dozen or so British bankers on holiday, a stodgy looking group if ever there was. Our row of seats was elevated slightly above the row in front of us so we could have a clear view of the proceedings. The warm-up act was a few naked girls, not a stitch on them, who came out with the house lights still up and relentlessly teased the bankers, providing for us high comedy at its best. A banker seated just in front of Stu and me reached for one of the naked ladies, whereupon she deftly swung a leg over his head, holding him in place while side-stepping the reach and leaving a smear of vaginal secretion that glistened on the dome of his balding head and trailed off into the fringe of hair beneath the dome. Stu and I nearly had to leave the theater to control our laughter, the banker unaware of the kiss and attendant garnish that had been bestowed upon his pate. The eye-opening main event was an experienced and hardworking couple who were very good at what they did. Were there an Olympic category for fornacastic gymnastics, then I would guess they were potential medalists. A sex-show, indeed, but it's the comedy provided by the naked ladies and the bankers that remains vivid.

→-←

WILBERT "MR. KANSAS CITY" HARRISON came with us as the opening act for the first European tour in April of 1970, when Creedence was still a quartet. A warm and soulful individual, Wilbert became a beloved member of our touring group. He had a joyful smile and an easygoing way about him, and it was clear that he enjoyed life and his profession. Wilbert was an ideal touring partner, performing as a one-man band and damn good at it too. He had a bass drum and a hi-hat cymbal with a tambourine attached to it, and a harmonica in a holder around his neck, Bob Dylan style. He played guitar and sang, accompanied by his array of instruments, all at the same time. Wilbert's grand claim to fame was the fifties super-hit, "Kansas City," a classic that no doubt sold in the millions and has been recorded by countless others, but Wilbert's version is considered the standard. He also authored and performed a fine song titled "Let's Work Together" that achieved a modest success. Wilbert enjoyed drinking, and he probably did more of it than may have been advisable.

This tour opened in Rotterdam, Holland, with two shows the same night. Fantasy Records head Saul Zaentz was along for part of the tour, a time prior to hostilities between the band and label. The hall was relatively new, built with acoustical engineering designed for a symphony orchestra. I wanted to hear what the band sounded like in this environment, and I took in the opening show seated in the audience with Saul. The sound was superb, even if over-driven by the CCR Kustom amplifiers turned up to ten. The midnight audience, well-oiled and anxious for Creedence, gave Wilbert a less than warm reception. A disrespectful audience generally pisses me off, and I felt bad for Wilbert, who didn't deserve their shit.

The following show in Essen, Germany, was about to start when Wilbert grabbed me backstage, pleading, "Brothuh, you got a taste?"

"A taste … a taste of what?"

"Whiskey, anything. I can't go out there without some help."

Shit. I could see he was really scared. The hostile second-show crowd in Rotterdam had destroyed his confidence and he was terrified that he'd get a similar greeting here in Germany. I grabbed a German fellow who worked at the hall and gave him 100 Deutschmarks, telling him to run out and buy some booze, "Schnell! The show won't start without it."

"Schnapps?" wondered the German.

"No. Bourbon, brandy, whiskey, something brown."

He was back in a few minutes with a bottle of brandy that Wilbert upended, doing about a quarter of it in one swallow. Soon he was ready. The arena crowd loved him and he responded with a superb show, his confidence again fully intact and remaining so for the rest of the tour. Bless the Germans for their love and recognition of American bluesmen.

※-※

AT SOME POINT MID-TOUR, THERE was an article published in *Rolling Stone* about the band on tour, and some not-so-nice things were said about the British tour promoter. He sued us for slander, the band, me, and Bruce. We learned about this in London and called our attorney in Oakland who told us, "Whatever happens, don't let them serve you!" An impossible task, trying to hide from process servers in a foreign environment. Hell, they would get us on stage at the Albert Hall if nowhere else. We nonetheless made a game of it for a couple of days, disguised with hats, dark glasses, and trench coats, each looking like a different version of Inspector Clouseau, leaving the hotel separately and hooking up afterward, sneaking around London like wanted criminals. They nailed us one at a time, in elevators, at a restaurant, in the hotel lobby and so forth. We didn't stand a chance, but it was a fun game while it lasted. The lawsuit was soon settled for a modest sum.

The Royal Albert Hall concerts were legendary performances with screaming crowds and stomping ovation demands that went on and on. Creedence by then had adopted a "no ovations" policy because it was thought that ovations had mostly lost any true meaning. Stage calls would be demanded again and again, even when the band thought they had played lousy. On some nights they had been called back to the stage a dozen times. These days they announced their final song, then closed the show with a 10-minute version of "Keep on Chooglin'," high energy, high velocity rock & roll that served as the evening's musical orgasm and grand finale. Most audiences, of course, didn't understand that the band wouldn't return to the stage, and Creedence, I think, ignored the adoration aspect of the demand. They could have come out, bowed to the audience and whistled Dixie and the crowds probably would have been happy. I thought it indifferent, even arrogant, not to acknowledge an appreciative audience, while band members thought it would have been phony of them to withhold songs, especially "Chooglin'," for use as a built-in curtain call. In some ways, CCR could be too honest for their own good.

Frank Sinatra once weighed in on the matter: "An audience is like a broad. If you're indifferent, Endsville."

A band called "Hawkwind" appeared with Creedence at the Albert Hall, their appearance arranged by the promoter. Their music and visual presentation is maybe best described as psyche-delic. After the show they presented us with a gift, several joints of their private-stash cannabis.

After the usual post-concert party and indulgence, I went to bed but couldn't find sleep. I laid there for what felt like an eternity, tossing and turning, my mind racing. What kind of weed was that? It was after four in the morning and I was reading, still restless and unable to sleep, when a quiet knock came at my door. It was Bruce and he had Bob Fogerty with him. Bruce wanted me to help him explain to young Bob that everything was okay, we were still on planet Earth, and that he was indeed still Bob. Poor Bob had been kicked into another reality after a few puffs on a Hawkwind joint, suddenly finding himself without compass or bearings. We went out and walked the streets of London, talking philosophical bullshit until the sun was fully up and Bob's feet had returned to Earth. Never again did I ever experience anything quite like the Hawkwind private stash. I don't imagine Bob has either. I always wondered what else might have been in there.

The tour ended with a couple of shows in Paris at the Olympia.

What an intoxicating town. Stu and I played tourist to the hilt, visiting every landmark, museum, and palace we could squeeze in, cruising around Paris in our Cadillac limo. We felt like we were on top of the world, even if only Eiffel's tower. During the sound check at the Olympia, Bruce spied a microphone dangled out a small window in the sound or lighting booth and told the theater people they weren't allowed to record the performance. Argument ensued and the mic was eventually withdrawn. But during the show, there it was again, snaking down the wall. Bruce ended the argument with a pair of diagonal wire cutters.

At tour's end, Wilbert, a little numb from the night before, but looking very cool in his dark glasses, hat, and trench coat, managed to set himself on fire lighting a cigarette at the airport in Paris. He was oblivious to the flames billowing from a nylon scarf he carried over his arm when Bob, standing nearby, rushed over and beat them out. "Damn!" declared an unbelieving Wilbert, "Where'd dat fire come from, brothuh Bob?"

❧

SUMMERTIME WAS THE PRIME TOURING season. No one wanted to tour in winter, unless to a country where it was still summer. We had a few days off from touring and we were hanging out in Memphis before the next dates on our schedule. Tony Joe took us fishing in a nearby Mississippi river backwater. Jim Marshall was along to document the day with his cameras. We had rented several aluminum skiffs with oars, each about 12 feet in length. They had a flat front end, up-swept, rather than sides that come together in a frontal peak. Jim was alone in his skiff, and at one point, he moved forward, one foot resting on the front of the up-swept bow to get a particular shot and view. There was no motor to weigh down the stern. We watched, first with alarm, then with laughter, as the rear of the skiff slowly lifted from the water, becoming completely upright, dumping Jim and all of his cameras into the swamp. He shinnied up the nearest tree stump, soaked and terrified by the thought of water moccasins. Then the thought of his cameras at the bottom of the swamp brought on a crushing grief. Cosmo was the hero that day. A superb athlete, he dove again and again to the bottom of the murky water, eventually retrieving all of Jim's cameras, apparently not at all bothered by the thought of water moccasins.

We cooked our fish in Tony Joe's backyard, playing music, trading stories, and passing a bottle while fireflies dotted the landscape on a warm summer evening. Billy Swan came from Nashville to join us for a night on the town. Billy was a remarkably warm and open individual, and somewhat of a musical legend as well, writing a song for Clyde McPhatter while still in his teens, producing Tony Joe's "Polk Salad Annie," and authoring his own mega-hit "I Can Help." At the various venues in Memphis, the band and Tony Joe were invited on stage for a musical free for all, swamp music ruling the night.

❧❧

"YOU BOYS MEAN TO TELL me—gospel truth, now—that y'all've been here in Little Rock for half an hour an' no one's been laid yet?" A limousine driver bringing us into town from the airport, either commenting on local morals or impugning our cocksmanship.

❧❧

I OFTEN POSTED MYSELF OUTSIDE the dressing room door when the band was tuning up and getting ready for the show, making sure they weren't disturbed by the uninvited and keeping track of the stage call. They had to tune their instruments by ear, using a harmonica for pitch, the electronic and digital tuners of today not yet a reality. On a night in Shreveport, a deputy sheriff came down the hallway, then suddenly made an abrupt turn and started into the dressing room. I grabbed his shoulder and spun him around, "Hey, you can't go in there!" That's a mistake in Louisiana. The high sheriff and a few more deputies were following. Two of them grabbed me and slammed me up against the wall, forcefully holding me there while cops surrounded me wondering how I'd like to spend some time in their jail. I won, though. The bastards never got into the dressing room.

On reflection, I wondered if they were attempting a surprise raid in hopes of making a high profile drug bust. Drugs were never a part of a Creedence performance. Stu and Doug once told me of a time, early on, when some Grateful Dead guys brought some spiked punch into the dressing room at the Avalon Ballroom in San Francisco. They thought these Creedence guys were a great band, but maybe they could use a little mind shift. Cosmo said he started having hallucinations on stage, but I guess it didn't matter—the entire audience was hallucinating along with him.

At a Madison Square Garden concert in New York, I was standing by at the dressing room door when I turned and noticed that, suddenly, all of the people who had been bustling up and down the corridor seemed to have disappeared. Stage hands, security, sound and lighting people—everyone was gone. Then, appearing like shadowy apparitions, three large and rough-looking men in Hells Angels garb made their way up the hallway to the dressing room as though they owned the entire building.

"We want to see Fogerty," announced the lead Angel. A little nervous, I explained that he couldn't see him right now, he was getting ready to go on stage. I noticed the handle of a revolver sticking out of his waistband, just under a leather vest.

"That's cool, man. We'll see him after the show." He said it as though fact. He wasn't asking for an appointment. I asked what they wanted to see John about, and they rolled out their plan for me.

The lead Angel was president of the New York chapter of Hells Angels, and this was a diplomatic—even patriotic—visit to introduce a plan that would make America a better place, and they wanted to invite Creedence Clearwater Revival to be a central part of their vision. They had opined that the youth of America were going down a wrong road, becoming "pussies, queers, and druggies," embracing shitty-sounding rock music that delivered the wrong message, essentially missing the boat to what America was all about. Allowed to go on unchecked, they explained, America was in danger of going down the tubes like the Roman Empire. For the Angels, Creedence represented the real America, who played real rock & roll music the way it was supposed to be played, and whose songs and images provided a message of strength and American spirit.

Amazing, I thought: These guys worship my guys. They wanted Creedence to join with the Hells Angels in supporting a nationwide program aimed at straightening out the youth of America. There would be radio and billboards, huge rallies and concerts, Creedence and the Angels leading the way, shining examples of what America stood for. In any event, that seemed to be the general idea and was my interpretation of what they had to say.

I knew, of course, Creedence wasn't going to join forces with the Hells Angels. Hadn't these guys heard of Altamont? I was nonetheless pleased by their adoration of the band and their reading of what CCR's music conveyed. But how was I going to be diplomatic and keep them away from the band? Though these East Coast Angels were scary looking, I never felt threatened. They seemed to have a certain sophistication and sense of dignity. They appeared to lack the utter ferocity I had seen firsthand in West Coast Angels when Stu and I—stoned again—had been together near the front of the stage at Altamont. Demoniacal Angels, running amok, terrified and panicked the crowd, killing one fellow.

I was at my wit's end on how to handle this situation when I was saved by a near-impossible circumstance I couldn't have imagined in my wildest dreams. Again, my stars must have been in perfect alignment. As my conversation with the Angels was coming to an end, up strolled Don Buchanan, our copilot on the Learjet, and he and the

Angel president looked at one another in disbelief, then greeted one another as though a long lost brother had suddenly appeared.

It turned out that Don had once had a close, non-romantic relationship with a woman who had been the Angel's one true love when she succumbed to a life-ending disease. Specifics aren't recalled, but Don had been a very close personal friend, maybe a relative. Years earlier, together with the now president of the New York Hells Angels, Don had nursed the stricken woman through her final episode of life, establishing a bond with the Angel that would last a lifetime, each a comfort to the other during this significant loss to both of them.

They forgot all about a meeting with Creedence. The Angels scooped up Don and took him with them to Angel headquarters somewhere in the city (Hell's Kitchen?). We spent the next two or three days in New York, staying at the Plaza and farting around, while Don spent the whole time with the Angels. He later regaled us with stories about his royal treatment at Angel headquarters. I guess their grand plan was put on a back burner, where it simmered and evaporated, eventually forgotten. We didn't hear from the Angels again.

❧

WE WERE HEADED TO NEW Zealand on a commercial jet with a stash of marijuana brownies, a bon voyage present from a friend, that turned out to be much too potent, something we weren't aware of until it was too late. One brownie would have been enough for all of us, but we each ate a whole one. I had to strap myself into my seat, so stoned I was afraid I was going to be sick. Stu, likewise feeling ill, was in the bathroom so long that a stewardess became alarmed and flushed him from the enclosure. It made for an uncomfortable first leg of the journey, which ended in Fiji. We were okay the next day, a little wiser now about our brownies. The band played a single date in New Zealand before we moved on to Sydney for the usual gathering of press, radio, and record company generals. After a half-dozen dates in Australia, we would head for Japan.

The first Australian date was in Brisbane, where we were treated to a cyclone that shut down the airport and flooded city streets. At one point during the concert, a beer bottle came flying up onto the stage, a potentially dangerous missile, and we were ready to shut things down if more were to come. It was as rowdy a crowd as I'd ever seen at a Creedence concert, rivaling an out of control night at the Monkey Inn.

After an evening that included the requisite meeting with press, radio, and local record people, Stu and Doug awarded me with an "above and beyond the call of duty" citation for my valor in bedding a not so lovely woman who was said to be an important player and critic in Australia's music press. Her reputation had been whispered to us by someone from the Australian record company, suggesting that she expected such a perk. Someone had to accept this role or risk her journalistic ire, and I was, after all, the band's diplomatic attaché. "Hired stud" could now be added to my job description. A forward and aggressive woman, if anyone bedded someone, then it was she who bedded me.

We had to make a run for the airport the next day, the weather allowing a brief window through which we could take off for our concert in Sydney. Getting to the airport was a circuitous route; many of Brisbane's streets were being navigated by boat rather than car. The band played to a crowd of twenty-five thousand the next day at a race track in Sydney.

→-←

IN MELBOURNE THERE CAME A request for John to visit a stricken fan who was hospitalized. We somehow understood that this was both important and the right thing to do. I went with John to visit the fan, a young woman who had little time left. She was nonetheless winsome and self-assured, a quiet acceptance reflected in her eyes and manner. The last thing she seemed was sorry for herself. Her boyfriend was with her and both were a little overwhelmed, not really expecting John's visit. She truly loved CCR's music, but wasn't strong enough to attend the concert.

John was gracious and friendly, but seemed to start off a little lost for words. What do you say to someone, a stranger, who's about to die, tragically, way before her time? Mine was the easy role, supplying introductions and a sometimes awkward dialogue. Ultimately, John was aware that fame is a poor substitute for solace, and he shed any pretense that might come with his stature, exposing himself as a caring person. All of the bullshit that swirls around us during our lifetimes stops here. I admired John's humility and the young woman's strength.

The concert was broadcast live on radio the next evening, and John dedicated one of his songs, "Up Around the Bend," to her, a song that takes the listener to a new and promising reality, up around the bend. John made it a habit to put new strings on his guitars for every performance. He did it himself, a time before every rock-star guitar-slinger had his own personal guitar valet. He played his ferocious music with an amazingly light touch and rarely, if ever, broke a string on stage. But on this night, just into the song's clarion-like introduction, a string snapped. He finished the performance, able to turn that musical switch in his mind that allows him to play the right notes on the remaining strings. John caught my eye while replacing the string. His expression of disbelief and wonder spoke volumes. In his mind, the song was hers and represented her embodiment in this lifetime. The guitar string represented her tenuous grasp to a lifeline. As the broken string released her into the hereafter, John found himself transported to the *Twilight Zone*.

⇒-⇐

LED ZEPPELIN STARTED OUT IN Perth when Creedence was at the opposite end of the country in Sydney. The twain would meet in

Adelaide, more or less the populated center of the continent, the steamship Proud Mary meeting the Zeppelin airship as they passed one another on tour. Both groups stayed at the same hotel. Creedence would play concerts Thursday and Saturday, while Zeppelin played their date on Friday at a different venue.

As was my habit at any new hotel, I checked with the dining room to see if there was a dress code that had to be observed. If so, we'd order through room service or find a restaurant. Jackets and ties weren't a part of our wardrobe. But there was no requirement other than being respectfully clothed, and having shirts and shoes. The Zeppelin road crew arrived while we were having lunch, looking ragged and unkempt, if not homeless, torn pants and shirts hanging open, barely, if at all, meeting dress requirements. They sauntered in and ordered up their lunch while I wondered about the necessity of my cautionary dining room habit.

Out in front of the hotel, a gaggle of Zeppelin fans lined the sidewalk, looking like the road crew, ragged and scruffy. They also appeared to be very young, and it suddenly hit home for me: a new generation was making itself known, establishing their exclusivity, and the music they embraced was part of what set them aside from the preceding generation. Led Zeppelin, more than Creedence, seemed to represent this younger generation. Creedence was a great *rock & roll* band who also could play rock. Zeppelin a *rock* band who could also play rock & roll, one genre blending into the next, the same way soul music seemed to replace the earlier rhythm & blues. Rock & roll will never die if you believe the songs, but you could write volumes on the deviations. To me, each band represented a slightly different genre. In coming years, there would be more outgrowths of what was originally rock & roll, even musical nerds and androgyny becoming cool.

We partied with Zeppelin and their road guys, along with our road guys and other invitees peripheral to the tours. Each band had their own exclusive floor in the hotel, and the party took place on the Zeppelin floor. Nothing got out of control or over the top. It felt to me like the two bands were sharing a mutual camaraderie and respect. It was especially intriguing to see John Fogerty sitting there on the floor next to Jimmy Page, two giants of the rock & roll arena, trading stories and laughing, while Cosmo established a bond with Zeppelin drummer John Bonham. John Fogerty was intrigued to learn that Jimmy Page had been the guitar player on the classic "Them"/Van Morrison recording "Gloria," a crowd favorite when the band would perform it during the Monkey Inn days, before they were Creedence.

Some of the Zeppelin guys got a little carried away, taking out a wall when they wanted a connecting room. Creedence guys didn't do that shit, although on our final evening in Perth, the last Australian venue, Stu and Bob stayed up all night and filled the hotel swimming pool with lawn furniture and empty beer cans. They were still at it and looking proud of themselves when I emerged from my room in the morning. Maybe something had rubbed off on them from the Zeppelin guys. It was Bruce and I, of course, who had to face pissed off hotel management and pay for damages.

※-※

GETTING TO TOKYO WAS A hard day's travel from Australia's west coast, nonstop for 24 hours. From Perth, across the Australian continent to Sydney, a brief stop in Hong Kong, then on to Tokyo, where we first learned to bow with our overly polite hosts. Arriving at the hotel, my first chore was to count out millions in Japanese yen, spending money for the band, a dizzying task in my weary condition. We were all exhausted when the Japanese promoter treated a few of us to the experience of an exclusive traditional Japanese bath and massage.

The bathhouse was a wonder of Japanese beauty and craftsmanship. Walls of teak and cedar enclosed a private room through which a man-made creek meandered under an arched wooden footbridge. A potted plum tree provided an outdoorsy touch. A cold pool and a hot pool were opposite each other and there was an air mattress on a shallow, basin-like floor between the pools. The combinations of wet, dry, and steam heat, each followed by an immersion into the cooling pool, were thought to reinvigorate the body and remove toxins through the sweat glands.

My personal attendant, young, lovely, and lightly robed, spoke no English, but bowed and smiled politely throughout each of the processes. She led me through the various sweat therapies, then had me lie on the air mattress and bathed me before leading me to a massage table where I underwent further toweling, a sprinkle of powder and the relaxing manipulation of body massage by skilled hands. I was wearing nothing through all of this, but if there was any self-consciousness or embarrassment at my state of undress, it was my own.

I was then to learn that the finishing touch to this invigorating process and tradition was the release of any semen my body might have stored away. When I fully understood what she had in mind, I thought to myself, well, good luck with that! The thought of an erection was a remote one. But my body was completely at ease and she had the hands of a milkmaid, expert in her craft and aided by a fine lubricant. To my astonishment, she completed her task in very little time, businesslike and matter of fact. It is, you know, a mechanical process that we males don't make too difficult or mysterious. Nothing she did was suggestive of a sexual come-on (I hear echoes of my pal Sheldon: "Are you tryin' to tell me that having your joint worked on isn't a come-on?"). On legs at first unsteady, I walked out refreshed, feeling like a king.

⇒⇐

THE ENTIRE JAPANESE CONCERT SCHEDULE had sold out in hours, a month ahead of our arrival. Similar to most countries, Creedence was a very big deal in Japan. The next day, I met Sachiko, head of the CCR fan club in Japan. She was cherry-blossom pretty with a sweet face that spoke to an inner innocence and appeared to be in her mid-twenties. She dressed her petite anatomy in formal business attire, a skirt and jacket. She had an excellent command of the English language and was so well-mannered, polite, and courteous you wanted to puke. We sat together at a press reception, drinking tea and talking about the band and the upcoming performances throughout the country. She had taken a leave of absence from her job, and paying her own way, had tickets to all the shows and would be at all of the venues. She was interested in everything Creedence, the Australian dates, future plans, me and my relationship with the band. She mentioned that she wanted to be staying at all the same hotels where we would be staying.

I guess it was the way she talked about wanting to stay in the same hotels. I had to ask her. I meant no disrespect. I simply wanted to know her intentions ... do you expect to stay with me? Never in my life had I seen such a combination of shock, revulsion, and embarrassment come over someone. I might as well have asked if she doubled as a hooker when she was done at the office. She got up to leave the table as the enormity of my faux pas became clear to me. Summoning all the honesty I possessed, along with the most sincere apology I could muster, I persuaded her to please sit down and let me explain. I told her that anywhere else in the world I had been with Creedence, if someone had said to me what she had, it would be interpreted in the way my question implied. "I am new to your culture and I need to learn. Please accept my apologies. I meant no disrespect." She was a single woman from a traditional Japanese family, still living with her parents. We each had much to learn about our respective cultures. From this shaky start we established a close bond built on respect and this remarkable band to which we were both connected.

John's girlfriend from Copenhagen, Lucy, was along on the tour. I thought her a sweetheart of a woman and always enjoyed her company. It was a time when John was exploring more traditional and country music, and he brought a banjo and a pedal steel guitar on tour with him, teaching himself the intricacies of each instrument. In Tokyo we found a club that featured country and bluegrass music played by very skilled Japanese musicians, and we went several times to enjoy their performances. Their playing was superb and their vocals mimicked traditional American song and harmony, even though they could never get the "r" quite right.

I invited Sachiko to join me, John, and Lucy for evenings of dinner and music. We had a driver and limousine, a grossly huge Cadillac that stood out like a gorilla on a ballet stage. The Japanese paparazzi followed us everywhere we went. Cruising down a boulevard, a photographer would suddenly appear outside the limousine window on the back of a motorcycle, snapping away with a camera. We thought it was fun and sometimes made a hide-and-seek game out of it. Sachiko's eyes were filled with excitement over these thrilling episodes of life in the company of a rock & roll star. Most nights when there wasn't a concert date, the four of us visited the clubs and restaurants, blending the cultures of Denmark and Japan with our own brand of Americana. Lucy and Sachiko enjoyed one another like sisters.

On a night in Tokyo, I offered our extra room to Sachiko so she wouldn't have to travel to the outskirts of the city to get home, and it was going to be a late night. We always had an extra room at the hotels, either as a party room or, should we say, a spare room for emergencies. I usually shared a room with Bob Fogerty. This night, however, Bob apparently had an emergency, and when we got back to the hotel, the spare room was occupied. Sachiko had informed her parents she would be staying at the hotel that evening and it was three o'clock in the morning when we discovered our plan had been undermined.

Since it was Bob who was occupying the spare room, that meant there was an extra bed in my room. What the hell. "You can stay with me tonight, Sachiko. It will be okay. You will have your own bed." Again, she registered a look of shock. She explained that if her parents ever found out she spent a night, unmarried, in a hotel room with a man, she would be disowned. It was truly a frightening prospect for her. I convinced her there would be no shame to her staying. No one will know but us.

It was a comical scene, getting her into bed. If modesty came in crates, then she was a truckload. I had to proceed her getting into my bed, then turn out the lights for her while she came from the bathroom, chittering away like a little bird, thanking me for my understanding and hospitality. Little by little, she was learning the ways of the West, understanding that, really, it was okay. The important part was intention and respect. Her honor, along with her maidenhead, would remain intact.

Perhaps a foreshadowing of what was to come, an earthquake shook the city while I was in the hotel lobby getting ready to leave for the Tokyo concert. People cried out and elevators banged and rattled in their shafts. A ripple like a small wave rolled across the lobby floor, lifting me up then setting me down as it passed beneath me. The epicenter was far enough offshore that major damage in the city was averted. The band arrived in the lobby, each member with his own tale of the quake, and we loaded into the limousine that would take us to the Budokan, the central Tokyo arena where the concert would take place.

Creedence poured it on at the Budokan, three playing as one, like a team of superb athletes who knew each other so well as to make blind passes exactly on the mark, effortlessly picked up by teammates synchronized like finely made clockworks. The audience left their seats and crowded into the aisles and pushed to the front of the stage, roaring their approval. Spontaneity rather than expectation ruled the night. After the concert, there was a riot by an over-amped audience unable to contain the energy of the music. Cars were set on fire, and raging Japanese youth squared off with police in revolt against the old ways. The world was changing here, too. We were hustled out of the arena through underground tunnels. I was thinking Japanese authority would no doubt again have their hands full when Led Zeppelin got there.

Sachiko came up to the room to say goodbye and rode down in the elevator with me to the limousine that would take us to the airport. A tear rolled down her cheek as she turned her face up to mine. It was a gentle embrace and kiss, on the mouth, for her maybe the first time ever. "I have but one wish," she said, "that one day you will return to Japan." I never did.

THE BAND WOULD FINISH THE recording of *Mardi Gras* and go back on the road for one final tour, a half-hearted attempt to promote a record that was doomed before it was recorded. John, Stu, and Doug agreed to disband as a group, and the house that Creedence built came tumbling down.

John and I, with Bob and Bruce Koutz, moved out of the Factory to a temporary office in Albany. Stu and Doug, together with Russ Gary, started a production company based at the Factory. Bruce Young seemed shell-shocked, so terribly saddened at seeing the end of the brotherhood he had poured his heart and soul into. He continued to work with Stu and Doug, but some of the light that had once shone from his eyes had dimmed.

We all managed to remain at least cordial and open with one another over the next few years, although I can't speak for John and Tom, whose relationship was outside of the one I shared with John. There were mutually beneficial wars yet to be fought and no one had yet so thoroughly pissed off one of the others, though that train was starting to roll, building momentum on a track that stretched out ahead of them, set to arrive somewhere down the line. I'm glad I wasn't around when the wars came between the band members themselves, animosity growing like a cancer. I regarded them as brothers. I cannot imagine having to take sides in battles that might require me to choose one brother over another.

6

OUTLAW'S ROOST WELCOMES JOHN FOGERTY AND THE ROLLING STONES

Nineteen seventy-three found Creedence a thing of the past and John Fogerty engaged in the process of feeling his way, unsure of what his future might hold. This chapter represents just one of the bumps in John's road as he reinvented himself, time and again, searching for the elusive path that would take him home. Like many other great and talented artists who were no longer a part of the group entity that had propelled them to stardom, John, too, would learn that the whole was greater than the sum of its parts. The magic entity that was Creedence Clearwater Revival, largely his own creation, was now but a ghost.

Max Halsey was a close friend of my dad's and had become family—very close to my brother and me since Dad's passing. About 25 years our senior, Max was both a brother and an uncle to us, always a reminder of Dad with his smiling, country ways. A late-blooming free spirit and genuine soldier of fortune, Max was determined that life would work for him on his terms. He was living in the remote village of Troy, Oregon, and on the lam from charges that he had been the ringleader of a marijuana grow in Idaho. Max was in California at the time of the bust and those busted all pointed to Max as the main man. I was working for Creedence when the law caught up with Max, and I enlisted John Fogerty's financial support to save Max from the clutches of Idaho justice. I explained the situation to John and he never hesitated, figuratively opening his wallet and telling me to take what I needed. John was always a warm and generous employer, and I admired his person as much as I admired his talent. I got Max bailed and hired legal gunslinger Carl Maxey, former Attorney General for the state of Washington, to represent Max. He blew Idaho's case against Max out of the water in short order. A couple of years went by before our connections to Max would lead to new and unforeseen events in our lives.

Following the breakup of CCR, John kept me employed for the next four years or so as his aide and personal representative. We were gone from the Factory, but hadn't yet developed a game plan. We would take things one step at a time. John was fed up with Saul Zaentz and Fantasy Records, harboring countless unpleasant feelings toward Saul and the label. We found a residential property in Albany, just off Solano Avenue, that was also zoned for commercial use, a fluke. John bought it outright and it became our new office and his studio. Before we moved in, I got a call from Max, setting into motion circumstances that would for a while have a significant impact on the life of John Fogerty and create no small changes for me as well.

Max explained that a local packer named Roger Wilson was going to take a string of mules up into canyons of the national forest that borders Troy. Max was going with him on horseback. Their purpose was to see how Roger's hunting camps had come through the winter and do a little clean up. The area contained one of the largest elk herds in North America. "It's wild back country," said Max. "The trail follows the Wenaha River all the way, one of the prettiest and cleanest rivers anywhere. We might see bear, deer, elk, big horn sheep, maybe even mountain lion. We'll catch some trout, too. Why don't you and John fly up here and come with us?"

The idea of getting on a horse and going into a back-country wilderness like this very much appealed to John. It would be mostly a new experience for him. John was enthusiastic about going, and I looked forward to seeing this country and spending time with Max.

The closest commercial airport to Troy is Lewiston, Idaho. Max met us in his angular Toyota pickup that looked a little like a military vehicle. We drove the two hours or so to Troy, making our way along a lower portion of the Snake River, up past the "Eye of Asotin" (a locally fabled sphere atop a marble column in a hillside cemetery), through high-country farms and wheat fields, then down steep and majestic mountainsides on a winding road called the Rattlesnake Grade that bottomed out at the Grande Ronde River, one of the tributaries to the Snake and the mighty Columbia. We followed the river's course through Washington, then into Oregon and Troy, about 20 miles from the grade on a gravel road. Towering canyon walls studded with rimrock rose all around us. Troy was also known as "Outlaw's Roost" in its earlier days, a notorious hideout for outlaws on the run.

The township of Troy (population 26) sits at the confluence of the Grande Ronde and Wenaha Rivers, nestled in canyons cut by the rivers over countless eons. The only business in town was the Troy Resort, run by Roger and his family. It was old and quaint, a two-story clapboard structure with a steeply pitched roof, western-style shutters and a hitching post out in front. The people who frequented the resort were visiting sportsmen and local country folk, cowboys, farmers, field hands, and loggers, people who worked with their hands. Tough, capable, and strong, they were a population who avoided big cities and heavily inhabited areas. Max fit right in. He was born in Anatone, Washington, at the top of the Rattlesnake Grade, where he had spent his early years farming and working with trucks, bulldozer, tractor, and other farm rigs.

Roger was a country boy, hayseed and easygoing, nonetheless

alert and savvy in his own rural way. Not what you'd call an academic, Roger was a mule skinner, someone who knew horses and mules inside and out. He was a shrewd buyer and seller of mules, and he knew how to train them and use them as pack animals. True to reputation, they were stubborn animals, but possessed a sure-footed ability beyond that of horses, making them a valued pack and trail animal. Roger had a magnetic personality and a charming, countrified cowboy personality. I liked him right away. I think he enjoyed tending bar and being an innkeeper, as well as working with animals.

On our first night in Troy, Max got drunk, something I'd never seen before or since. Why he saved it for our arrival was beyond my reckoning. Even so, we had a fun evening, strumming guitars, Max playing his harmonica. John and I got loose, maintaining a reasonable sobriety, while Max got sloppy and staggering, managing to fall over a dining room table and sprawling out onto the floor. Maybe John's fame and Max's gratitude for saving him from the clutches of Idaho justice overcame him. Troy didn't host many celebrities like John.

We got a late start on the trail, getting underway without enough coffee or beer to sustain us through the trip, Max nursing a mighty hangover. We were short on food rations as well. This may have been John's first time on horseback and he struggled with his mount. Roger gave him his personal riding mule, John remarking that the mule felt like driving a luxury sedan after wrestling with a jalopy. Bringing up the rear with his hangover, Max called out, "First one sees an elk gets an extra beer!" Then, typical of his subtle humor and desperately wanting a beer to soothe his pounding head, almost under his breath and directed to no one in particular, "Think I just seen one."

John and I were dazzled by the natural beauty and ruggedness of the terrain. The trail took us along rocky bluffs high over the river, an eagle soaring up the canyon beneath us. Then we descended to the river, crossing a waist deep tributary on horseback, wending our way farther upstream through wooded flats that gave way to rising trail before again falling to the next flat. We didn't encounter another soul the entire journey. Around a blazing campfire, we traded stories deep into the night, the bitter cold and ink-black dark closing in on us the moment we ventured from the fire. The scream of a mountain lion sent a chill and shattered the darkness around us. I shivered the rest of the night through in a lousy sleeping bag.

⋇

ARRIVING BACK IN TROY, THE Grande Ronde Social Club, headed by local rancher Lester Kiesecker, called for an evening of food, music, and dance at his ample backyard patio a few miles up-river from Troy on the Grande Ronde. Word had spread through the canyons and valleys that John Fogerty was in Troy! The local country people were fond of music, especially America's traditional roots music, and many were home-schooled musicians as well. John, of course, knew and enjoyed the same kind of music, and true to CCR's demographic, most knew John's music too. Lester himself was a live wire, playing fiddle, musical saw, spoons, guitar, and probably other instruments as well. His sons also played various instruments and his wife played piano.

That night's gathering hosted about a hundred people, men with bottles of bourbon and jars of "white lightning" in brown paper bags, women in gingham dresses piling the tables with food. Respectful of John's celebrity, people would come up to me and ask, "Is that really who they say it is? Doggone!" John got up and sang a few songs with Lester's son's band, and I chunked along with Max's 12-string guitar. People danced and laughed and had a hell of a good time in this festive country setting, a wild river running between high canyon walls, echoing a time and place long gone in the America John and I had come from. As we were dazzled by the terrain, we were also charmed and welcomed by the people. Their social life, along with the role music played in it, represented a natural existence that relied on the seasons and each other. We'd only seen this life before in the movies.

Roger was a charmer nonpareil and easy to like. He was also an experienced rodeo cowboy, capable and skilled. He was in his late twenties at the time and had never seen a large city. He wasn't an aggressive person, rather, you were struck by the warmth of his smile and his outright friendliness. He had ways that seemed to be right out of a cowboy western. One night I saw him leap over the bar at the resort, moving so fast I missed the fact there was a problem. He grabbed the troublemaker, a character known as "Bad-John," and knocked him through the front door and out onto the street with a right cross, just like Hopalong Cassidy or Roy Rogers. He was also shrewd in his own country way and he had a natural gift as a salesman.

Troy is in Wallowa County, the far northeastern corner of Oregon, where elk season is a paramount event. As many as fifty thousand hunters would descend upon Wallowa County for elk season, chasing a herd of elk estimated at about fourteen thousand head, maybe three thousand or so of those legal-to-hunt bulls. Of economic importance to the state and county, the hunters would each buy a hunting license and an elk permit, and they would inhabit local motels and eat at the diners, buy groceries and gasoline and sporting equipment, a major element of the local economy. In Troy they would hire Roger as a guide and a packer, using his tents, mules, and horses, and they would eat and drink at the Troy Resort. In this period of a few short weeks, Roger would bring in the majority of his annual income.

As it turned out, there was another business in Troy, not as visible as Roger and the Troy Resort. There was a rival packer whose operation consisted of a barn, some modest cabins, and a few lots at the backside of town. Roger worked his magic on John who was wide-eyed and intoxicated by all that we had done and seen in Troy. John then announced that he had entered into a partnership with Roger. He would buy out Roger's competition, expanding the packing business that John would now share in, and have some property on which to maybe build his own cabin. Except for Roger's benefit, it probably wasn't a great idea. But I looked at it as symbolic of John's desire to be a part of a world that had previously existed only in his broad and active imagination. We enthusiastically jumped on board in Troy.

➶◀

FOR THE NEXT FEW YEARS, Troy became a part of our lives. The partnership never worked quite the way John had envisioned, and he eventually extricated himself from the business and the real estate. In the meantime, David Geffen had come to town, courting John for his own label, Asylum Records, and he put together a deal that bought up most of John's remaining obligations to Fantasy Records. John busied himself producing his first solo album for Asylum, which never quite measured up to expectations, although I always enjoyed it. I still hear in it the heart and soul of John Fogerty, even if lacking that magic that was Creedence Clearwater Revival. John seemed every bit as interested in establishing himself in Troy and becoming a hunter as he was in pursuing his musical career.

We returned to Troy for elk season, along with John's brother Bob, equipment man Bruce Koutz, and Harvey Graham, a carpenter and builder of exceptional skills, equally adept as a hunter and backwoodsman. Harvey had originally done some remodeling work for Doug Clifford and was then passed around to the other CCR members. Personally appealing as he was skilled, Harvey was a man of great honesty and individual character, and he would find in Troy his personal Shangri-La, a place that offered the natural environment and outdoor sports he valued most in life.

My family, too, came to hold Troy in high regard, especially my daughter, Tracy. In Troy she found her own very special place in the world, filled with natural wonder and memories of growing up. She and Roger's daughters became good friends and would set out together up the Wenaha River trail on their own camping trips, Roger's German shepherd, "Duke," outfitted with saddlebags and trotting alongside the girls. I bought a rustic little cabin on the Wenaha River that provided a place for the family, a serene setting with the river for a soundtrack and providing that intangible sense of ease and comfort that comes with gently moving water.

I was not especially keen on taking up hunting again, remembering too well the hunting accident that had taken Dad's life, and not very anxious to kill anything at all. But I enjoyed the camaraderie of bivouacking in the back country with all the boys, passing a bottle around a campfire and bullshitting while the night sky, unblemished by light pollution, filled with brilliant stars and surrounded us with a primal darkness. Max and Harvey would make it an especially memorable experience. With any luck, I wouldn't encounter anything to shoot at, and maybe it wouldn't snow on us, both wishes coming true.

Back in Troy, informal music sessions featuring traditional and country songs were a part of many evenings at the resort. When John played, sometimes joined by other skilled musicians, it would be a special evening and the resort would fill with people and joyful music. The café would fill beyond capacity and Roger would sell a lot of beer. John found a 400-acre parcel just across the river from Troy, and plans were made to build a house fronting the Grande Ronde, a country retreat for John and his family.

John was a great one for experiencing life, reaching for things that had been only dreams in his youth, learning much of it on his own. He once learned how to fly an airplane, getting his pilot's license and doing a solo flight, and then, to my knowledge, never flying again. His musical skills are exceptional. Throughout the Creedence years and beyond he would teach himself to play whatever instrument might be needed to make the record he had in mind. Starting with his *Blue Ridge Rangers* project and continuing for years, he was adamant about making his records by himself, playing all the instruments. He was a hard worker, capable and bright, and he would undertake whatever he deemed necessary to make his visions a reality. In Troy he would learn to hunt and fish. Now he would learn how to build a house. With Harvey in the lead and the guys who worked for him (me, brother Bob, Bruce Koutz, and John himself), we would build from scratch his country home on the Grande Ronde River. A water witch ("dowser") came with a willow branch to locate the well. It was a great eye-opener and learning process for me as well.

Max was also on the team and had started Ho-Hum Construction with Charlie Allen, a local roustabout and hired hand. Along with their laughable slogan, "Don't Call Us—We'll Call You," they had a tractor and an old dump truck and not much more. Whenever I'd run into Charlie in later years and ask what he was up to, the answer was always the same, "You know, man, just ho-hummin' it." Charlie also joined us in elk camp. During a cold spell, Max and I moved into the cook tent where we could light a fire and warm things up. But come two or three in the morning, we were freezing again: "Pssst, Halsey. Hey, Max ... why don't you get up and build us a fire?" "Why don't you, brother?" It was too cold for either of us to get out of our sleeping bags.

While the house project was in progress, we would travel from our Bay Area headquarters on a regular basis, coming to Troy for weeks at a time to work on John's house. Harvey would stay for extended periods, getting things done on his own. It wasn't an easy commute. Troy is some 900 miles from the Bay Area, no matter the route, and there are several. I came to know each intimately. That was a big part of Troy's appeal: It was so remote and hard to get to that it remained mostly in its natural state.

→-←

AS JOHN'S PRESENCE IN TROY became part of the scenery, Roger would let it be known in the outlying communities of Lewiston, Idaho, Clarkston, Washington, and Enterprise, Oregon: "John Fogerty's playing at a street party in Troy!" The once informal café sessions turned into rock & roll barn dances held in the old tack room, an outbuilding of the Troy Resort. A couple hundred people might squeeze in there, and the ancient, wooden structure would creak, bounce, and sway in time with the music and gyrating bodies of the weekend party folk. There would be a pick-up drummer, often a bass player whose name was Rex Bennett (who wasn't at all a bad singer), me on a rhythm guitar; sometimes CCR recording engineer Russ Gary was there and joined in on guitar. John, of course, kicking major ass, looser and having more fun than I'd ever seen him have on the professional stage. I have a cassette recording of this band doing "Mule Skinner Blues" in the old tack room. What it lacks in sonic detail is made up by energy and vibe, recalling the best of old time rock & roll. Roger prospered, John's celebrity swelling the population of Troy beyond capacity and bringing Roger more customers than he'd ever seen.

Roger was no dummy and every time a party was eminent, like a concert promoter, he would get the word out. The parties in Troy became legendary, sometimes even scary as people would overdo the party spirit, alcohol and testosterone, overcoming common sense. The village bad boy, Slim, a rangy logger whose fame was limited to his ability to savagely beat an opponent into a pulpy mass, would lead a charge into any arena, looking for a fight. Sometimes he carried a gun, but as far as I know, the only time he ever used it was to kill his dog, whose corpse he drunkenly threw out a cabin door and into the street. I sometimes wondered where Darwin would have Slim stand while charting the "descent of man."

≫-≪

BACK AT OUR HEADQUARTERS IN Albany, John, by himself, went to work on a second album for Asylum, *Hoodoo*, an ill-fated venture into synthesizers and disco rhythms. An admiring and humble Rick Nelson came to see John about producing an album for him. I guess John felt he had too much on his plate at the time and declined, although he was honored by the request. I thought John might undertake the project; I knew he could do a good job of it, and it might give him a break from what I sometimes looked on as the drudgery of making records all by himself. John admired the music of Rick's teen-idol days when he had a hot band led by the superb guitarist James Burton, elevating Rick's music well above the Frankies and Fabians. But it wasn't to be, and Rick was lost to everyone in a plane crash about a decade later.

Soon we'd be back in Troy, still working on the house. Asylum Records had arranged for a story about John to appear in *Rolling Stone* magazine. The journalist, wonder-kid and the "Almost Famous" Cameron Crowe, was scheduled to come to Troy, together with a photographer, to do the piece on John. It fell to me to see that they had somewhere to stay when they arrived. I called Roger and reserved two of his little cabins:

"We'll need them for a couple of nights. Some guys from *Rolling Stone* are coming to Troy to see John," was roughly how I put it to Roger. It didn't occur to me that Roger, unfamiliar with music media, wouldn't know that *Rolling Stone* was (and is) the preeminent journal of rock and popular music. This is what Roger heard:

"The Rolling Stones are coming to Troy to see John!" and word went out on the Roger wireless.

I was driving to Troy in my Peugeot 404, choosing the central Oregon route. Forty miles out of Bend I noticed the temperature gauge starting to climb and pulled over to have a look. Shit. A stream of coolant was coming out of the water pump; a seal had ruptured. I knew exactly what this meant: call a tow truck to get the car into Bend, overnight in a motel, find a garage capable of replacing the water pump (which I knew would have to come from

California), and rent a car to get me to Troy. All was accomplished and I pulled into Troy in the early evening of the following day.

Max had told me about Troy's history as "Outlaw's Roost." Troy provided a secluded hideout for an outlaw on the run, and there were several escape routes. There were two main roads in and out, one through Oregon, the other from Washington and Idaho, and two or three lesser-known routes through canyon and forest. When the outlaw got word that the sheriff's arrival was eminent, he could choose among the several exits and make a clean getaway.

Troy was still known for its outlaws, but I guess the thought of the drug-addled international bad boys, the Rolling Stones, was too much for local law enforcement, who had picked up on Roger's announcement. I was driving a rented Ford and came into Troy through Enterprise, Oregon, and down the Flora Grade, about 10 miles of steep gravel road with multiple switchbacks. When I reached bottom, coming into town on level road alongside the Grande Ronde, I saw flashing lights up ahead and found that the road was barricaded. There were several patrol cars, and when I pulled up, about a dozen cops surrounded my car with flashlights, searching everywhere their beams would penetrate. I presented myself to the cops, calmly, as a part-time resident and answered all their questions, noting they seemed disappointed in both my sobriety and legitimacy.

A similar roadblock was set up on the road in from Washington and Idaho. The cops were waiting for the Rolling Stones.

John wouldn't even arrive until the following week. Nonetheless, there were a couple-dozen early arrivals who made it through the roadblocks and who had come to party. For a band they got me on guitar, a somewhat loaded Charlie Allen on mandolin, and Rex Bennett on the bass guitar. Not quite John, let alone the Rolling Stones, but at least Rex could sing. As it dawned on me what had happened, I could only laugh and explain the reality of what was going on to Roger, who I assume then corrected the accuracy of his press release. Later, the following week, I took Cameron Crowe and the photographer up on "Fogerty Mountain," a part of John's 400 acres, where we laid waste to empty pop bottles with Max's .22 magnum Ruger single six.

※—※

As we came close to completing the house in Troy, a call came in from John's lawyer, who had been in touch with Joe Smith, the head of Asylum Records. John got in touch with Smith who told him he didn't think they should release the *Hoodoo* album because they thought it wasn't up to what John could do, no better than the prior album, which had not done well by CCR standards. At the time I thought it a crushing blow, but John, after dealing with the initial impact, remembers thinking they had made the right decision, as though he had been too close to the forest to see the trees. He no doubt had different expectations when he turned it in.

John then began in earnest to wrestle with his inner demons, none of which included alcohol or substance abuse. Adding to the stress and anxiety, John and the other the Creedence members had discovered that the offshore trust that held their millions, Castle Bank & Trust, was a scam, some said a CIA front. When their attorney, Barrie Engel, arrived in Nassau for meetings with bank officials, he found an empty building with chains across the door; only scattered furniture and shredders remained. Even *60 Minutes* did segments on Castle Bank & Trust.

In the months that followed, I could sense the tension and strain building in John. It was a time of gross uncertainty marked by an underperforming record release, the non-release of *Hoodoo*, waiting for unknown edicts from the IRS, as well as multiple legal maneuvers aimed at recovery from the legal teams who had ushered them into the tax havens to begin with. I had nothing to do but audit royalty statements and push papers around.

I knew it was coming. In May of 1977 John came into the

office and he didn't say good morning. "There's no easy way to do this ...," he said. He had me write myself a generous severance check and wished me well. Thus ended a relationship that went back to high school and contained within it a lot of trust, mutual support, and marvelous times marked by life experience beyond anything I could have imagined. Another eight years would elapse before the world again heard from John Fogerty.

➺-➻

I STILL VISIT TROY, THE town still sleepy but changed from the old Troy we first discovered when horsemen tied their mounts to the hitching post in front of the resort. The old Troy Resort was lost to a fire and Roger and his family moved on. Some years later, a less than welcome head of a motel chain discovered Troy and proceeded to buy up and tie up as much of the local real estate as he could. A self-serving and aggressive asshole, many took a strong dislike to him. I was sitting in prison at Terminal Island when I got a letter from him telling me that unless I deeded him a right of first refusal to purchase my Troy property, he would shut my water off. The waterline was a gift from the prior owner of the new resort, the folks who came after Roger, and who then sold it to this guy. I made the mistake of keeping the waterline. I should have told him to kiss my ass.

The back country remains pristine to this day, and I relive earlier years each time I hike into it, knowing exactly where the best pools are hiding the biggest trout, keeping a keen eye out for wildlife, a wary one for rattlesnakes. I laugh when I remember the contests I'd have with Charlie Allen over whose was the bigger fish. Whenever Charlie would lose, he'd claim his fish had been out of the water longer, thus shrinking from its original, winning size. John eventually sold all of his property in Troy, that bump in his road coming to an end.

The early days in Troy remain special in my memory. Going

to Troy was like stepping back into an earlier time, when life was simpler and more relaxed, a natural existence where values had real substance, a slice of the America that once was.

I read somewhere that John spent something close to a million dollars painstakingly producing his superb *Blue Moon Swamp* CD, which finally earned him a Grammy award. There was a time when the John Fogerty I knew would have considered such expenditure "vulgar," always proud that the Creedence albums were made in a week's time for a minimal amount. Maybe million-dollar productions are what are required to win a Grammy, an award representing an industry that, more often than not, seems to thrive on vulgarity.

I will always be grateful to John as a generous employer and a valued friend. My gratefulness extends to Stu, Doug, and Tom too, the boys who made the noise, for their friendship and the opportunity to come along when they conquered the world.

BOOK 3

PRELUDE

1

HONORABLE ASSOCIATIONS

ALL MY LIFE, WORK HAD FOUND ME, BUT NOW I HAD TO GO LOOKING for it. Instead, I found the business of illicit drugs, the dope trade. This is not to suggest dealing dope is not hard work. It is. When opportunity presented itself, financial reward provided a blinding opiate. Finding honor among my new associates, I convinced myself I still traveled a righteous road. I knew better, but buried that knowledge in favor of my empty pocketbook. Drug use, our hangover from the sixties, was still something that separated a lot of us from the "establishment," the ruling class phonies who told us mostly lies about its dangers and had waged the awful, shameful war in Vietnam. What follows is the story of my participation in the drug trade, the way I found it and how it entered my life.

I think it's too bad that everyone's decided to turn on drugs, I don't think drugs are the problem. Crime is the problem. Cops are the problem. Money's the problem. Drugs are just drugs.

—Jerry Garcia

The months following my discharge from John's employ were hard ones. I was living with a bright and engaging woman in San Francisco, estranged from my wife and family, and I was floundering. What would I do next? I had no idea. I prepared a resume and started looking around. I talked briefly with Bill Graham, but nothing ever came of it. I looked into some automotive positions. But my heart wasn't in any of it, and nothing appealing came my way. I found asking for a job an awkward experience, and I was fast running out of confidence as well as money. I collected unemployment for a while and worked on the side for my brother and Sheldon. Together they had purchased a unique Berkeley property they called the "Castle," a crumbling, art-deco-like remnant of an earlier era that resembled a 16th century Norman fortress, though decidedly smaller. I moved out of San Francisco and, for a while, into the Castle.

While I was running around the world with Creedence, and later working for John, my brother had become successful in various business ventures, mostly on Maui, and equally successful at selling marijuana and, more recently, cocaine. Sheldon and some friends had established a successful real estate investment company, buying, renting, and selling residential properties in Berkeley. My brother and my best friend, my two closest confidants, both who formerly worked for me, were doing well and tossing me $75 a week to be the caretaker at the Castle, for which I was grateful. The property straddled a major earthquake fault and was in need of a lot of care from decades of shaking. Between the unemployment benefits and caretaker income, I could see to the needs of my family without using up what I had managed to save. At one point I went to Maui with my son, and we spent several weeks working on the construction crew for a home my brother was building in Olinda, high on the slopes of Haleakala. It was a close and healing experience for both of us. Between working on the home and visiting with Mom, we spent generous time at the beach and on the basketball court.

I badly needed something to do with the rest of my life and unemployment benefits weren't going to last very long. Mom urged that I come to Maui and learn the real estate trade. She had recently sold a 40-acre property to Mick Fleetwood and even touted my availability to his attorney, but I knew that wasn't likely to lead anywhere. If I possessed abilities and experience that could be called a trade, it was in the automotive service business. I had worked in my father's service departments from the time I was 13 until the time of his death, after which I was soon managing the entire business, something I did for about six years.

An old friend several years my senior, and who had started in the automobile business working for Dad, became the Toyota dealer in Berkeley. Somewhere I heard he was looking for a parts man. I visited with him and toured his dealership. He was once a good-time Charlie ratfucker, slick and capable, who delighted in corrupting me plenty when I was in my teens. Now he was an adult, a serious businessman whose eye and efforts were solidly fixed on bottom-line profits. He wanted my solemn pledge of permanency. I didn't like the idea one bit, but it would be legitimate employment, if lacking the glamor of my previous positions.

My brother, bless him, was incredulous: "You don't want to do that," he said with a dismissive wave of his hand, like Obi-Wan Kenobi using his Jedi mind control. "Stick around. Opportunity will show up ... by the way, do you have five grand?"

I had five grand and not much more. "Give it to me," he said. "You'll get back fifteen inside a month." That sounded welcome. I gave him five grand, knowing that he respected my interests and wouldn't be careless with it.

The scam worked like this: One of the partners had a connection in Peru. A cruise ship traveled a route on the west coast of the Americas that called in Lima. Pure cocaine was purchased there for twelve thousand dollars a kilo then stashed behind a secure bulkhead in a suite on the cruise ship. The same suite was reserved in another name for the following cruise. When the vessel returned to San Francisco, the cocaine remained in the bulkhead. The ship was refurbished and made ready for the next cruise, prior to which there was, by tradition, a gala send-off party. Revelers by the hundreds came aboard to see their friends off and a couple of them left the ship with the cocaine in backpacks, free from the threat of customs, inspections, and so forth.

Voila! What cost twelve thousand dollars a kilo in Peru would fetch about sixty-five thousand a kilo, wholesale, in the US. One hundred thousand dollars was put up by partners and investors to purchase eight kilos of cocaine and cover expenses. Once the cocaine was sold in the US, it would return five hundred, twenty thousand dollars. Investors, who also included the partners who pledged their own cash at various levels, were paid three times their investment, three or four general partners splitting the rest. Turn-around time was about six weeks. It was understood that if something went wrong, you would lose all your investment.

Nothing went wrong, and in no time, I had some breathing room, plus I was given a twenty-five hundred dollar bonus for sitting on the load. The partners figured there could be no place under less scrutiny than my home in Orinda. I had moved back with my family, and it was a quiet, if uneasy, peace between Jeanne and me.

⊱⊰

I CONTINUED AS THE CARETAKER at the Castle, almost a full-time job. Everything there needed patching or fixing. Arriving to work one morning, there was a Latino man, who I learned was from Colombia, waiting at the Castle. He spoke very little English and had a wicked scar running from ear to chin on one side of his face. He was seeking one of Robbin's partners who, like Robbin, would be out of town for another 10 days or so. My junior high Spanish class was about to pay big dividends. I invited him into the Castle, and in clumsy conversation, I was able to learn that he had ten kilos of pure cocaine for sale at fifty thousand dollars (*cincuenta mil dolares*) per kilo. It was already here and there were no other parties to consider. I did some rough math in my head and convinced him, "Bring the cocaine to me!" And he did, starting with two kilos.

During the prior investment load, I had been introduced by my brother to one of his key distributors, a trusted associate called the "Professor," partly because he used modern laboratory testing equipment to determine the purity of the cocaine. I knew my brother and his associates prided themselves in quality product and never adulterated or "cut" the cocaine. If at all, that was done further down the line. Nonetheless, it was always tested for its purity.

I took the two kilos to the Professor, who examined them and spooned a miniscule amount into a small, hollow glass rod, which he then placed into a heating device that registered the temperature to which a sample was heated. It was equipped with a magnified window through which you could view the sample during the process. When it reached the prime temperature at which pure cocaine would melt, the sample instantly dissolved into a clear liquid leaving no discernible residue. The Professor's eyes gleamed, a smile crossing his face. "Let's do it," he said.

I didn't think of cocaine as a dangerous drug. It had been prevalent and socially acceptable throughout the music world. It was sometimes given to me as an introductory gift by various people who used it to express their cool. I used it on occasion but never thought much of it. If there was a single drug I thought powerful and to be respected, it was LSD. No one we knew used needles or had any experience with heroin, a drug we more or less thought of as evil. I remember my disappointment the first time I used cocaine. Some friends and I went to see the film *Easy Rider*, and we sat there and fidgeted. Fifty bucks for that? What a gyp!

Even though a rank rookie, I was entering the business on a relatively major league level. I understood the financial mechanics of the game. Purchasing in kilo quantity, we usually sold product in pounds and ounces, although amounts were measured on a metric scale. Our ounce was 28 grams; a pound of 16 ounces equaled 448 grams. So rather than 2 kilos, I left the Professor with four pounds, each weighing 448 grams and priced at $29,500 for each pound. There was over 200 grams left, about seven and a half ounces. The seven ounces would fetch another $13,000 and the half-ounce became personal stash, split among the partners. After I paid the Colombian his $100,000 for the first two kilos, there was a profit of $31,000. The same would have been true if I had sold the cocaine at $65,850 per kilo, but I guess $29,500 per pound had a better ring to it. Marketing wasn't limited to TV or selling cars.

This was in 1977, and cocaine was breaking into the American psyche, gaining in popularity and becoming a socially popular drug. *Time* magazine featured a cover with a martini glass filled with cocaine for its story about the drug's social proliferation. The drug cartels were still in their infancy. Cocaine was expensive and street-corner crack vendors were yet to be commonplace in the ghettos. "Freebase" and "crack" cocaine, the smokable variant, was initially unknown to us. Pure cocaine was in short supply and greedily scooped up by a rapidly expanding market. Those plying the trade, at least the ones I would meet in that first year or so, were honorable outlaws who operated on trust and a "do unto others" approach. Most had been involved in the marijuana trade and some still were. No one used weapons or participated in violence. It was implicitly understood: You didn't lie, cheat, or steal, and if you somehow got caught, you didn't rat on your brothers. I enjoyed being a member of this fraternity of smart and honorable people. There was also a female member who fit right in and handled herself well in this male-dominated business. Most were as interested in getting her into bed as into a business arrangement. To her credit, she was able to handle any such approach like a professional, keeping emotion and business separate matters.

When I went to collect the first payment from the Professor, he gestured to an adjoining room where there were a couple of full-sized brown paper grocery bags on the floor, filled with cash. "Take what I owe you," he said. I counted out approximately $130,000 in $5,000 bundles with rubber bands securing each end of the bundle. I laid it all out on the floor, but he hardly looked at it. There was an accepted belief that I would do what was right. I welcomed such open honesty and personal trust.

Over the next week, I saw the Professor and the Colombian almost daily, completing the entire transaction, all ten kilos. When my brother got back into town, I handed him and his partner over $50,000 each in cash, sticking a like amount into my own pocket. They were, of course, elated at this unexpected windfall, and I had arrived.

I recall no internal debate about moral values, risks, or what I would do next. I had made a clear and deliberate career choice. The thought of becoming a Toyota parts man vanished from my mind. My entire adult life had been about providing for my family. The automobile years without Dad were mostly about keeping the business afloat, along with the family. Though I had a comfortable income during the years with Creedence and John, I never managed to have much left after living expenses. After 20 years of just getting by, even if in reasonable comfort, there was nothing quite like having cash, lots of it, even if it wasn't kept in a bank.

⇒-⇐

SOME WEEKS LATER, SUCCESSFUL OUTLAWS met for dinner at the Kula Lodge on Maui, a prelude to an evening of celebration and camaraderie. I marveled at my lack of concern about how much things might cost. The waitress brought a plate of fine-looking spare ribs to the table and set them down in front of Ricardo. Before Robbin could fall on them, an event as likely as the change of seasons, Ricardo readied himself to fend off Robbin's boardinghouse reach, and hovered over his ribs like a protective mother hen. When Robbin reached for a rib, Ricardo blocked the attempt and commenced to spit on the dinner plate ... tooh, toof! toof! ...

a defensive maneuver thought to make the ribs inedible to others. Robbin nonetheless managed to dart in with a deft stab, grabbing the tastiest-looking rib of the lot, much in the way a wading heron spears a hapless frog. He dangled it over the table and dabbed at it with his napkin as to remove any would-be spittle, then attacked the rib like a contestant in a corn on the cob eating contest at a county fair in Iowa. "Animal!" scoffed Ricardo. Seated at the next table Maui's mayor, Hannibal Tavares, a tent-like aloha shirt covering his considerable girth, looked on, his face contorted into a grimace, as though reviewing a fee statement from his lawyers.

Finished with their entrees the outlaws, one by one, slipped off to the *lua* (*lua* is Hawaiian for "pit," a place to eliminate bodily waste) for their much anticipated after-dinner snort of cocaine. Each carried in his pocket a small bottle of prepared cocaine crystals, habit routine as wearing a watch or packing a wallet. Some bottles have a small spoon attached to the bottle cap by lanyard of miniature chain to assist in the pageant of consumption. Others simply make a fist and spill the crystals into the cavity between thumb and forefinger, then raise it to the nose, where a quick sniff propels the crystals into the nasal cavity. Snifters of cognac completed the dinner. Robbin grabbed the check, added a generous tip, divided by the number of outlaws present, and assessed each their share. Bills of various denominations rained on the table like falling autumn leaves. Robbin added up the litter on the table and asked the assemblage, "Who's short?" and more bills fell on the table, each outlaw covering an unknown shortage by an unknown someone. "Whoa, that's plenty," said Robbin, signaling that the money spigot could now be closed.

Later, after hours of cribbage, laughter, and good-natured gamesmanship, accompanied by more cognac and plenty of cocaine, most were disbelieving that the soft glow visible in the eastern sky was indeed the light of day, just beginning to peek over the rim of Haleakala.

⤐⤛

I WAS STILL AND ALWAYS have been drawn to music, and suddenly, I had plenty of extra cash. I thought music might provide legitimate opportunity to make a living, while also offering a means to dispose of illegitimate cash, a built-in convenience common to the music business. As it turned out, the reality of earning a living through music was still twenty years down the road for me.

Through an acquaintance of Sheldon's, I was introduced to a singer/songwriter named Roger Salloom, who was looking for management to help establish him in the music world. I was attracted to Roger's friendly smile and apparent integrity, as well as his music. He was levelheaded, sober, and serious about his career; his songs were clever, melodic, and he sang them with a rich voice. He had a great sense of humor and was delightfully playful as an entertainer, teasing his audience with clever comments and stories. Like his idol, Bob Dylan, he was right at home in the role of troubadour, accompanying himself on guitar and harmonica.

Together with Robbin and Sheldon, we agreed to bankroll a demo recording to see if we could attract interest from a substantial label to market and distribute Roger. We enlisted Stu Cook, who remained a pal and who had studio production experience, to produce the demo. Stu, too, could hear the potential in Roger and came aboard as a partner. He was also working with a fine and talented quartet, The Valley Boys (later shortened to Valley), and they made a great backup band for Roger.

Unfortunately, our efforts fell short of our intentions, the music business a fickle and erratic platform that required more of us than we could give. Stu produced a fine demo with a half-dozen of Roger's songs, but we got only compliments, no serious takers. And the drug business, of course, demanded constant monitoring and swayed my attentions from the other business at hand.

Roger, nonetheless, remains a friend to this day, and I'm happy that he finally has earned at least some of the recognition and respect he so richly deserves, his recordings and performances reaching wider and wider audiences. He also starred as himself, the "world's best unknown songwriter," in an award-winning documentary, *So Glad I Made It*. Roger always believed in himself and has persevered in a business that rivals the drug trade for its ruthlessness and reputation for chewing up and spitting out many a good soul to die an unheralded death in an unmarked grave.

2

BUSINESS AS USUAL

A NEW ASSOCIATE APPEARED ONE DAY, A LARGE, JOLLY MEXICAN FELLOW whose name was Henry, the introduction by way of Sheldon, who had met him through a real estate transaction. Sheldon could spot an outlaw at a hundred paces. Henry had connections and ways to move cocaine through Mexico and land it in the US. We had the connections and ways to turn it into cash once it arrived. We raised the required $100,000 or so with investors, most of it coming from ourselves. The load arrived on time and was transferred to my brother and me in an unnecessarily clandestine handoff in Tilden Park. The hungry market readily gobbled it up. I was now a full partner, and on completion, we each stuck $76,000 into our pockets. We called this load the "Spirit of '76."

Henry was a social gadfly who loved to party and always seemed ready to celebrate. His idea of celebrating our recent success was to buy Sheldon a pet monkey, a token of his appreciation for the introduction to my brother and me. What a blockhead move that was. Giving someone a monkey is appreciated in the same manner as would be a gift of syphilis. "Charlie" wasn't some cute little squirrel monkey, but rather a sometimes ferocious South American woolly, who probably weighed in at about 25 pounds. Instead of refusing the gift, Sheldon's idea of handling the matter was, "Take care of him for me, wouldja, JR?" My first chore was to build him a cage at the Castle, where I had continued my duties as resident handyman, newly acquired wealth notwithstanding.

I think I was the only one to establish a companionable relationship with Charlie. He seemed to know I was the boss and he followed me around the Castle, playing with the tools in my toolbox as I worked on various projects. Charlie and I developed a respect for one another. When it was time for me to go, I would have to put him back in his cage and he sometimes objected with a show of his formidable fangs. I knew that if I let him back me down I'd lose control, so on those occasions when Charlie proved difficult, I would steel myself to the task, talk to him firmly, then pick him up and put him in his cage. He never once bit me. But he did bite others, and he would get especially over-amped by females, no doubt a by-product of his own sexual frustrations. We learned that a menstruating female would set him off into a frenzy.

The first time Robbin met Charlie he had his girlfriend with him. When he let Charlie out of his cage, ostensibly to play with him, the monkey took over. Charlie didn't bite anyone that night, but he was no doubt excited by the female presence. He ran around the Castle using the stairway and balcony railings as his jungle-gym, swinging from overhead light fixtures that dangled on chains, generally raising hell and having his way, intimidating Robbin with his fierce teeth whenever he'd try to get him back into the cage. The frantic phone call came to me in Orinda, "Jake, get over here quick and do something with this fucking monkey!"

Some months later we were meeting with Henry at the Castle. The meeting concerned a second load we had financed and that was overdue. Henry's line of bullshit about the load bothered us. We somehow got our money back, but I always felt that Henry had cut us out, teaming up with some other distribution partner. He no longer had our trust, and he was also due a payback for Charlie, a little monkey karma. During the meeting, Charlie was out and occupying himself with some of his toys behind the sofa when Henry got up and crossed the room to get a beer from the kitchen. Charlie bolted from behind the sofa, a fierce ball of fur on the fly, grabbed Henry by the leg, and gave him a nasty bite. Scared the hell out of Henry, who let out a painful-sounding yelp.

During the time Henry was around, he introduced us to his brother-in-law, who had a scam of his own. He came by the castle one day with a heavy, oddly-shaped hunk of metal about four inches thick, two feet across, and weighing about fifty pounds. What the hell is this? He explained that it was a piece of the mechanical action from some industrial manufacturing equipment, a part from some huge commercial textile loom. Did I know someone with a drill press? We ventured out to Dog Patch, the home of a friend who had all manner of metal fabricating tools and equipment. The brother-in-law produced a template with half a dozen holes in it that fit the shape of the hunk of metal, a treasure map indicating where to drill.

After the holes were drilled, the hunk of metal fell away into two identical halves. Concealed inside were two and a half kilos of cocaine. The halves had been bolted together, the tops of the bolts counter-sunk, welded over, and ground smooth with the rest of the surface. Close inspection revealed none of this. It was a clever way to get the coke through customs. But our distrust of Henry soon extended to his brother-in-law, whose machismo-fed Latin ego made him loopy on his good days and nitwitted on others. This one episode was our sole interaction with him. Years later I read about Henry's problems with the feds, multiple arrests and charges likely to add up to a mountain of time behind bars.

Charlie once escaped and bit a little girl in the neighborhood, who had seen him and wanted to play. Thankfully, it wasn't a serious wound. The Animal Control people gathered him up, and we found him later at the shelter. It was becoming clear that Charlie was more of a handful than anyone wanted to deal with. One of our friends from Maui wanted him, and he took Charlie home with him. We all thought he would be better off in Maui's tropical climate. But Charlie soon administered a savage bite to his new owner's bare foot and, as I heard it, ended up in the Honolulu zoo.

⯈⯇

THOUGH I NO LONGER NEEDED employment, I went to work for the real estate company belonging to Sheldon and his partners, running the office and handling real estate transactions. Sheldon had fallen into a life that included plenty of cocaine and party girls and wasn't much interested in putting in time at the office anymore. I enjoyed the experience, learning the nuts and bolts of the real estate trade, and I liked the people I was working with. But cocaine was always around, showing up in my life. We had established a network of outlaws who provided a reliable outlet and, generally speaking, easy money. At least it seemed that way at the time. If we didn't have our own load happening, someone else usually did, Stephen Green among them. It became an integral part of my life. I was always meeting new people and hustling more cocaine. And starting to use more of it than I had in the past.

Green called me at the real estate office one day, wanting our participation in a load that had just arrived. He asked me to meet him in Orinda. He'd bring the goods with him and we'd go to my house to conduct the transfer. He arrived in his Porsche with several capped, white PVC tubes, about four inches in diameter, sticking up all around him in the car. Roof panels on the Porsche had been removed, allowing a couple of the cylinders to protrude beyond the roofline.

"Let's get going," he said. "I'm loaded to the gills!" He was anxious and on alert. I took note of the expression he used, "Loaded to the gills." Where the hell did that come from? It sounded a little fishy to me.

It was the strangest load of coke I'd ever seen, packed into these white cylinders. A lot of it was still wet from processing and difficult to get out of the tubes. It had a strong chemical smell to it and it wasn't consistent in color. We normally wouldn't have had anything to do with it, but at the time it was the only game in town, and we felt some sort of stupid allegiance to Green, the exalted "Mr. Big," who we foolishly elevated to some lofty podium as a senior member in our imagined brotherhood of spice merchants. Green was very good at selling himself, and we were taken with his bluster and bullshit.

Green once asked me if I'd keep a suitcase for him while he went on vacation. He said it contained over a million dollars. I declined. He hardly knew me, although he had known Robbin for a few years. I wondered at the time if it was some sort of test he had devised for me, but he seemed to know I was trustworthy, a Boy Scout with a merit badge in honorable coke trafficking. Green left the load with me to dry out and weigh on my own.

I spread the coke out in trays and put it in my attic where it sat for days, drying out. When I finally bagged and weighed it, we owed Green over half a million dollars. I took some of it to the Professor where it checked out reasonably well, but there was still something odd about its composition. The Professor wanted only the best of the load, the whitest with the best cosmetics. The rest sold at lower prices, but eventually it all sold, and I paid Green everything he was due.

Because of the poor cosmetics, some of it even appearing lightly browned and opaque as though too long in an oven, and the overall suspicious composition, I called this particular load of cocaine "Baked Alaska."

A client of one of our associates, someone I didn't know and never met, bought several pounds of Baked Alaska through the associate, paying cash for his purchase. It was packaged in three separate bags. For reasons unknown to me, he mixed all the bags together. It's possible he was "cutting" it by adding some sort of diluent—and the whole thing, all three bags, turned a vivid pink! Over a hundred thousand dollars' worth of pink cocaine. An alarm went out and chemists were consulted. I heard he had some success taking the pink out of part of it and heard further that even the pink stuff eventually sold as soon as the markets had dried up.

In the middle of the pink cocaine/Baked Alaska fiasco, our friend BL brought in a load of prime Bolivian cocaine that everybody wanted. It was much easier to sell than Green's Baked Alaska. At one time, I added up our obligations to Green and BL, noting that our lines of credit exceeded a million dollars by a considerable amount.

➤-◄

ANY POSSIBILITY OF REESTABLISHING MY family life and relationship with Jeanne had been skewered by champagne and party life. We remained cordial and civil with one another, our relationships with our proud and loving children our remaining link. I realized with no small amount of guilt what yet another separation meant to our children, but the loving bond we had established over the years would hold strong.

Robbin decided we should celebrate our success with what he called a "love boat" cruise down the Mexican Riviera. We brought Max along and invited our mutual pal Stu Cook to join the party. We brought along enough cocaine to fuel a field of race horses. Max claimed each time he snorted a line of coke he would become a few years younger. "Man, I feel like I'm fifty again! Can't wait to see what forty-five feels like." The times were festive, free, and easy.

Pulling into port at Mazatlán, Stu noticed that the evening's shipboard activities included a talent contest, and he was determined we would enter. He and I went into town and bought a couple of cheap guitars at the central marketplace. Max always had a harmonica with him. Robbin wasn't musically inclined, but we got him a tambourine to bang against his ass, counting in time, one-two-three-four. At rehearsal we met a delightful middle-aged woman seeking to join up with someone as a singer or dancer.

Perfect. We included her as our dancing lady. We would perform as "The Famous Flying Tomato Brothers & Sister Rose," the name inspired by The Flying Burrito Brothers, the Maddox Brothers & Sister Rose, and the color of my guitar, a gaudy reddish-orange. Stu's guitar was identical, but an eggplant purple. Tomato brothers won out over eggplant brothers. I told corny jokes and introduced the band members ("When Max was born the doctor slapped his mother!"). The audience loved us and we were the hit of the show.

We had such joyous times we tried later to duplicate them with a Caribbean cruise. Although mostly entertaining and fun, it lacked the magic of the Tomato Brothers cruise. Max was uncertain about setting foot in Florida, convinced it was a hotbed of thieves and red-necks. Robbin talked Ed Olson into coming along. Ed hated being cooped up on a ship for days on end. The only table for him there was in the casino, where one night he got drunk enough to spill a drink all over the roulette table and belligerent enough to have security escort him to his cabin. Then we had to put up with an older man, "Crazy George," who was coming apart at his mental seams and had somehow gravitated to us. He was taken off the ship mid-cruise, strapped on a gurney belonging to a waiting ambulance.

Ed taught us a new trick: Stu and I climbed around a partition between our shipboard suites and "short-sheeted" Robbin's bed, folding the top sheet back inside the covers, and remaking the bed. Anyone trying to climb into a short-sheeted bed bottoms out halfway in, especially aggravating when you're loaded, which we always were. Our steward, Winston, a charming and playful Jamaican, got loaded with us most nights. We ran out of cocaine two nights before the cruise ended, putting a no-more-coke damper on festivities. Winston especially missed our nightly escapades.

We were having too much fun to notice the storm clouds building on the horizon.

3

THE JOURNEY OF *WHITE BIRD*

OUR FRIEND AND FAMILY MEMBER MAX, EVER THE SOLDIER OF FOR-
tune, had left his life in Troy and was building a new life of
adventure on Maui and the high seas. He parlayed his skills as
a bulldozer operator into a living and bought a modest sailboat,
learning to sail and navigate. He eventually teamed up with Maureen, who was also a sailor and would become his partner in life
for the rest of his years. One day they happened on *White Bird*, a
sleek 42-foot trimaran capable of world voyaging. Max saw there
his life's dream. Its cost was beyond what he could handle, but in
a partnership with me and my brother and Stu Cook, we bought
the handsome sailing vessel along with a mooring at the Lahaina
roadstead, where Max lived aboard with Maureen.

❖❖

IN THE SUMMER OF 1980 Max and Maureen sailed *White Bird* across
the Pacific to the San Francisco Bay, where Max would oversee
some refurbishing, purchase some new sails and rigging, and get
the vessel shipshape, spending a few months at the task. Afterward,
we planned to voyage down the coast into Mexico. Max and Maureen would sail home to Maui from Mexico, and I would fly home

to Berkeley from La Paz. Stu and I met them at their landfall in Santa Cruz and sailed up the coast with them into the San Francisco Bay, eventually putting in at the marina in Berkeley.

I arrived one day at the marina to visit and plan our journey. I spied *White Bird* in a temporary berth and started down the dock. Just as I approached the vessel, a silver missile flew from the open engine hatch and plopped into the marina, followed by a stream of curses, "When the goddam hell is someone going to invent a flashlight that works?" Max was below deck trying to install a new cable for the knot-meter and having a rough go of it. He climbed out and greeted me, still cursing the flashlight.

"Maybe the gods have determined we don't need a knot-meter," he said. Max had an abstract way of looking at things, as though maybe everything was the way it was *supposed* to be, broken or not. When he'd encounter something beyond repair or his ability to alter it, then it *must* be the way it was supposed to be.

"Oh yes we do need it, Max," said Maureen, coming up the stairs out of the galley. "It could get tricky trying to navigate without it." Maureen held the captain's license and did most of the navigation. "Hiya, Jaker," she said, smiling her greeting. Max was always a ladies' man, the pretty Maureen nearly 30 years his junior.

"Okay, Maureen, I'll get 'er done in good time," said Max, "... soon as I find a flashlight that works." He showed me the new pilot's chair and rigging, the new dodger stretching across the center hull, near mid-ship in front of the compass and wheel, guaranteed to keep heavy seas off the helmsman. New hardware sparkled everywhere, stainless steel clips, pulleys, and stanchions. "Don't ever bring no black iron aboard *White Bird*," said Max, as though a curse portending serious consequence. I gave him a hand replacing the cable, and we found its length had somehow been stretched by the prior installation attempts. "Must've needed stretching," said Max.

We spent the afternoon planning our voyage to Mexico. I would meet them in San Diego. I invited an old high school friend,

Freddie, to come along, and we hooked up with Max in San Diego to start our journey down Baja's western coast.

I'll always remember being stopped in my tracks when I saw the headlines in the San Diego newspaper racks on the day we set out: John Lennon had been killed, gunned down in front of his New York apartment by some crazy punk. His death stunned me, and I enlisted inner defenses to blunt and desensitize the shock of loss. It felt personal, as though I'd lost a friend, similar to the way I felt when the Kennedys were killed. I buried the knowledge somewhere deep inside and busied myself with the chores of preparing for the voyage. Through his music, Lennon was special, to me and to most of the world. Thirty-two years after his death, an absurd line of John Lennon "fashion" clothing gets released, aimed, I guess, at people who somehow feel their social ranking is elevated by aligning themselves with a celebrity through clothing. Spectacles around your tits, hand-prints on your crotch. Just imagine.

❖

MAX WOKE ME AT MIDNIGHT. It was my watch on a quiet night in calm seas. There was no wind to propel us and we were motoring parallel to the Baja coast with the sails dropped. *White Bird*'s sturdy little diesel engine pushed us along at about eight knots. I was alone at the helm, the big wheel in my grip, holding to a compass heading, and keeping an eye out for other vessels. Moonlight played off the water, highlighting the ripple and splash of our wake, alive this night with the plentiful phosphorescence found in the sea, electric and mystifying.

I heard their high-pitched clicks and squeaks before I saw them, a pod of dolphins. Then the vessel was surrounded, far too many to be remotely countable. They surged around our bow, keeping pace and weaving back and forth among themselves, their numbers spilling out and down each side of our 42-foot length. We were being escorted, carried along in a spectacular sea of dolphins, playful, sleek, and galvanized by the phosphorescence, their silhouettes distinct and outlined in an eerie glow as though each animal was defined in its own neon signage. Now and then an individual would leave the pod to capture a bait fish, speeding out ahead or peeling off on either side, then rejoining the group. The pursuers left a zigzagged trail of phosphorescence that mapped the chase and capture, like the tail of a crazed comet out of control in the heavens. The quarry had no chance once locked onto by these hunter-missiles of the sea. I was mesmerized by this stunning show of nature, unable to do anything but drink it in. By the time it occurred to me to wake the others so that they, too, could experience this unimaginable show of light, beauty, and grace, the pod was gone, moving on to their next order of business.

In the morning, we saw enormous dolphin pods moving across the sea in side-by-side formations seeming to stretch a quarter-mile across—thousands of dolphins in motion like a Serengeti migration, moving away from us. Their splashing, jumping, and diving was visible for 10 minutes or so before eventually falling off the horizon. We came across a sea turtle that morning, in apparent distress and being harassed by circling game fish. Freddie insisted we come to its aid. Max maneuvered *White Bird* into position and I held Freddie by his legs as he lay on the deck and leaned over the side and grabbed the turtle on each side of the shell. When he tried to lift it, the turtle panicked and started splashing the surface with its flippers, creating a pretty good ruckus. Almost immediately, sleek dark shadows knifed through the water at remarkable speed just beneath the turtle, sharks, maybe makos, investigating the commotion. I don't think Freddie saw them, but I held on a little tighter while he managed to haul the turtle on board. The turtle traveled with us most of the day, and we took turns keeping it wet and cool with buckets of sea water. When we released it in the afternoon it seemed to have regained its strength and stamina.

I put out a bone and feather lure on a trolling line and we soon had a couple of small barracuda for dinner.

Two nights later, Max and Maureen were engaged in a heated argument concerning our position. It was nearing dark and the sea was turning angry. White caps appeared all around us and waves started to break over the bow. The wind was noticeably picking up. "We should have seen that beacon by now," hollered Max, busy reefing the main sail. We were searching the ever-darkening horizon for a rotating lighthouse beacon that was supposed to be visible for two seconds at 60-second intervals, marking the southern end of the Baja peninsula.

"I think we've passed it," said Max, not at all pleased with the lack of information on where we might be. "I think we should head east." GPS was in its infancy, beyond our budget at the time. We instead relied on charts, sextant, and compass, technology unchanged for centuries.

"It's too dark, Max," insisted Maureen. "We could run into the Baja peninsula, if not the Mexican mainland." Stormy skies obscured the moon and stars.

Max moved to the bow and began hauling in the foresail, hanging onto the rigging for dear life, swinging around the deck like a rag doll in the closing darkness. "What balls!" said Freddie, standing back at the helm with me, watching Max wrestle the sail. The wind continued to rise and seas turned increasingly rough.

"C'mon, Maureen, let's head east!" called Max.

"No, Max, we can't! It's too dangerous!"

Max wondered if they had navigated one stretch of our course in kilometers instead of nautical miles, throwing our reckoning to a miscalculated guess. The sound of their argument was getting lost in the howl of the furious wind. I feared the stalemate over our position would lead us to a possibly dangerous path eastward or leave us with an uncomfortable and scary night at sea. Then it began to rain and we were pelted with cold, heavy raindrops driven by the wind, stinging our faces. Just when it couldn't get any worse,

I saw a brief flash on the eastern horizon out ahead of us, faint, like a candle at a distance.

"Beacon ho!" I called. All eyes turned to where I was pointing. Soon it flashed again, still dim on the horizon, and Max began tracking it with his watch, timing the flash and sequence.

"Sure as hell!" he cried after a couple more flashes. All of the stress and heaviness of the previous hour was left behind as *White Bird* headed east and into calmer seas.

When the sun came up, we were passing the coast and beaches at Cabo San Lucas, close in. Then we headed north, up into the Sea of Cortez, and followed our charts into the bay that fronts La Paz. Back on dry land after several days at sea, the ground wouldn't stop moving, but we soon recovered our land legs. Freddie and I left Max and Maureen on *White Bird* and headed into La Paz. Once settled, we went looking for what we had known since high school as basic Mexican trade commodities: cherry bombs and switchblades. Then we tried to buy some uppers and downers at a pharmacy. We couldn't believe it. There were no cherry bombs or switchblades for sale anywhere, and the pharmacy wanted to see our prescriptions. What the hell has happened to Mexico?

❖-❖

AT THE BORDER COMING HOME, I was watching the immigration officer's face across the counter from me. Something told me I should pay attention to him. He was entering my particulars into his computer, the screen filled with numbers and characters reflected in his glasses. Suddenly, his eyes visibly widened and his expression changed from routine to alert. He moved from his post and motioned for me to bring my belongings and come with him. We went to the back of the room where he had a few private words with an aggressive-looking customs cop who locked onto me with his eyes, holding me in his gaze. If central casting was ever in need of a nasty-looking SS lieutenant, here was the guy.

With a few clipped commands, the cop had me remove everything from my pockets and gave me a thorough pat-down. He went through everything I possessed with an exhaustive search, removing the contents of my wallet and ordering me to wind the unexposed film in my camera onto the spool so he could open it. He shot curt questions at me, treating me like the criminal I was, though I wasn't engaged in any crime at that moment. Then they pulled Freddie out of line and brought him to the back of the room with me, giving him the same hard time and treatment.

"Why's your hand shaking, pal?" the snotty bastard customs cop asked Freddie.

"My hand's not shaking," asserted Freddie, thrusting his hand out in front of him, rock steady. "Let's see yours," he said.

The cops finally relented and let us go, obviously displeased with our lack of any criminal contraband. As cool and belligerent as Freddie was with the customs cops, he then had an onset of acute paranoia for the rest of the journey, picking out people he thought were following us, imagining our every move under surveillance. His imaginings continued into the days following our return, becoming a genuine pain in the ass while I was trying to make sense of what I had learned.

They weren't supposed to know I was a bad guy. Who the hell told them? There was no question that something clandestine was going on with the feds. My cover as an innocent taxpayer had been blown: The feds had a file on me, flagged in their computers as a bad guy. Almost a year would go by before they arrested me, during which time I could only look over my shoulder and wonder about the source of their knowledge. What should have been obvious to me was a mystery. Amazingly, I never thought of Stephen Green as the root of it. His name had been suggested, but no one advocated silence more than Green. Even so, I never dreamed that words out of someone's mouth, accusations from a drowning man trying to save his own ass, could be evidence enough to convict someone of a crime, not in this country. There was no victim, no smoking gun, no dead body, no drugs, no money ... just words that chronicled a time gone by in which a hundred pounds of blow had changed hands. The law and the feds, of course, looked on society as the victim, and as far as they were concerned, that blow was real and a lot of it was deemed to have been found in my possession, adding weight to the conspiracy charges against me. Again the hard way, I would learn more about the feds than I ever wanted to know.

⇒-⇐

WHEN THE FEDS FINALLY LET the hammer drop, my brother and I found ourselves in a period of turmoil and uncertain future. Defending ourselves from criminal charges was new territory for us. The idea that the evidence against us, and others, was the word of one man, was unacceptable. Among other things, we feared that the feds might try to confiscate *White Bird*, depending on what Stephen Green might have told them. It was an unlikely scenario, given our histories as taxpayers with legitimate income, as well as Max's and Stu's interests, but these were times of less than reasoned judgment, fueled by a fear of prison and the unknown. I got in touch with Max and suggested that it might be a good time to visit the Marquesas and Tahiti, possible adventures we had discussed in the past. Max was in agreement, and *White Bird* was on her way within the week.

We counted ourselves lucky that *White Bird* was still afloat. One summer earlier, my family and I, along with Max and Maureen, ventured off for a week aboard *White Bird* to visit Moloka'i and Lāna'i. During our absence at the Lahaina roadstead, where dozens of private vessels are normally moored, a pissed-off Samoan named Benjamin Ko, angered that his passage to Tahiti had been withdrawn by a vessel neighboring ours, threw a fit of rampage and mayhem. He commandeered a large double-decked dinner boat that catered to the tourist trade and roared through the roadstead at full throttle, ramming every vessel he could get in his sights, sinking many. It was said that crew members on the tourist boat, attempting to allay the mayhem, sneaked up behind him at the wheel and broke an oar over his head, which didn't faze him at all. The massive Samoan grabbed two of them and threw them overboard and went back to his version of nautical bumper cars. When the aftermath was tallied, Benjamin faced something like 130 felony charges. I wondered if the dinner boat was filled with terrified tourists during the rampage, but I think Benjamin grabbed control before the dinner passengers came aboard.

After the initial landfall at the Marquesas, and throughout the following months and years, *White Bird* visited numerous island groups across the South Pacific, then headed to Australia's northern coast, then northwest through the Indian Ocean to Sri Lanka, ever westward to the Gulf of Aden, then north through the Red Sea and Suez Canal into the Mediterranean, where they again headed west before passing through Gibraltar and turning south, following Africa's western coast to a southwest crossing of the Atlantic into the Caribbean and through the Panama Canal, following the western horizon all the way back to Maui.

The journey of *White Bird* wouldn't be over until Max and Maureen had sailed her around the world, arriving back at their starting point, equaling in time my journey through the federal maze of trial, appeal, prison and eventual release. While in prison, we'd get occasional letters from Max telling us about his adventures. What a grand reunion awaited us at the end of our journeys, each of us indelibly branded for the rest of our lives by the people we'd met and the places we'd been, always looking forward to the next horizon.

Portions from a few of those letters from Max are excerpted below. In them I again hear his deep, warm country voice and remember his smiling face. Max died in Hilo in 1997, age 78 years.

Aboard *White Bird,* the Red Sea, March 1984.

Dear Brothers:

It's a hard push up the Red Sea. We left our last anchorage against strong northerlies, but it got too bad and we turned back. We've followed coastline since the Gulf of Aden, crossing from Yemen to Sudan and Egypt. Each stop along this coast features desert, camels, dust storms and flies. We keep an eye out for pirates and the Mini-14 at ready. We have some 600 miles to go before our next stop-over target, Cyprus. Egyptian military has been none too friendly, so we hit it again, right into crashing seas and 40-knot gale winds. Day and night with no relief, no moon to guide us. We got separated from our "buddy-boat" sailing partner, 45 hours without sleep, the main sail in tatters.

We finally spotted the Egyptian coast and headed for some shelter where we could lick our wounds. I was taking stock of everything that needed fixing when I paused to let the smallest of farts and completely shit my pants. I took them off and tried to throw them off the stern, but they hung up on the VHF antenna where they stayed, flying high, our disgusting flag and symbol of the last 48 hours. We heard on the radio that our buddy boat had gone on the shore in North Yemen and was waiting for a commercial tug to come and pull them off.

Heading out again, this time into calm seas, winds NNW at ten knots. It's warm, the sea is flat and I'm happy. Your brother, Max

❖

Aboard *White Bird*, Cyprus, July 1984.

Dear Brothers:

The smooth sailing up the Red Sea and through the Suez Canal didn't last very long, a repeat movie of 40-knot winds and high seas, lots of big ship traffic. We had to take on a pilot who brought along his prayer rug and kneels to pray to Mecca several times throughout the day. We finally found some shelter and the steering cable broke just as we dropped anchor. I jury-rigged it and we made it to Suez through one hard blow. I wanted to go to the pyramids, but felt the need to keep going on to Cyprus and make *White Bird* new again.

Cyprus at last! The sun shines, the people smile and the food is good. *White Bird* is safe in the marina. Coming into Cyprus at night, we were blown off course toward Lebanon where we saw flashes of shell fire and war ships. We raised a French aircraft carrier on VHF and they wanted to know what the hell we were doing there. They wouldn't give us a position fix, but did give us a bearing on Larnica, Cyprus. They launched a plane that made a low pass over us, and then followed us for two hours to be sure we were leaving the war zone. We'll be in Cyprus for some time, doing repairs and getting things shipshape. Your brother, Max

❧

Aboard *White Bird*, Adriatic Sea, September 1984.

Dear Brothers:

Anchored in a protective cove tonight, making slow northerly progress between storms. Looks like about 175 miles to Venice. The thread in the main sail is rotten and we blew out the lower seam, but were able to take one reef and get by. This morning we blew out the next one up, and we're now running with a double reef. The cloth is still good, so it's just a matter of getting to a good sail-maker for restitching. There are hundreds of islands along this coast, so we have good stops each night. We'll cross over to Yugoslavia before long. Once we reach Venice, we'll find a winter home and *White Bird* will get the VIP treatment, awaiting the next leg of our journey in the Spring. Your brother, Max

➵⳺

Aboard *White Bird*, Venice, Italy, December 1984.

Dear Brothers:

As we moved across the Pacific, from island to island, we never stopped for more than a few weeks before we were on our way again. Most of these stops meant working on the boat, getting her ready for the next leg at sea and new horizons. The longest stop to date was Sri Lanka. We were there for four months, waiting out the hurricane season. I was always frantic to move on when the horizons had become too familiar.

Now it's winter and we must stay here in Venice until the spring, and already I am restless. I want to go to sea, keep moving westward until I can drop my anchor where I first picked it up, a complete circumnavigation. To ease my restlessness, I have lowered my line of sight to things closer around me, trying not to look at those distant horizons. Venice is a unique city and there's plenty to see, so, between excursions and getting the boat back in shape, I'll hang on until spring. Last week we took the train to Florence, stayed a day or two, then went on to Rome. The Holy

Father wasn't there to greet us, so we didn't stay too long.
Your brother, Max

Aboard *White Bird*, Los Christianos, Canary Islands, November 1985.

Dear Brothers:

We're trying to get it together for the Atlantic crossing,
but pushing does no good as my speed around the world
is governed by #1, my income, and #2, the seasons and
weather. Direct to Florida from here is not a good route for
us. We will go south, down the African coast as far as the
Cape Verde Islands, then start our curve west, depending
on trades, Atlantic currents, and possible hurricanes. We
should start across the Atlantic early December and expect
landfall in Barbados or St. Lucia after about three weeks at
sea. I have no complaints and no fears. It's been a great sail
and I'm looking forward to the green, green grass of Maui.
Love from your brother, Max

P.S. Still believe in miracles.

4

THE DOWNWARD SPIRAL

I WAS EVENTUALLY TO LEARN THAT COCAINE BRINGS WITH IT A KARMA ALL its own, and it rubs off on those around it. The huge financial rewards attracted the kind of people who were as willing to cut your throat as look at you. What I had once seen as a business that ran on honor and respect became a murky world filled with paranoia and unseen dangers. Use of the drug was itself a slippery slope, especially in the long-term, when it became an everyday habit. "Poverty will keep you from going snow-blind," says one song, but that didn't apply to us. Money was never a problem and we had our own supply trains with enough "free" residual leftovers to keep us supplied all the time. Then many who had been regular users began to freebase, a powerfully addicting process. The Professor fell into its clutches and could no longer function in the real world. Freebasing seemed to hide people away in their closets, coming out only to obtain more cocaine, the pipe their only friend. I had once seen cocaine as generally harmless and benign. Now I was beginning to see that it dismantled people's lives. It is an insidious substance, sometimes masking itself as an empowering wonder drug before dragging you into its downward spiral.

For the great majority of us, when we were doing pot or psychedelics, things were headed in a fairly interesting direction. When we started doing coke and heroin, things went to shit.

–David Crosby

The world of the "honorable outlaw" I had once embraced was crumbling all around me. It started with an armed robbery at the Castle, gangsters in search of a big score, out to steal a "load." Drug dealers and outlaws, people who live outside the law, can't call on the law when they might need it. They become easy targets for these vampires. A woman who was visiting at the Castle innocently opened the door one night and let them in. I was in the upstairs bedroom attempting to reach financial accord with "Brucie," a client who owed us a lot of money and whose drug habit had rendered him broke and incompetent. I heard the woman call my name and came out to find her bent over in a headlock, a revolver held to her head. She and the assailant were halfway up the stairway. I assured the punk with the gun he could have whatever it was he wanted and implored him not to shoot anyone. I briefly considered a heroic gun-grabbing lunge as I passed them on the stairway, the punk appearing to be easy game. Instead, I called to Brucie to come out and stay cool.

The punk blindfolded me and Brucie and made us lie face-down on the floor, where he tied our hands behind us then threw a rug over us. He blindfolded the woman and seated her across the room. Then the two main characters arrived. They put a gun against my head as they interrogated me, insisting there was a load of cocaine in the house. I knew by their voices—no question—that they were black men, although the punk was a white boy. They roughed me up some and banged their pistol against my head a couple of times, I suppose so that I'd know they were serious, but

I wasn't hurt. I sensed they intended to scare rather than maim. I knew I had to stay calm and deal with these guys in a manner they would find credible. Like a blind man, I was acutely aware of the physical surroundings.

At their insistence that I "give it up!" I told them, straight ahead and unapologetic, "You're in charge here ... look around. If there was a load here, you'd own it." I was businesslike. I had truth going for me and I refused to let them think I was cowed. I was apparently convincing. They took only my wallet and an ounce of what we called "Bing Wong" I had picked up earlier that day. Bing Wong was a reconstituted cocaine, washed under laboratory conditions. It was impurity-free, a sparkling, flaky snow white, and highly prized among cocaine devotees. Were we wine merchants, Bing Wong might have represented a prized Bordeaux from a legendary estate and vintage. We named it after a Berkeley dry-cleaning business and rarely sold it. It was personal stash and status symbol, reserved for our very best associates.

Poor Brucie had picked the wrong time to visit. He was terrorized but not physically hurt. Lying there tied up beside me, he peed in his pants, some of his urine flowing my way on the uneven surface of the Castle floor. Feeling the wet on me I at first wondered where Brucie got the glass of water to spill. The gangsters left as quietly as they had arrived.

I knew with little doubt who the responsible party was. We had only one black client, the "Ghetto King," our sole connection to the black drug market. He never required a "front," always showing up with a briefcase full of cash. He was a big operator in the Oakland drug trade, personable but steel-hardened by his rise to the top of the game in the ghetto. I got along well with him. We even played some basketball together. He turned serious when we were negotiating price and quantity, but was otherwise easygoing, pleasant, and smiling. He never personally used the drugs he sold, but he lavished them on his women.

The attempted theft was within the rules of his world, a place where life was a cheaper commodity. I had no significant cash in my wallet, but they had my ID and could show the boss they'd done their job—they weren't after my credit cards. I had mentioned the possibility of a new "load" to the Ghetto King only a week before, and he had once visited the Castle. It also nagged at me that the assailants didn't seem mean enough; I don't think the Ghetto King would want to hurt me. *Don't insult my ability to reason, Satch, you lowlife sonofabitch. Don't tell me it wasn't you behind the hit.*

"No man, it wasn't me," he pleaded. What else could he say? He was sympathetic in his denial, and he knew he was under no threat of retribution from me. "Okay," I said. "That's the way it will be ... tell your boys I said thanks for not shooting me."

That essentially ended our relationship until I bumped into him on a basketball court at Terminal Island a few years later. I was thirty pounds heavier than when he'd last seen me.

"You say you know Jake?" he wondered.

"No, Satch, I am Jake."

He took a closer look and smiled, his eyes laughing. "Man, you sure been eatin' well." Even though certain I was a victim of his gangsterism, I could not bring myself to dislike this man. Our relationship continued, but mostly on the basketball court.

❧ ❧

ONCE RELIABLE CLIENTS WERE FALLING by the wayside, some acquiring habits that involved freebasing, consuming great amounts of product then unable to pay for it. One friend and client was set up by a woman he thought cared for him. He was ambushed by gangsters who beat him, stealing his drugs and money. Adding insult to injury, they tore a hair piece from his scalp, a woven affair, exposing what Robbin had once teasingly called his "perfect Friar Tuck." Stephen Green, the trusted "Mr. Big," was set up by an insignificant client who had been "rolled" by federal drug cops searching for a bigger catch. He was arrested in a sting at the San Francisco airport, his empire reduced to ashes. Mr. Big, he who more than anyone else preached the gospel of tight lips, went to trial and got 20 years, then turned major rat, taking down his best friends, associates, and family members so he could resume his freedom. We never saw it coming.

Another good friend and reliable associate, Richie, was involved in an auto collision just after picking up a kilo on a stormy night. He was arrested with it after some Good Samaritan witness saw him stash something in a nearby dumpster while waiting for the cops and was unable to keep such knowledge to himself. Write-offs were becoming major money and it was only because of prior successes that we were able to take care of our own obligations. Richie was a principled friend and he eventually paid us back after serving some minimal state jail time, thanks in part to having San Francisco heavy-weight Willie Brown a part of his legal team. But he, too, would learn things the hard way, some years later acquainting himself with the feds. He showed up at the Lompoc camp just about the time I was getting released. He asked if I got the thirty grand he said he gave to my ex-girlfriend for me. Of course I did, Richie, in your dreams.

Going to trial was no picnic, stressful and nerve-racking, but the nearly two years I spent on bail pending appeal were the worst of my life. I was still in business, an unthinkable recklessness on my part. And I was clinging to an unsatisfying relationship fed by a constant stream of drug use, treading water while waiting for the hammer to drop, as I knew beyond any doubt that it would. I gained the thirty pounds of unhappiness the Ghetto King had noticed.

≫-≪

THE GUY WE KNEW AS "T," one of the smugglers from the early days, contacted me with a plan to buy ten pounds of cocaine in Los Angeles. The seller was the uncle of another trusted friend and associate. T had once met the uncle a few years earlier. Both T and the nephew had been partners in the Peruvian cruise ship scams. This amount of coke being sold by the pound rather than by the kilo was the first warning sign. And it was being offered at a price far under market. I told T it sounded too good, that he could be getting set up. I should have listened to myself more carefully. T assured me otherwise then proceeded to get set up with my thirty grand, a down payment on the load. We had agreed that the money would remain hidden in an airport locker until he could inspect the cocaine and confirm everything was on the up and up. But T was sweet-talked by the honey-tongued "Uncle George," lulled into a sense of security from the longtime connection to the nephew. He brought out the cash beforehand, which in turn brought out the .357. There was no coke. Uncle George was as unprincipled and vicious as they come. What was T supposed to do, call the cops?

Following the rip-off of my thirty grand, Uncle George somehow found out where T lived, a rural home in Sonoma County. A month or two later, he showed up with two gunmen, seeking further hoard from someone he thought couldn't call the police. This time, however, he made a miscalculation.

T's property was enclosed by a high redwood fence with a gate. He was lucky to have been upstairs that morning when he saw Uncle George's Cadillac pull into his yard, two men with guns and wearing gloves getting out and closing the gate. T recognized Uncle George and the Cadillac right away. He grabbed a 12-gauge shotgun and pumped in a round, letting the Cadillac have it broadside. The men with the guns returned the fire while at the same time managing to reopen the gate, and they made a hasty get away. T had no record, drugs, or warrants. He called 911 and reported the attempted home invasion, describing the Cadillac, its passengers, and the gunfire. The highway patrol stopped the Cadillac, arresting the occupants. Uncle George, incredible weasel that he was, faked a heart attack and went to the hospital rather than jail.

None of us ever signed up for this shit, but as I was learning (again the hard way), coke's karma can deal a vicious consequence. Uncle George never knew of me or that the money he had stolen was mine, a fortunate circumstance for me. He assumed T was the financier and thought he would be an easy target for more. When T told me what had happened, I hired one of the better private investigators in San Francisco to find out as much as I could about these evil bastards.

Surprise, surprise: The two gunmen were off-duty Los Angeles police officers. Cops and robbers, in league with the low and unscrupulous Uncle George. LAPD Internal Affairs got involved, and the case against the cops was transferred to LA and, as far as I know, effectively hushed up. I doubt they were criminally prosecuted, T in no big hurry to be a witness in any prosecutions. Sonoma County law enforcement knew this was a drug hit. Even though T had no record, he was considered an uncooperative witness. Sonoma County was no doubt happy to transfer the case against the cops to LA. I remained a phantom principal, unseen and unknown by all the other players except T. The case against Uncle George was drawn out until he really did have a heart attack that killed him. There were no tears or sorrow from our quarter to see this nightmare of a man meet his maker.

❧⤏

WHEN MY TRIAL CAME AROUND I was paired with John Viljoen, the fun and friendly South African, as my codefendant. Two days before the trial was scheduled to start, he came to see me. "I can't go to trial," he said, "and I can't stick around. I'm not a citizen. They'll crucify me then deport me to South Africa where I'll be crucified again."

I never understood how he got bail under this circumstance, but obviously he did. I assumed the feds held his passport, as they did my own, but John was smart enough to maybe have a spare. I sympathized with him and knew that his status as a fugitive wouldn't reflect on me. I guess it might have had they known I gave him a couple thousand dollars to help him on his way. When Viljoen didn't show up for trial, the prosecution delayed the proceeding and paired me with Bump, who usually appeared to me as standoffish and sullen, lacking Viljoen's perky smile and esprit de corps. I never learned of Viljoen's fate. For all I know, he's still a fugitive.

More than eighteen months after my trial, I was still out on bail, sick of drugs and the lifestyle that came with them, sick of what this "honorable" business had turned into, sick of holding off the inevitable, sick of clinging to an unsatisfying relationship fueled by drugs. I actually felt a sense of relief when my appeal was denied, anxious to alter my circumstance. Even though still wary of prison. I was more than ready to end this chapter of my life.

I did my last line of cocaine ten days before surrender, concerned that they would throw me into the hole on arrival if my urine tested dirty. After years of abuse, there were no withdrawal symptoms, but I noted that it took a threat to compel me to quit. I felt I would be okay in prison, confident I'd be able to fit in where I chose. I wished only I could join my brother at the Lompoc camp rather than having to check into the medium-security prison at Terminal Island. Eventually, the camp would become a reality. I would deal with the shame and guilt, and pay the debt I owed, thankful for the love and nonjudgmental support from my family and friends. Though my banquet had been underway for some time, there were still many courses yet to be served.

BOOK
4

ROOTS

A FORTUNATE SON

We are here on Earth to fart around. Don't let anybody tell you any different.

–Kurt Vonnegut, *A Man Without a Country*

THE WHOLE TIME I WAS GROWING UP I NEVER MET ANOTHER KID WHOSE name was Jake. The only Jakes I encountered as a kid were characters in cowboy westerns. Today they're all over the place. My grandfather, all his life a Missouri farmer, was Jacob, known as Jake, and I was named for him but not on my birth certificate. I guess mom and dad wanted something a little more upscale. I was baptized James when I was six or seven and remember my disappointment when nothing of spiritual significance happened following that ceremony and ordeal. I never knew that name until I had to use it on legal documents. The feds, of course, used it on my indictment.

Growing up I always thought of Mom and Dad as among the best there could be, an opinion I still hold. Dad was a Missouri farm boy with a dozen brothers and sisters. Mom was from a small, quiet family in Northern California. Both were born in 1914, at the start of the First World War. They came of age during the

Great Depression and learned the value of hard work and a dollar. As parents who had known hardship, they were determined their children would not. In later years, Dad would instill in me a work ethic similar to his own, while Mom would push her children to be industrious and take their education as a serious matter, even though we seldom did.

I arrived in August of 1943, right in the middle of the next World War. My sister preceded me in January of 1942, and more brothers would follow in 1945 and 1951. Dad was exempted from military service because of vision deficits and further exempted on arrival of his dependents. Learning the automobile business, he soon started his own, buying and selling used cars. It was a great business to be in during the war years, because there were no new cars; the auto manufacturers instead supporting the war effort. Dad was a charismatic salesman with a perceptive ability to make money and he made more than just a living. He invested in real estate and became modestly well off for the times. Perhaps extraordinarily so for a thinly educated Missouri farm boy whose sun-darkened skin had earned him the racist grade-school nickname, "Nig."

➳‑❦

WITH EVENTUAL PROSPERITY, MOM AND Dad built their fantasy home in Kensington, an unincorporated and largely white East Bay community bordering Berkeley, Albany, El Cerrito, and regional park lands. A more exciting place for a kid to grow up is hard for me to imagine. We had climbing trees and frog ponds and our own spring. Sometimes in winter a lower portion of the backyard would flood, providing a tree-lined lake for us to pole our homemade rafts around in. Tree forts, underground forts, hiding places, and rope swings were all part of the landscape. The wonder of the natural world was all around us: deer, raccoons, opossum, birds, frogs, snakes, lizards, minnows, and creatures of the ponds. We could walk to school, just across the street and up the hill, where there were basketball courts and a baseball diamond. We picked wild blackberries by the basketful, and grandma would bake us wonderfully delicious tarts and pies. Neighborhood friends were abundant. This golden environment, together with the love of my parents, convinced me that I was among the most fortunate of sons.

From a second grade reader, the first book ever to captivate me, I felt a close bond with the young boy who was the lead character. He wore bib overalls, was very fond of blueberry pie, and had a pet crow. One day I discovered a crow in a pet shop and talked mom into buying him for me. I had also developed an appetite for blueberry pie. I named the crow Jamie, after the crow in the book, and tamed him to sit on my shoulder and eat from my hand. Together we won the "Most Unique Pet" trophy at the Live Oak Park pet show in Berkeley. Accepting the trophy on a stage with Jamie on my shoulder, he shat a copious crow turd on me, part of it running down my back.

Across the street from our house was the community church, a place where I never felt at ease except for during one period when Mom taught Sunday school and I learned about Moses. Otherwise, my brother and I refused to attend any of the classes set out for us, even though we had been appropriately dressed and deposited. Dad told me of a Sunday morning I came running down the driveway, followed by my younger brother, and when he asked why we weren't in church, I exclaimed, "Bobby escaped!" as though trying to aid in his capture but out ahead of the quarry in the chase. Looking back on it, I felt about as foreign and out of my element in church as I did in the US district courtroom, as though the "elders" held a similar view of me as did the judge and prosecutor.

⇥⇤

MY BROTHER AND I COVETED recreational explosives, firecrackers, and the like. We weren't interested in "safe & sane" fireworks, sparklers, and lawn fountains. We wanted things that went boom! Things that when ignited under a tin can would send it sixty feet into the air. Bursting sky rockets and roman candles that shot balls of fire. When we'd visit relatives in fireworks-legal Missouri, we always came home with a bounty of firecrackers, cherry bombs, and rockets. Even as such, we reached adulthood with all our fingers intact.

When we'd blown them all to hell, we'd get Grandma to take us to San Francisco on the F-train that then crossed the Bay Bridge, long before BART was around. Grandma was overbearing in her approach to looking after us, and learning this, we were skilled at disobeying her. We'd end up in Chinatown where bootleg fireworks were available if you knew the secret places to buy them. Poor Grandma probably turned frantic when Robbin and I ignored her orders and disappeared into the bowels of Wing Duck Liquors, through a cellar door and down a rickety stairway into the nether-land among the boxes and crates and dusty, exotic smells, where the bespectacled Chinese vendor in his grocer's apron spoke to us in grunts and gestures, then opened a cupboard against a wall exposing the treasures we sought: packets and bundles of firecrackers wrapped in cellophane through which we could see brand names and brightly colored labels, Camel, Black Cat, Scorpion, Zebra, and Chinese Dragon, in all sizes, tiny ladyfingers all the way up to four-inch salutes as thick as a stick of dynamite, clusters of bottle rockets, cherry bombs, and torpedoes in boxed cases. We were the one-eyed cats, peeping in a seafood store, carefully selecting the choicest morsels. We spent every dime we had and then found Grandma out on Grant Street. She scolded us to no end, but we never told her what we had in our bags. Second only to firecrackers was our fascination with knives, especially switchblades. We collected those too.

WHEN THE SIXTH GRADE IN grammar school was reached, my classmates and I found ourselves, finally, at the top of the ladder. Now we were the oldest and the biggest kids on the playground. After years of being pushed around by those in the grades above us, now we could do the pushing. Together with boyhood friends Mike Doyle and Dave Grace, we became the "Swade Gang," ignorant that suede wasn't spelled like it sounded. The Swade Gang was Mike's invention and he was Swade, as smooth as his namesake material, the brains of the outfit. Dave was "Spike," so known for the hobnails in his pretend stomping boots. I was "Curvy," because (of course) I could never go straight. We were proud criminals, inhabiting a make-believe criminal world. We even had a mascot, "Sneed" the duck. We found Sneed one day at Jewel Lake in Tilden Park and brought him home with us, where he lived in my backyard with the rest of our menagerie.

Mike and Dave were both natural comedians, smart and inventive, as funny as the days were long. We had some cruel pastimes, pulling malicious raids on the nearby Blake estate, running from the gardeners who sometimes gave chase. Sometimes we'd engage in telephone games, blindly calling people with the old "I'll give you three guesses who this is!" routine. Invariably, the guessing would start and someone would claim to be an early guess and carry on fabricated, counterfeit conversations. Then we might look up a name in the phone book, say, someone named Parrot, like the bird. When we confirmed we had Mr. Parrot on the line, we'd let out a mighty "squawk!" and hang up. Mean kid stuff. We also did some mean, intimidating stuff to other kids, too, but quickly outgrew our need for that when we started to pay attention to girls. Nonetheless, I'd like to offer up belated apologies from the Swade Gang to Doug Houser, Gary Tuley, and a couple of others whose names escape me at the moment.

➹⭅

INTEREST IN MUSIC CAME INTO my life first fueled by a friend of Dad's, Joe Gaeta, who could play hot shit boogie-woogie piano, the real deal. On those occasions when the families came together at our house, Joe would play and I would be swept up in the energetic rhythms of the driving left hand that created a foundation for the right hand chords and repeating hot licks. Boogie-woogie piano touched something deep inside me and became a goal and musical destination. I thought being left handed would give me an advantage because of the strong left hand rhythms and patterns.

Mom started me on piano lessons, where a graceless and stern old woman demanded that I learn to read music and memorize the scales, teaching insipid songs and pasting little colored stars into my music book whenever I managed to learn something. I had to memorize a wimpy song called "The Big Brown Bear," and play it at a formal recital in a dark, stuffy hall somewhere near the Berkeley campus. I hated the song and still remember some asshole out in the audience who snickered at me when I began my piece. I would later be thankful for at least this rudimentary introduction to conventional music. As soon as I could muster the will to stand up to my mother's urging that I continue, I quit, but not before I had memorized the scales in all of the keys.

A couple of years later, Mom learned of Chuck Dutton, who had a piano studio in downtown Berkeley, an easy bus ride, and taught his students to play by ear, teaching boogie-woogie and popular music classics. I took less than a dozen lessons from him but learned a lot of progressive and down-home chords, 12-bar blues, hot licks, and the way things went together. These were piano classes I found thrilling, and ol' Chuck was a very cool guy.

❧⋅❦

BILL HALEY AND HIS COMETS arrived before Elvis and other great rock & roll pioneers of the mid-1950s. His music had all the energy and urgency I found in boogie-woogie. One of the leading questions of the day for me and my friends was, "Is Bill Haley a colored man?" He, of course, was not, but his music so stood out from what else was offered to a white audience in 1954 we thought he might have been. Even back then, Bill Haley and His Comets sometimes caused an actual riot by an audience unable to contain the fierce energy of his music.

My sister, two grades ahead of me in school, became my musical mentor. She introduced me to the music she and her friends were attracted to, letting me hang around with them, learning what was cool and what was crap. Most of what was cool was black music, rhythm and blues, doo-wop, even some jazz by performers like Sarah Vaughan and Nina Simone. Ray Charles had just arrived. The Bay Area, Oakland in particular, had a rich heritage of black performers, many of them unknown outside their own communities. A show business idiom of the time was: "Think you're good? Play Oakland," a genuine dare if you were a performer. An Oakland audience demanded more than just competence.

Our favorite radio station was Oakland's KWBR (later becoming KDIA), broadcasting the music of the best black performers of the day. It was hosted by "Big Don" Barksdale, a former NBA player, and "Bouncin' Bill" Doubleday, recently inducted into the Bay Area Radio Hall of Fame. Our record store was Reid's Records on Sacramento Street in Berkeley, away from downtown, closer to the black neighborhoods. They had an impressive inventory of our favorite black performers, and we bought 78 rpm records, soon to be replaced by 45 rpm singles and 33 1/3 long play albums. We bought white pop records at Hink's Department Store in downtown Berkeley. They even had private audition rooms with windowed doors in an upstairs balcony where you could listen before you bought. Private rooms just for the purpose of auditioning records! What a concept.

One day I called KWBR and talked to Bouncin' Bill and made my first dedication: the Danleers would sing "One Summer Night," from Jake to Patti. She lived at the Russian River and wouldn't hear my message of affection, but that was okay. I was proud of myself for dredging up the courage to call Bouncin' Bill and make the dedication. A few minutes later, there I was on the radio, Bouncin' Bill leading me through a brief interview and the dedication, my voice and everything! Another day I won the "Mystery Group" contest, correctly identifying the performing group of a brand new unreleased record and was rewarded with a free record certificate from Reid's Records.

When the blues music of Jimmy Reed came along, it reached out and grabbed me. Then I actually got to spend part of an evening with him when my sister and her friends took me along with them to see Jimmy and several Oakland-based rhythm and blues performers at Sweet's Ballroom in downtown Oakland. We were among the few white people in the audience. I was all of 13, but I wore a coat and tie and drank a near-beer, thinking it would add some years to my appearance. I thought the beer was awful, like it was mixed with rusty water and poured from an old shoe.

Jimmy was out with the audience before his own performance, loaded but reasonably in control. I walked up and introduced myself and I guess he recognized me as a true fan. He was surprisingly warm and welcoming. He took me out to the parking lot to show me his brand new Mercury, a 1957 hardtop with bright, mirror-like chrome standing out against an elegant two-tone paint job. Now and then Jimmy would swig from a bottle in his pocket. Coming back inside, we went into the men's room together and peed, side by side, at the urinals. Imagine that, standing there peeing right next to Jimmy Reed! My respect for Jimmy was such that I didn't even peek at his pecker. Then we stood together out in front of the stage as Johnny Fuller and his band played, followed by Jimmy McCracklin's band, Jimmy Reed treating me like family. It wasn't a concert with reserved seating or anything like that. We were standing on the dance floor. There was a guitar player whose name I don't remember and who backed up all of the bands that night. He would play with Jimmy, too, when he performed. Jimmy pointed him out on stage, telling me, "Tha's one ghee-tar playin' sum'bitch!"

When Jimmy's first long-play album came out, I bought it and took it with me along with a portable record player to a vacation cabin at Rio Nido on the Russian River. My good pal Dave Grace had moved to the river area and we'd get Mom to bring us there for brief holidays. There's a song on that album titled "Can't Stand to See You Go," and right in the middle of that recording someone laughs out loud. I guess Jimmy and his producer liked having it in there even though it's right up front in the mix. I was alone in the cabin, hearing this song maybe for the first time, when I stepped out of the shower and someone laughed at me! I was sure I was being spied on and I wrapped a towel around me and searched the cabin and surrounding grounds for the Peeping Tom. Plainly, I couldn't find him and didn't discover until later that it was just Jimmy having some fun in the studio.

❧❧

ONE MIDSUMMER EVENING FOUND ME huddled around the radio in my bedroom with a neighborhood friend listening to the white pop station out of San Francisco, KOBY. The game was called "Hit or Miss" and the disc jockey was soliciting opinions and votes for a brand new record, which he then played on the air. We decided we didn't like it. My friend Ron made the call. Sassy and commanding, he told the DJ, "Never play that fucking piece of shit ever again or we might blow up the station." The phone was between our heads and I was listening in. There was a brief period of silence followed by a stern, businesslike voice that said, "Operator, you may trace this call." Ron slammed the receiver down, ashen faced. Two scared and guilty boys spent the rest of the night waiting for the FBI to knock on our door.

Unbelievably, the FBI actually did come looking for me a year or two later when I was a freshman in high school. The hall monitor brought the pink slip into my algebra class (which I managed to fail), summoning me to the dean's office. The secretary ushered me into the inner sanctum, where two humorless looking men in suits and hats sat opposite the boy's dean, Richard Lovett. The dean stood from behind his desk, saying, "Jake, I want to introduce you to so-and-so and so-and-so. They're Special Agents from the Federal Bureau of Investigation and they want to talk to you about this," pointing to some scrap of paper on his desk. I leaned in and took a look. Oh no! Where did they get it?

There on the desk was a facsimile of a twenty dollar bill I had made on a copy machine at Dad's office. The paper had a brownish hue and was printed on one side only. Cut into the oval normally occupied by Andrew Jackson was the facial image of my pal Dave Grace from one of those 25-cent arcade instant-photo booths. He had both fists raised at eye level, middle fingers extended in a double-barreled bird (perch!), accompanied by the silliest, goofiest expression imaginable. Dave was probably the funniest guy I ever knew.

The dean looked at the bogus bill and couldn't contain his mirth, letting out a chuckle he discreetly tried to smother. The agents weren't amused. They wanted to know how many of these I had made and let me know in no uncertain terms that printing or duplicating US currency was a serious offense.

The idea that this cartoon bill was remotely passable as real, or that a couple of fourteen-year-old kids having fun with a Thermofax copy machine could endanger our country, was (and is) ludicrous. That two Special Agents from the FBI apparently had nothing more pressing to occupy their energies boggles the mind. Why weren't they out there chasing commies?

Okay, I promised I wouldn't do it again, but they wouldn't tell me who gave them the evidence or told them my name. I was only a freshman in high school and already someone had snitched me off to the feds. Early on, I had reason to look at federal authority with a certain disdain.

I was no more than eight years old when Robbin and I experienced our first "arrest." A few of us went to explore an old deserted homestead in the hills beyond the school. One of the kids who joined us was called "Bubblegum," a goofy kid who was rarely part of our social group. On his way to join us, he cut through someone's property, and when the resident took him to task for trespassing, he apparently told her he had matches and would burn her house down, or something along that line. She called the cops.

The cop arrived at the old homestead and put us all into the cop car, confiscating Bubblegum's matches. The cop wouldn't say a word, just posing his dour cop authority. After we'd driven several blocks, in my mind on our way to jail, near to tears and in a quavering voice, I asked him if we could tell our mother where he was taking us. He still wouldn't answer, but then drove us home and let us go. I can still remember my relief when it dawned on me that I wasn't going to jail.

His silent dominance was chilling to us kids. He could have smiled and come up with some sort of interaction we could have respected, along with cops in general. Instead, he chose to be an asshole, terrorizing seven- and eight-year-old kids, flaunting his stern authority and making all cops who came after him have to prove themselves otherwise.

⤜⤛

WITH THE DISCOVERY OF MUSIC came the discovery of girls. Sponsored by our grammar school, Carol Cayley held her social dancing classes at the church and community center across the street from our house. My friends and I would put on our best clothes and line the walls as Carol demonstrated the steps for the fox trot and the waltz, along with some be-bop steps for faster tempos. Etiquette and manners were also taught as a part of the classes. She could sometimes be an ill-tempered, mean bitch of a woman. Anyone who fucked up, and we did a lot of that, got yelled at in her harshest, most unforgiving tones, a shameful public embarrassment.

Most of the time our dancing partners were selected for us, a matter of where you physically happened to be, and changed from dance to dance. Once in a while, the boys had an opportunity to select a girl and then the girls had a chance to select a boy. It wasn't a matter of casual asking. Proper invitation and acceptance were required, the extending and taking of the offered hand, returning your partner to her seat when the dance ended, and with a slight bow, thanking her before returning to your side of the room. One of my friends once asked me, "You ever get one that stunk?"

The classes required two nights weekly to accommodate everyone who wanted to learn social dancing. To my dismay, the girl I had my eye on was in the other class. But these were things we didn't acknowledge out loud at age eleven. Love's first glow was largely kept secret. Though we didn't share the same dance class, we soon attended the same birthday party hosted by one of my neighborhood friends, where spin the bottle was played. I was sure I caused it to happen by my fervent wishing, or maybe there was an intervention by a cupid angel. When it came to her turn, she delicately spun the bottle while I looked on with great and breathless anticipation. The bottle turned its several revolutions then came to rest ... pointing right at me. OMG!

To execute the kiss, we were allowed to excuse ourselves from the party room to the privacy of the parlor, to where I walked on a cloud, her hand in mine. Arriving at the appropriate place, I looked into her wondrous eyes, my hands delicately at her waist ... and planted my first and best kiss firmly on her cheek. Music played and a warm rush of emotion flowed through me like an involuntary spasm. The immediate stirring in my groin, the unbidden turning of the worm, surprised and amazed me. I think I realized from that moment on I would love and adore women for the rest of my life.

Our romance was something even we didn't speak to each other about. All we had to do was look at one another and hearts beat faster. Nearly as pleasing as the rest of her, she could play baseball, too, really well for a girl. We once went on a formal date with my best friend and hers. Populating those scenes from Norman Rockwell's vision of America, we put on our best clothes and took the

Number Seven bus into Berkeley, where we sat side by side at the United Artist Theater and watched the movie and then had ice cream sodas at Edy's. We would end up dancing together at other parties and playing baseball at the school playground, sometimes having lunch together, and that was the sum of our romance. At the end of the school year, we drifted apart, hardly acknowledging one another when we moved to junior high school in the fall.

It's said that love springs eternal and maybe it does, the memory of my first love firmly affixed after all these years. All the other women who would one day find a place in my heart would have to share it with this one, who first lit the spark.

MATING RITUALS

IN TERMS OF WIDE-EYED EXPLORATION AND INITIATION, I WOULD FIND little difference between federal prison and junior high school. Each was a brand new world filled with wonders and dangers new to my experience. Interest in sex came along in my 10th summer when the older sister of the guys I was palling around with at a family summer camp came into the tent and dropped her swimming suit. In no hurry to clothe herself, she sat on the bedside with her legs apart (she even had hair down there!) then put on her shoes and socks first. She somehow managed to get my attention. Viva la difference!

> Teenage boys, goaded by their surging hormones, run in packs like the primal horde. They have only a brief season of exhilarating liberty between control by their mothers and control by their wives.
>
> –Camille Paglia

Junior high school, grades seven through nine, was a revelation after spending grade school tucked away in Kensington. I suddenly had a separate teacher for each subject, each in a separate class-room. This rarely allowed the close bond sometimes established with a single instructor, but it also ruled out the possibility of get-ting stuck exclusively with the teacher from hell for a whole school year. The sound of slamming lockers, ringing bells, and the rush and clamor of students getting to their next class in the few min-utes allowed became the new soundtrack for my education.

I don't recall a single black student attending my grammar school. Now there were lots of them, along with Mexicans, Asians, and shapely girls with noticeable breasts. There were guys who shaved and a few who even drove cars. Then, daily after physical education, I was required to take a shower in the middle of the day with about 200 other guys.

What a strange new world it was. Tough-looking guys with greasy hair and who smoked cigarettes and wore their blue jeans low on the waist roamed the terrain like dangerous animals. Each had a particular slouch and style, as though daring someone to fuck with them. Some had metal "taps" on the soles of their shoes and they would drag their heels to produce clicks and scraping sounds with each step, as though warning people of their approach (they weren't dancers). Each seemed to be known for his purported fighting abilities. The toughest of them all, according to reputation, was Mike Friddel, who was only in the eighth grade. But he didn't even look dangerous, more like a big, happy farm boy. He smiled a lot and didn't put on the tough guy front like most of the others. I imagined he didn't need it.

It was also a time in our society when educators could physically punish out of line students without the threat of legal retribution. At Portola Jr. High School that meant they could wallop the shit out of you. The dean, Mr. Scott, kept a leather razor strop in his desk, and he would lay it on with a will to any deserving smart-ass sent to him for insubordination. Without a trial, he would bend you over and let you have it right there in his office. It happened to me once when I was guilty of being a punk-ass 7th grader, challenging the authority of a teacher. I don't know how much good it did, but I was never anxious for more. He stepped into the arc of his swing like the Mighty Casey. I can still recall the emitted grunt of his effort. He set your ass on fire.

The majority of kids in junior high were 12 to 15 years old, a terrible age for most of us. Surging hormones accompanied by pimples, sexual awakening, and peculiar body hair growing in strange places were all part of pubescent onset. It was all too much, all at the same time. There was so much that had to be learned on your own, the stuff you weren't taught at home. No one gave us a pamphlet explaining how to find our place in this strange new world, how to act around our peers, especially around the mysterious opposite sex. How did it all fit together? No wonder so many guys turned primal, putting on a tough exterior and turning to physical combat as a means to assert and protect themselves, a way to hide shortcomings, imagined or real. Many didn't know how to behave otherwise.

Racism flourished, particularly anti-black, sometimes anti-Asian, left over from World War II. Geographically ignorant, no one seemed to think there was any difference between the Japanese and the Chinese. One black fellow with some Asian features was denigrated by other blacks: "We call him 'Ling Ting' 'cause he look like a Jap." A Japanese guy was denigrated by whites, "Feed that Chinger some rice!" Black people were "spades" and "spooks" and worse, so called by the whites, mostly behind their backs. There were also some genuine transplant redneck hillbillies, one such known as "Mississip'," was hailed as a famous nigger-fighter and whose name spoke to his former home.

Across the street from the campus was the Boys Club, a franchise of the American institution, Boys Clubs of America. "Behind the Boys Club" was the preeminent battleground if you had been "called out" (challenged to a fistfight). Inside, there was a central room with a small stage, a pool table, boxing, Ping-Pong, game rooms, and a Coke machine. On Friday nights there was sometimes a dance, occasionally with live music. The first group I saw there called themselves "The Honky Tonks." The guitar player had sideburns and a waterfall of hair that spilled down his forehead, and he played the great guitar anthem from Bill Doggett's *Honky Tonk*. The girls looked on with dreamy eyes, sometimes even a muffled scream. I thought then it might be cool to learn how to play a guitar.

When Elvis arrived the girls really learned how to scream, now accepted social behavior because they saw it happening on TV. There was something indecent and sexual about having the power to make young girls scream. That's what rock & roll seemed to be all about: a mating dance, the bird of paradise with the gaudiest display, the guitar a phallic extension, a beat, rhythm, and energy to get your pulse up. Rock & roll was the platform for those with the talent to strut and spread their feathers, every young boy's dream, a holy grail with the promise of sexual reward.

❖❖❖

ONE DAY THERE CAME A hushed urgency, like an electric current, that spread through the school. I had no idea what brought it about, but the word on campus was that there would be a gang fight after school, white against black.

"Gang fight" was not an apt description for what took place. White boys lined one side of the street, blacks the other. All the biggest and toughest-looking guys were there. Taunts and insults were traded. Rather than opposing gangs fighting it out like sometimes seen in the movies, this turned out to be more like a medieval jousting tournament. A champion from each side met in the middle of the street, in the center divider, and punched it out. No one used weapons other than their fists. Onlookers like myself stood outside the throng of toughs. There were a few females as well, girlfriends of the tough guys who had undeserved reputations as whores among the socially elite classes.

Out into the center of the street strode the white champion, Mike Friddel. How he was chosen or just who was running this show was as much a mystery to me as was the event itself, but I guess everyone knew of Mike's reputation as a fighter. He was met by an equally big and capable-looking, youthful black man, and both raised their fists and circled each other. A feint here, a feint there, and it was all over in about 30 seconds. The black man lay on his back where he had been knocked to the ground by a single punch. A cheer went up from the white side of the street.

Then the first black man was replaced by another who was equally tough and capable looking. Again, the same ritual ensued, the circling and feint, and the black man was quickly knocked to the ground, sent there by a single punch from his white opponent. And the second black man was replaced by a third, with an identical result. Mike had won the day for white America and he wasn't even breathing hard. Congratulations and backslapping took place on the white side of the street, while those opposite slowly made their way toward the other side of town.

The fighters probably didn't even know each other by name. It wasn't a personal grudge. They were simply representing their races, the same way Olympians represent their countries. The contest was representative of the racism that existed all over the country. Black people were still very much engaged in their struggle for human redemption, Martin Luther King still years away. If a black champion had won in the South, he would have faced serious retribution. I always wondered what would have happened if the white champion were beaten here in El Cerrito. It was over as quickly as it began, and I don't recall another similar confrontation while in junior high.

❧•❧

"NINE-NINE!" EXCLAIMED T.C. WALKER, ONE of the physical education coaches, a stop watch in his hand. T.C. for Thomas Calhoun, although among the boys he was known as "Terrible Cock" for the rumored monster between his legs. Nine point nine seconds was a new 7th grade school record for the 75-yard dash. "Where did you start from, son? Are you sure you were at the starting line?" he chided the panting boy.

The runner was Larry Halls, a perky, cocky, smiling, handsome, devil-may-care kind of guy who was also a superb athlete. If Mike Friddel was known for his fighting prowess, then Larry was known, at least among his peers, for being the fastest runner who could do the most pushups, climb a 20-foot rope faster than anyone else, and who excelled in all the sports. He was slender with tight muscles that rolled under his skin, and he had rugged good looks with jet black hair and a sloping nose that looked as though it once might have been broken. He could do a "kip" from flat on his back to a standing position with just a kick of his legs and a push from his hands. He earned his "green trunks" the first time out, nearly scoring gold. The color of your trunks, the shorts you wore for your physical education classes, was a status symbol determined by your score in a series of decathlon-like events. You started out with gray, then moved up to blue, red, green, and gold. Only a handful of guys, mostly 9th graders, had earned their gold trunks. The girls all loved Larry and he loved them back. If ever there was a model for Johnny Cool, the Prince of the Hop, or a Bad Motorcycle, it was Larry.

We came to know one another mostly through sports, always, it seemed, playing against each other on various intramural teams. I admired his abilities and he could at least appreciate my competence. Somewhere during his education he was held back a grade, I believe due to a serious childhood illness. He was close to a year older than me. We soon started hanging out together, then going out evenings, spending the night either at his house or mine. Sometimes on weekends we'd hitchhike without destination, just to see how far we could get. We were headed wherever the car that picked us up was going, then we'd let our thumbs find us a way back.

What do 13- and 14-year-old kids do at night? All of our heroes smoked, so we thought we'd take that up. The whole country smoked, a symbol of maturity for juveniles. Cigarettes were available from vending machines for a quarter, and we had discovered Drucquer & Sons, Ltd., a Berkeley institution first founded in London in 1841.

Drucquer's was on University Avenue in downtown Berkeley, just a few doors from Chuck Dutton's piano studio. A fine and exotic tobacconist, they sold quality tobaccos, cigars, and cigarettes from all over the world. Mr. Drucquer had no problem selling his wares to us, even though the law said you had to be at least 18 years of age to purchase tobacco. Larry and I bought all sorts of cigarettes from him, French Gitanes, colored Dunhills in a flat box that when opened displayed a rainbow of cigarettes with gold filters, aromatic Mapletons, along with our usual Pall Malls. He was a distinguished-looking gentleman who spoke with a British accent and was always nattily dressed.

One day I stepped up to his counter to make my purchase and was stunned when Mr. Drucquer said to me, "You don't look quite 18 to me, son. Do you have a note from your parents or something?" "But ... but," I stammered, "you just sold me ..." He leaned toward me over the counter, and in a low, conspiratorial tone out of one side of his mouth, he said, "Got to watch out for the old bag, you know," indicating some matron in the shop who might take offense to juvenile tobacco sales. "Well, it's okay this time, laddie," he said in normal tones with a wink, "but tell your mother to call me before her next purchase."

Larry and I enjoyed playing sports of all kinds, and we both played on the community Pony League baseball team, but foremost in our minds was girls. We stayed up late at night smoking cigarettes, talking about girls, fantasizing about our first conquest. We weren't smart enough to discuss pregnancy, disease, or the responsibility therefor. We just wanted to get in there and learn what it was like. We had a running bet on who'd be first. Larry had three girlfriends to my one, and I knew he would win, but I bet him anyway. It was more than a year before the bet played out, and as I imagined it, Larry won. I had to take his word for it, which I did, happy that any pressure was now off.

Most of us never came close to sexual conquest during the junior high years, but that didn't stop us from carrying a condom around in our wallets. Rather than the use for which it was intended, it served instead as the mold for a design that soon emerged on the outside of our wallets, indelibly struck by the pressure of being sat upon, our circular badge of puberty.

Unlike cigarettes, condoms weren't widely available from vending machines and had to be purchased at a pharmacy. We drew straws to see who would make the purchase. One day our pal Sheldon was the winner or, thought some, the loser. Overcome by embarrassment at making the purchase, he pointed an emphatic finger at me, loitering nearby, telling the pharmacist, "Really, they're for him!"

✦✦

As 7ᵗʰ graders, Larry and I attended a classmate's birthday celebration, an early evening swimming party at a public pool in Albany. Kenny, whose birthday we came to celebrate, was a strange kid. He was a bully, robed with an insecurity that required him to put on a constant tough guy act. He wouldn't mess with anyone who looked like he might be a match for him. Anyone like that he considered his pal. Others, who he read as lesser than himself, he would push around and cajole, daring them to fight him as though on stage for onlookers (Puddem up, puddem up!). On this night, though, he made a tactical error.

Also in the pool was a chunky kid from another school whose name was Mervin Pizzagrante. He was shorter than Kenny, and

Kenny imagined him a target. He started in on him with his tough guy routine. "You wanna go outside?" dared Kenny. "Sure," said Mervin, "why not?" All of his party guests had gathered around. There was no honorable way out for Kenny.

Mervin was as fearless a kid as ever there was. He was a little heavy at age 12, but he made up for any lack of a muscular physique with nerves of steel and a powerful punch. Mervin wasn't afraid of anybody. I once saw him wrestle two cops to the floor when they tried to arrest him on a juvenile warrant in the Albany Bowl. Mervin wasn't yet 14. "Help me, you fools!" cried one of the cops at a few of us who were standing there watching Mervin go to town on them. "Don't think so. Good luck." Mervin's disrespect for law and authority was out front and apparent early on.

So when Mervin came out of the dressing room to square off with Kenny, all of Kenny's party guests were there to watch. Mervin's nonchalance and confidence were unnerving enough, but the look in his eye turned Kenny to Jell-O. He stood frozen in front of his "target." Mervin hit Kenny just once, and Kenny fell to his knees, whimpering, "Please, no more." Mervin just smiled. "Sure," he said and walked off into the night. Larry and I exchanged knowing glances. It couldn't have happened to a more deserving guy. But I think Kenny learned an important lesson from his encounter with Mervin, and as a result, a lot of the bully in him seemed to magically disappear.

About twenty years later, Sheldon happened to run into Mervin on the street one day. He told Sheldon he had just been released from San Quentin for, "Killing a nigger," said Mervin. "Shot him three times in the chest. Niggers don't die easy … they're hard to kill."

➤-➥

DURING THE SUMMER I TURNED 13, Dad started bringing me to work with him, where I would wash the rows of used cars, dragging a long hose around the car lot with me. I was instructed on the importance of clean windows, the use of the chamois, and cautioned to always make sure I hosed off any soap film before the sun could bake it dry and ruin the finish. I would work for a few hours and then someone—sometimes my older cousin Joe-Boy—would drive me home. Once, on the way home, he wanted to know if I'd ever "dipped my paint brush." I told him, no, but I was working on it, and one day I'd be a great artist.

This was the summer of the "runaways," Linda and Carolyn, two neighborhood girls who liked to come by the house on summer afternoons when I got home from work and tease me with sexual innuendo and batting eyelashes. They were skilled in the use of the powerful tools wielded by pubescent, developing girls. Linda, especially, was physically mature for a twelve-year-old, and she had lovely, deep, dark eyes. Each knew the power of her charms and how to jerk a guy around, way before they were ready for any sexual exploration. I was, of course, an easy mark. They'd climb into my tree fort with me, 30 feet up in a large, spreading pine, and go to work on me with questions and stories about sex, coquettish and pretending they didn't know much. Just how much I might have known was also in question, but I pretended I knew it all. Once during our playtime I got a boner, and the little vixens caught me trying to hide my condition, which my embarrassment took care of all by itself.

Carolyn once showed me her small, developing breasts, and Linda and I would make out, even French kissing with our tongues and such. She would unbutton the top of her blouse and put her mature and alluring cleavage on display, but I was denied anything beyond that; good evidence, I think, that female is the smarter gender. P.G. Wodehouse once wrote, "At the age of eleven or thereabouts, women acquire a poise and an ability to handle difficult situations, which a man, if he is lucky, manages to achieve somewhere in his seventies." I think Mr. Wodehouse was on to something.

Sometime near the end of that summer, Dad woke me in the middle of the night, telling me I had to get dressed and climb up into my treehouse. Two local girls had run away from home, he explained, and the cops thought they might be hiding up there. I hadn't seen Linda or Carolyn for a couple of weeks, but I knew that's who they were looking for. One parent or another had obviously heard about the treehouse. Dad and I made our way to the base of the pine tree where two cops were giving it another try. With their hats, guns, and equipment belts still on, and wearing shoes with smooth leather soles, they had no chance to get up that tree. One cop made it up about three feet, and we watched him slide back down and fall on his butt when he hit bottom, Pop having a little chuckle at them. The cops were laughing at themselves too. I scampered up the tree like a squirrel and came back down to tell them that the runaways weren't there. I had to assure them I wasn't covering up for the girls.

Linda and Carolyn were gone from their homes for two or three days. I never learned where they had gone, but it was clear they were in full rebellion against parental controls. My parents never put much in the way of controls on me. What they got out of the deal was love and respect without ever having to ask for it.

That summer of huckleberry days, the runaways, and the treehouse came to an end, slowly fading into the distance like a summer fog burning off the San Francisco Bay. School started again and we melted into our new surroundings and social circles. We brought with us those memories and lessons learned some 30 feet above the sod, where life was explored in an environment of our own making, free from adult expectations and rules that governed life on the ground.

→-←

AT 15 AND A HALF, Larry got his driver's license, followed by a '51 Mercury coupe that he would turn into his personal chariot. Door handles and unnecessary identifying trim were removed and the car was painted a color called "dusk plum." Spinner hubcaps, dummy spotlights, Naugahyde upholstery, and any number of custom accessories were added. Soon we'd be "dragging the main," joining the parade of cars on central boulevards, filled with young people looking for adventure. It was a four-wheeled mating ritual, driven by the energy of the extraordinary rock & roll music of the day. Reputation as the toughest fighter was replaced by reputation for the coolest and fastest car.

It was during this era that Larry's mom and step-dad planned a weekend gambling trip to Carson City in Nevada, and Larry and I were invited to come along. We couldn't gamble, of course, but with Larry's new driver's license, his parents' car would be ours for most of the time we were there.

The name of the whorehouse was "Moonlight Ranch," and it didn't take us long to learn how to get there. My 15th birthday was still a couple of months away. A black woman answered the door. I guess she was the madam, but she looked more like a housekeeper, maybe filling in on the early evening shift. With hands on her hips, she took a step backward and made an appraisal, staring at us with raised eyebrows and the most incredulous examination imaginable. "Well ... I guess you's old enough," she said, leading us to the wares.

The working girls were thrilled with our youth. They gathered around us, petting and cooing. It wasn't my first time, but might as well have been. There's something to be said about having a professional as a guiding partner. Her fee was only five dollars and I gave her a two-dollar tip. Unknown to me at the time, she gave me a tip of her own: pubic lice, known as the "crabs."

It took a few weeks for those little devils to form a community and start making me itch like crazy. I couldn't figure it out. Is this what Elvis meant when he sang, "I'm itchin' like a man on a fuzzy tree"? Had I somehow gotten poison oak all around my dick? Then, lying in bed at night, I did an examination. There appeared to be some grains of sand around my pubic hair, maybe from a recent trip to the beach, but when I tried, they wouldn't brush off. I plucked one of the grains and looked at it very closely on the tip of my finger ... holy shit! It was alive and had tiny legs that waved in the air! Crabs! I knew it had to be. I got into the bathtub and sat there for an hour, trying to drown them. I poured a harsh mouth wash all over myself, trying to chemically incinerate them. All without positive result. How could they be so tough? What could I do? I felt I was diseased. Dad was away on a hunting trip. No way could I go to Mom and tell her I'd been to a whorehouse. Mom would have taken it in stride, just a warm-up for what was to come, but I wasn't ready to go there.

I got to Larry's house first thing the next day. "Larry! Larry! I got the crabs! What can we do?"

This is how uninformed we were: All we knew about crabs was it was some form of venereal disease, one of several, but right up there with syphilis and the clap. We started calling pharmacies, talking to the pharmacist, asking if they had anything for venereal disease. I still remember the concern in a pharmacist's voice, "You'd better see a doctor, son. Right away."

I was saved when Larry's step-dad got home. An ex-marine, he knew all about crabs. "Har, har," he laughed at my distress. He went into the bathroom and came out with a bottle of a common household medication that had an oily base. "Here, put this on them. That'll do the trick." Sure enough, dead crabs dropped like dandruff flakes, filling my undershorts. Before long, I had enough dead crabs to bread a veal cutlet.

➤⋅◄

JUNIOR HIGH SCHOOL CAME TO an end when I entered the first freshman class at El Cerrito High School in the fall of 1957. Prior to this year, high school had started as a sophomore. There I was again, at the bottom of the ladder, and feeling cheated of a year at the top. When I got my school "letter" in B-team football, my graduating year (1961) was also featured on my school sweater, and I was teased mercilessly by upper classmates who regarded that year as impossibly far off, as if we were serving a prison sentence. Larry, though, lived in another district and was shuttled off to a new high school in Richmond. Our brotherhood would remain intact for a couple of years, slowly drifting away as we found new friends and new activities to fill our lives. But the bond I felt with Larry remains to this day.

In recent years, I attended a reunion of my high school class, hoping to find some news of Larry. I found there Larry's 7th grade sweetheart, Irene Chavez, who told me Larry had died years earlier, a cancer victim. I hadn't seen Larry in over 40 years. Nonetheless, a hollowness enveloped me, a sense of loss I could never replace. I was troubled by never having had closure with Larry, never sharing what we had become and how we got there. The times we had made plans to get together in later years never seemed to work out. But there would always be next year, until there was not … *do it now, brothers.*

I later learned that Larry had lived the last years of his life with the sister-in-law of an old high school acquaintance. He told me that the sister-in-law had inherited Larry's "business" from him. I asked about the business and learned that Larry had been a bookmaker, mostly sports betting, and had what my friend called a "high-level weekly book." It was almost too perfect. Larry as a later-day bookie fit my image of him perfectly. I knew, too, that he had tended bar on a professional level, probably providing a platform for his other business. "He might have smoked and drank himself to death too," said my friend, and I suppose that's what Larry would have done, although bone cancer is what killed him. "His hair was always immaculate," he continued, bringing up as comparison some guy from a TV show I'd never seen.

But I knew Larry, the man and his pocket comb. I pictured him running it through his jet-black pompadour with its Jack Nicholson widow's peak, every hair obeying, just like the Werewolf of London ("His hair was perfect!"—Warren Zevon). Arching eyebrows over confident hazel eyes, keenly aware of his appearance, always ready to present himself to the next pretty lady or as a challenge to any nearby male. But there was nothing behind those eyes that ever hinted at malice. For Larry life was a sport, may the better man win. And I thought of Jack London who claimed he would rather be "a superb meteor, every atom of me in magnificent glow, than a sleepy, permanent planet."

Without ever intending it, Larry taught me to reach a little higher, to try a little harder … and when I encounter that bowl of cherries on life's highway, to reach out and pluck one for myself.

THE BOYS FROM EL CERRITY

A la ka-zip, ka-zip, ka-zam
Sonofabitch, god-damn
Horse's ass, cow's titty
We're the boys from El Cerrity!
Yeah ... weasel shit!

*—A party chant adopted by the boys,
defining turf and maturity*

HIGH SCHOOL HIT ME RIGHT BETWEEN THE EYES AND PROVIDED A social structure that invited rebellion. Where does a freshman fit in? At the bottom of the ladder, of course. I ran smack into a social class mentality that seemed to pervade the entire experience, the elite spending their time looking down their noses at those beneath them, each class assuming a position of authority over the underclasses. The pinnacle of the social register was represented by the fraternities and sororities, membership in which would allow you, too, to look down your nose at those less than you. As a freshman, I was acutely aware of my lowly status, often reminded of it by those not so loftily positioned within their own class, but taking opportunity to assert themselves at the expense of the underclasses.

It is, of course, how a pecking order works: downhill. The poor freshmen had no one beneath themselves upon whose shoes they could piss. Membership in the fraternities was reserved for the social elite: the best athletes, the cheerleaders, the coolest cats, musicians, social and class leaders, the wealthy and best-dressed, and so forth. Underclassmen need not apply. It didn't take long for this reality to sink in and piss me off. Faced with exclusion, at least until I would be an upperclassman, I did what a lot of teens did at 14, I rebelled against the machinery that dictated life in 1957 white America. The great rock & roll music of the era, itself an explosive expression of rebellion against convention, fueled our hard-headed determination to be other than what had been laid out for us.

Propelled by ignorance and raging hormones, along with a persnickety attitude, the boys and I would choose our own path. Lack of a driver's licenses was accompanied by pimples and an uncomprehending mindset. We were just learning how to think and having a hard time with it, empty-headed and unclear on many concepts. Anything forbidden had to be tried, at least once. A joy ride in a stolen car provided new thrills, ignorant of how close we came to carnage and jail. We learned most things the hard way, finding that the cheap, sweet fortified wines could make you engagingly stupid and engrossingly sick.

A bus ride into the bowels of Oakland's sordid downtown nightlife could provide a drunk or a predatory homosexual to buy us some more wine. A sleazy live burlesque show invited our attendance in a tattered and raggedy theater, unconcerned about our age. If you had five dollars to spend, a new tattoo was available from 'Frisco Bob on 7th Street. If you didn't have five dollars, two dollars would get your name tattooed across your arm somewhere in case you forget how to spell it. It was rumored that 'Frisco Bob had a "B" tattooed on each cheek of his ass, and when he'd drop pants and bend over it spelled "BoB." The walls of his dingy little shop were covered with the in-vogue tattoo designs of the day:

daggers, panthers, dragons, skulls, roses, hearts, buxom women, cartoon characters, scrolls with "Mom" in them, and so forth, an art form all its own. I had a cartoon kitty wearing a sailor's hat tattooed on my shoulder (where it was easy to hide), chosen because I'd heard one of the older, cooler guys with the same tattoo talk about how it got him laid. The women, he said, loved it. I guess I never showed mine to the right girl.

Before I acquired the kitty tattoo, Sheldon and I and some of the boys one night decided it would be a smart thing to tattoo each other. With a sewing machine needle and some India ink, we set out to enhance the natural beauty of our bodies. I awoke the next morning with a make-shift scroll running through a capital "J" tattooed on the inside of my right forearm, scared to death of what my parents might think. I wore only long-sleeved shirts for the next couple of weeks. Then I learned of a folk-remedy that removed tattoos ... it was easy! You get some salt and lemon juice and rub the salt into the area of the tattoo, diluting it with lemon juice so that it becomes a workable abrasive. Once the skin is opened by the abrasive, the lemon juice will penetrate the tattoo and melt and wither the ink, making it disappear in no time. I worked on it for what seemed like hours, but the result was only to fade the tattoo, making it indistinct and anyone's guess as to what it might be. "Cool scorpion, Jake!" said some. A further result was a nasty infection I feared might turn into blood poisoning, whatever that was. I knew I had to see a doctor, and now I had to confess my indiscretion.

It was early morning before school and Dad was still in bed. Mom was horrified, mostly, I think, about the infection, but nonetheless shocked her darling boy had gotten himself tattooed. "You have to show your father," she said. Standing by Dad's bed, Mom announced, "Howard ... our son has gotten himself a tattoo!"

Dad rolled over, shaking the sleep from his head, "Let's have a look at it," he said, and I showed him the mess on my arm.

"Next time," he murmured, rolling over to resume his sleep, "get yourself a barber-pole." It was his way of saying that my tattoo was equally dumb and senseless as would have been barber-pole stripes tattooed around my pecker. That was all he ever said about my tattoo.

❧-❦

WORD ONCE GOT AROUND THAT "Wild Bill," a homosexual bus driver, welcomed all the boys to his apartment on 17th Street in Oakland, where he would provide us with all the wine we could drink. "All you gotta do is show him your dick," said one of the boys who'd been there before. "He's harmless." I wasn't concerned about him doing us harm, but not so sure I liked the idea of putting my private self on display for him. Nonetheless, there I was among half a dozen of the boys, having a laugh, and putting down glass after glass of Thunderbird wine.

Before the question of showing him my pecker ever had opportunity to present itself, the room had started to spin, and I knew there was about to be a great exodus from my stomach, the contents in full retreat up the path it had come down. I barely made it to the toilet where it all gushed out in a horrible, stinking discharge of undigested hooey and grist. My head hurt something terrible, and the taste in my mouth was unspeakably foul and bitter. And still the room wouldn't stop spinning. I made it to one of the twin beds in a section of the apartment that could be closed off from the main room. Gratefully, I went into an alcohol-induced slumber, consciousness leaving for parts unknown.

Maybe an hour had passed when I awoke to the sound of Wild Bill's voice coming from the other room, "Where's that big boy from Arkansas? Come along with me, boy." He led the big boy into the room where I lay and to the twin bed just across from me, where the two participated in what appeared to be a consensual (if indeed a minor can consent to anything) buggery, the big boy at the helm. It wasn't hard for me to feign my unconscious state, keeping my eyes mostly closed to the goings on, trying to block out the grunts and groans coming from the participants.

I guess Wild Bill picked the right guy. It was said that the big boy would fuck a wood pile if he thought there was a rabbit in it. Sheldon and the Jayhawk once caught him masturbating to images in a magazine in the restroom of a dental office waiting lobby. The sight of bare-breasted African women in the National Geographic he had picked up sent him into a state of arousal. Just how he could become aroused by the backside of this short, middle-aged, bald, and chubby bus driver was beyond my imagining.

The evening at Wild Bill's ended without further fanfare and we caught a bus back to El Cerrito. My head was still pounding, my eyes glazed and largely oblivious to the panorama of San Pablo Avenue rolling by outside the windows of the bus, the entire way wanting to throw myself into the San Francisco Bay to somehow cleanse myself of the rank disgust that had welled up inside of me.

➤◄

NORTH OF THE BAY AREA, almost to Napa, in the middle of a pasture, was a venue called the "Dream Bowl," an outsized honky-tonk with sawdust on the floor and through which passed some of the great performers of the day. Some of the boys and I would attend various shows, usually in the company of my sister and her friends, all of them a few years older than us and who would do the driving. One night the great and sometimes crazed Gene Vincent and His Blue Caps was the headliner. Gene was performing with a plaster cast on one leg, all the way up to his crotch, rigid and kicked out to one side while he held onto the mic stand, growling out his songs with authority and his trademark reckless abandon. According to his drummer, who was accessible and friendly during a break, Gene had broken his leg playing chicken with a freight train on his motorcycle. He wasn't what our parents would call an exemplary model for the youth of the day, but we loved his music and searched for the dirty words hidden in his lyrics, imagined or real. We thought "Woman Love," the B-side of "Be-Bop-a-Lula," contained some especially naughty reference. Some of the fun provided by rock & roll was trying to figure out what the singer had sung. It wasn't until the internet came along and spelled it out for me that I could finally make sense of the opening line to Huey "Piano" Smith's "Don't You Just Know It." Other nights at the Dream Bowl featured the likes of Fats Domino, Brenda Lee, and Jerry Lee Lewis.

At the Dream Bowl I also learned that sloe gin could be every bit as ruinous as the cheap, fortified wines. Though I escaped the major ravages I had experienced with Thunderbird wine, never again did those particular beverages find their way past my lips. Funny how we remember the awfulness of something as it comes back up so much different than on the way down.

Another Dream Bowl night, alcohol clouding what limited judgment I then possessed, I was goaded into a senseless parking lot fight against an adversary chosen by my sister's older friends. I managed to acquire a black-eye, multiple abrasions, and bruises from rolling around on the gravel, bitten, punched and scratched by my scrappy opponent. It was hard to tell who looked worse when we were done. Street fighting immediately lost any appeal it may have previously had. A few "older" women, maybe in their late teens, took an interest in me after the fight, doctoring my wounds and vaunting my prowess as a parking lot fighter. We danced the two-step on that sawdust floor, the girls passing me around like a reefer. Following the parking lot experience, I would picture myself a lover, not a fighter.

❧❦

MY YEARS AS AN UNDERCLASSMAN couldn't pass soon enough, but I somehow managed to survive them. By the time I got my driver's license, near the end of my sophomore year, I had assumed a new maturity. I had a serious girlfriend with whom I spent most of my free time, a lot of that at the drive-in theater where we seldom watched the movie. Alcohol was still around, but had ceased to be a main attraction. I had my own car and access to many. Gas was only 30 cents a gallon, but I had to buy my own. I worked a steady schedule, after school and Saturdays, in the service department at Dad's auto business.

Sometime during that year the boys and I hooked up with members of a renegade fraternity from neighboring Berkeley High School. They were called "Saxons" and had been expelled as a fraternity from that school for reasons now lost in the mists of the years. The invitation to join their fraternity, where we could have our own jackets, pins, secret codes, and other such exclusive accessories, had a strong appeal, even though we knew we would be outcasts at our own school. Mingling student bodies within a fraternity was a brand new idea. As far as we were concerned, we had already been cast out. None of us fit existing social requirements for invitation to join the sanctioned fraternities at our school. We would sanction ourselves. The further thumbing of our noses at existing social conventions seemed an okay idea. Why not a fraternity for misfits and the socially challenged?

At first we had to take the expected crap from those who felt threatened by our boldness. We had shat upon their exclusivity, essentially serving notice that, not only do we not need you, our preference is otherwise. That may have seemed high-minded at the time, but the Saxons would thrive in their new incarnation, eventually becoming entirely an El Cerrito social body, creating our own exclusivity and morphing into something very close to what we sought to overcome in the first place.

By the time my junior and senior years arrived, all the social exclusivity that had once made me feel an outsider seemed to melt away. I was now a part of the whole, among my peers, and gaining respect from the upper class. Having been looked down upon quite enough, most of us were void of any need to look down on anyone else.

I attended my senior social activities with my soon-to-be wife, Jeanne, together with our then embryo son, conceived one night in the generous front seat of my '59 Chevy Impala. I was all of 17 and ready to take on the world, much of my confidence flowing from my father. I was always trying to grow up too fast, thinking it cool to pass for 21 at the local bars, ready for marriage and fatherhood without much thought to the realities and responsibilities that came with them. I was ruled by the three bad kings: smoking, drinking, and fucking. The benevolent king, thinking, would be kept in the dungeon for a few years yet to come. I was comfortable with the idea of marriage and very fond of Jeanne. This child was our responsibility and we would accept it head-on. A sobering moment came when my former "serious" girlfriend arrived at a party on the arm of the fellow who followed me as president of the Saxons. The Saxon mantle was now his, but it hit me right in the gut that I wasn't ready to relinquish the other, an impossible longing that stabbed at me inside, confidence momentarily turning to helplessness.

❧⚜

UNTIL I ATTENDED COLLEGE CLASSES the following year, I was a crappy student, barely getting by, thinking that homework was unfair and meant for somebody else, not me. I managed to learn proficiency at the typewriter, a skill that has always served me well. I excelled only at physical education and metal shop, where the instructor, Dick Grimm, took a shine to me, and in my senior year, installed me as the foreman in three of his classes. I essentially had my own way, doing as I pleased. I was also his "ringer" and played left field for the short-handed faculty baseball team, which he managed. All I had to do was pass the civics class in order to graduate, which I somehow managed to do. Baseball and football had been a part of my curriculum in my freshman and sophomore years, abandoned when interest in cars and women came along, bringing with them a need to earn money rather than practice after-school sports.

Neighboring the metal shop was the wood shop. The instructor was "Duke," a man of large proportions with a dour expression and a craggy face, lined as though with a chisel. If he ever smiled, I missed it. He often walked around looking as though he might be in a trance, like maybe he was getting in character for a role in a zombie movie. I would have entertained the idea of a woodshop class, but the thought of Duke as instructor was unappealing. One afternoon Sheldon was in a back corner of the shop supply room, kneeling at a drum of machine oil while filling a container from the spigot for the metal shop. Duke walked in and, looking around, missed the fact that Sheldon was there—whereupon he lifted the lid on a barrel of glue, stuck his head all the way in, and helped himself to the intoxicating fumes with a mighty inhale. Hah! So it wasn't a zombie movie after all. He then spied Sheldon and gave him a look that said, *breathe a word of this to anyone and you'll curse the day you set foot on this campus.* Sheldon returned to the metal shop, trembling a little from the arrant weirdness of the encounter. It was a few days before he told the boys about it. Duke was likely a full-on "glue head" with a free and generous supply of his chosen elixir.

❧⊰

IN MY JUNIOR YEAR ONE of the boys, Dan Heikka, was relocated to Stockton in California's Central Valley, where he lived with his mom and step-dad. We missed our good friend, and together with Sheldon, who we called "Balls" (a designation we'll leave to the imagination), the "Jayhawk," Mike Lasher, whose family had roots in Kansas, and my brother Robbin, who we called "Louie Young-Kid," we planned a road trip to Stockton to visit Dan. The boys usually called me by my initials, JR, sort of boring when compared to the colorful names of my companions. It was a part of the plan that Dan would return to the Bay Area with us for a visit of his own.

We arrived in Stockton in my car of the moment, a '58 Plymouth Fury, a cool car in its day, a sporty two-door hardtop with outsized Cadillac-style rear fins. It had two big four-barrel carburetors sitting opposite each other on a ram-induction fuel system that fed a huge "hemi" V8 engine. The speedometer registered all the way up to 160 miles per hour. I'll mention it again: Gas was only thirty cents a gallon. It had a three-speed automatic transmission that could be manually controlled with push buttons located on the dash, left of the steering wheel. The front suspension was lowered, giving the car a stylish "rake," and it had dual exhausts with glass-pack mufflers that announced our presence with a bad-ass rumble. Dan climbed aboard, bringing with him a chrome metal shaft about two-feet in length with an 8 ball on one end, once a floor-mounted gearshift lever from some hotrod, a talisman that might also serve as a weapon.

We went in search of Dan's pal the "Beaver," who Dan wanted us to meet and who would hang with us that evening. We soon caught up with the Beaver (whose front teeth explained his name) and he climbed into the back seat, making six of us. A car like the Fury, with a "floor box" manual transmission, would have then been considered the pinnacle of cool.

The ruse wasn't planned, seeming to happen on its own. The 8 ball gearshift lever was sticking up between Dan and me in the front, and as we pulled out into the street, I grabbed the 8 ball and went through motions of shifting through the gears, letting up on the accelerator between gear changes as though I had a clutch, each gear change enhanced by the glass-pack mufflers and exaggerated by the powerful torque of the engine. I was at the same time manipulating the gear changes in the automatic transmission with the control buttons, pretty much out of sight.

The Beaver's bulging eyes did little to conceal his envy and approval as he exclaimed, "Oh, man! I really pin to your punk!"

Sheldon and I exchanged uncomprehending glances. This was a new language for us. To our amusement, we learned that to "pin" was to dig or covet, while "punk" was Stockton teen vernacular for a car. We kept the floor box scam going for a while, then I took off from a stoplight and handed the 8 ball and shaft to the Beaver in the back seat, telling him it was his turn to go through the gears. We all had a good laugh on the Beaver, whose pinning of my punk was diminished only slightly.

We were to find that nightlife among the youth of Stockton included a lot of stupid and reckless punk (not the car "punk") stuff that held little appeal for the boys from El Cerrito. Evening activities included stealing spinner hubcaps and Appleton spot-lights (actually, they weren't lights at all, just dummies that would mount on either side of a car hood near the windshield and that were thought to look cool). Then, to keep the evening interesting, they thought it might be a good thing to roll a couple of skid-row drunks, not for money—just to beat them up. Then, if we were really lucky, maybe we could stir up a gang fight with the "beans," a derisive term for Mexicans, many of whom inhabited Stockton and California's Central Valley. The beans occupied a lower rung on social ladder, similar to the blacks in our city.

Dan returned from a foray into the street where he tried to rip a dummy spot from a parked car, but got only a handful of razor blades, stuck under the bottom rim of the spot as a theft deterrent. Blood poured from the wounds on his fingers. "Motherfucker!" he cried, cursing the owner of the spots. Few were clear on the concept of karma in those days.

Downtown, a lot of kids were out on the streets. One fellow, who I guess was designated the "bean counter," was busy counting the Mexicans on the next block, then tallying the white boys in our immediate area, declaring it about even, "Twenty, maybe 21 beans, and 20 of us." The idea was to spur some sort of gang fight, not our idea of a good time. We suggested to Dan that we were ready to head back home where we might undertake to rehabilitate him from behavior we considered unbecoming of a Saxon. For us, Stockton would forever become "Punkton," inhabited by punks of the nonautomotive sort.

We got back to Dan's house only to learn that his step-dad, Morton, had decided that Dan wouldn't be allowed to return with us, in our minds an unfair withholding of what had already been agreed to. Morton, a cold and stiff man with the soul of an insurance executive, was exercising his authority over his step-son, claiming he hadn't finished his chores or some such shit. Dan's gangster friends would instead be allowed to spend the night at his house.

Morton had recently acquired a new Ford Falcon, and he kept close track of his fuel consumption, wanting to be certain that he was getting his share of promised miles for each gallon of gas. We went out and bought a couple of cases of beer, using a phony ID to make the purchase. We managed to drink all of it in the next several hours, each of us going out to empty our bladders into the gas tank of Morton's Falcon throughout the evening.

The following morning Morton drove to Sacramento, returning in the early afternoon to report with a great deal of satisfaction and pride that he had just documented his best mileage result ever. He was so happy about this he relented, allowing Dan to come back to El Cerrito with us. Go figure. I imagined he would have serious car troubles as a result of all that piss in his gas tank. Our urine must have been octane-rated.

✦✦

THE NEIGHBORING UNIVERSITY OF CALIFORNIA at Berkeley was a citadel we were always aware of, and we would sometimes visit just to get the feel of the campus. "Big Game" week, when the Cal Golden Bears played their annual football game against their archrivals, the (then) Stanford Indians, was always a time of spirited hijinks and celebrations at both campuses. Rallies, bonfires, parties, and celebrations were taking place every night leading up to the Big Game. The Stanford ax, a symbol of the university with a history dating to the 19th century, had become the perpetual Big Game trophy, the winning side each year getting to possess the ax until winning it back on the gridiron. Over the years, there were many clandestine cloak and dagger episodes of one side stealing the ax from the possessing side of the moment, spirited gamesmanship and hijinks that would earn front page stories in the local papers. Spurred by example, and not wanting to be left out of the fun, we set out to develop a game of our own.

El Cerrito's archrival was Richmond High School. We were the Gauchos, so named for the Spanish heritage reflected in the name of our city, and they were the Oilers, so called for the presence of the Standard Oil refinery located nearby. The symbol of our high school spirit was the "pep jug." When the head cheerleader removed the cork from the jug, great clouds of school spirit were said to flow forth, enveloping the cheering crowd. The Oilers' symbol was, of course, an oil can, which I guess was used to grease up the crowd, allowing school spirit to rub in all over. The idea of breaking into the school to steal the oil can was discussed, but ruled out as being too heinous a crime to undertake in the name of school spirit. There was, however, an alternative target.

Out in front of Richmond High was the "Richmond Rock," a good-sized boulder that, I guess, might have represented their steadfastness. Out in front of our school was a sundial on a stone pedestal that might have represented the timelessness of our institution, again guessing. Both represented the schools themselves, symbols of pride and spirit. A few days before the Big Game against the Oilers, under the cloak of night, we would paint the Richmond Rock green and white, our school colors.

John Peralta and I were in the front seat of his '55 Chevy, Balls and Louie Young-Kid in the back. We had a can each of green and white house paint. John pulled up in front of Richmond High School and he and I bolted up the walkway to the rock and dashed it on either side with our school colors. Take that, heathen Oilers! We could have done a neater job with brushes, but we were out in the open and didn't want to stick around any longer than necessary. Two days later, of course, we arrived at classes to find our beloved sundial bathed in blue and red, the Richmond school colors. We had started a war and school officials were not at all happy about it.

At a school assembly before the Big Game, the principal and dean condemned the acts, promising to find out and punish those responsible. The student body, giddy and supportive, cheered their approval of the destructive hooliganism. John Peralta and I were nearly pushed to the fore as heroes, many knowing who the responsible parties were. I knew right away the jig was up. We'd been careless. Too many people had knowledge of who did it. Thinking about this, I told John it might be to our advantage if we turned ourselves in. There was no way we wouldn't be found out. John agreed, and that afternoon, we visited the dean and confessed to the crime. Balls and Louie Young-Kid were never mentioned. We each served a three-day suspension from classes and paid fifty dollars for the cost of sandblasting, the mild sentence representing our cooperation for informing on ourselves.

⇒·⇐

MY SEVENTEENTH YEAR WAS MUCH too fleeting. Carefree, adventurous days, romantic interlude and freedom from adult responsibility passed me by like a meteor in gravity's grasp, replaced by real life duties and social obligation. If there is one overall emotion that expresses what I felt at seventeen, it would be joy. Radiant, dumbass teenage joy, unhampered by a worldly view, social and civic responsibility, or the dark times that would soon be coming. Mine had been a blissful ignorance, sheltering me from the realities I would soon be handed.

Together with my old and dear pal Sheldon, we recently attended our 50th class reunion. A lot of the boys were there, still and always the boys. Many of the girls as well. In contrast to the boys and girls, others seemed adult, formally dressed and groomed, graduates of El Cerrito High School, Class of 1961. Nonetheless, I remembered most of them fondly. Sheldon and I visited the haunts of our youth and visited the "Castle," the scene of so many debaucheries and headquarters for our outlaw commerce during the drug years. Sheldon had the balls (of course he did—isn't that what we called him?) to simply knock on the door and make our introduction. The current resident greeted us graciously.

At the reunion I was reminded of the joy I once knew, now tempered by knowledge, and unavoidable in this setting, a lingering sorrow I felt for those who didn't make it this far, the many memories of them always a part of me. Recollections flooded my thoughts, the joyfulness of that special time ... before the fortunate son and the America of his youth both lost their innocence.

NEWLYWEDS

A
LL OF A SUDDEN, THERE WERE A LOT OF PLANS TO BE MADE, A HOME to be found, budgets to be considered, healthcare to be arranged, and on top of all else, my wife and I had to learn how to live with one another. We went from high school to marriage to parenthood in the blink of an eye, like learning how to swim by being thrown into the river. But life had a way of rolling easy when we were 17.

> **Mom and Pop were just a couple of kids when they got married. He was 18, she was 16, and I was three.**
> **–Janis Joplin (quoted in *Pearl* by Ellis Amburn)**

Married life started with two teens playing house, one with child, the other ready to take on adulthood and the world. Work was nothing new for me. I'd been steady at it throughout high school. Our first home was in Albany, and now work was just a short walk down the street and across San Pablo Avenue to Howard's Motor Sales. My parents wanted to see me continue my education and Dad's business would pay my tuition. Was this son fortunate? You bet.

In the fall I enrolled in morning classes at Berkeley's Armstrong College and still worked a 24-hour week in Dad's service department. We managed just fine on about $90 a week in 1961. Family expectations were idealistic and we adapted to them. We had everything we needed.

We were still in high school when one of Jeanne's friends recommended a cooperative doctor who would confirm the pregnancy without her parents' consent. Neither of us wanted to take our situation to our parents until we were sure. After talking to us, he advised that we should "assume pregnancy." Jeanne's confidence in this doctor wavered a bit when she spotted someone in the waiting room apparently bringing in a parakeet to see the doc. Nonetheless, the pregnancy was confirmed and we chose the day on which we would simultaneously break the news to our folks.

I had bought wedding rings and presented the engagement ring to Jeanne at one of the graduation dances. My parents had confidence in me and were cool and supportive. Mom later told me how sure and confident I was when I told her about my coming family. As far as Dad was concerned, it sometimes felt like I could do no wrong, and I always aimed to please. If he had any reservations about my situation, I never knew of them. Dad actually influenced my relationship with Jeanne. Shortly after we first met, she and some her sorority sisters came to our house one Sunday to plan a party with the Saxons. After introductions, Dad said to me with a wink and smile, "I'll take the brunette."

Jeanne wasn't too sure how her parents would take the news. Late in the afternoon on the day we had chosen, I went to Jeanne's house to face the music, whatever it might be. Her dad, Les, answered the door: "Jake! You old dog!" He was all smiles and handshakes as he stepped out onto the porch with me. Jeanne, he said, was upstairs resting, and if I could, I should come by a little later and maybe we'd celebrate. He was thrilled about us! How fucking cool can it get? I didn't know that Jeanne had yet to tell them the whole story. She was sneaking the information in piecemeal to lessen the impact. So far she had only announced our engagement.

It was a different Les who, with Jeanne's mother, came to our door later that evening to make the acquaintance of their daughter's in-laws-to-be. Les' shoulders were stooped as though he'd been punched in the stomach, all the life gone out of him. The wedding was only weeks away. I was disappointed that I'd have to work my way into their good graces all over again.

Even with high school diplomas and our parents' consent, because we were just short of our 18th birthdays, we were required to sit in an interview with a superior court judge before the county would issue our marriage license. It felt to me as though I'd walked into a church to be examined for worthiness by the head elder. Rather than offer encouragement, good wishes, or the wisdom of his years, this bastard judge just wanted to dress us down about what he considered our unacceptable behavior, like taking a ruler to the knuckles of naughty children. I've always had a hard time with disrespectful authority. What did this worthless sonofabitch think he would achieve?

→·←

FOR OUR HONEYMOON, DAD LET me take his demo, a brand new model from Peugeot, the 404. I had sold my hotrod '59 Chevy Impala, needing the money to start married life. Twice on our honeymoon, we were stopped by highway patrol cops—not for driving irregularities, but for their personal interest in the car I was driving. The cops were polite and apologetic for delaying us. They just wanted to take a look at this new model from Peugeot and ask a few questions about it. They probably thought it was okay to stop us because of the dealer license plates, opportunity to offer a sales pitch.

Our honeymoon destination was Santa Catalina, an island 26

miles off the Los Angeles coast, according to the dippy hit song about it. It felt to us like we were visiting a different country. We were walking the promenade at Avalon early one evening when some guy felt the need to give my new, pretty wife an amorous look and let out a wolf whistle. My reaction was to challenge him to a fight, as though he had insulted her rather than paid her a compliment. Such was my 17-year-old view of chivalry. The wolf puffed out his chest and asked me if I knew karate. I admitted not, and he warned that we'd better not fight then, because he might really hurt me. Not an apology, but close enough. I was content to let that dog lie, even though I didn't think he knew karate either.

About 40 years later, on another island, Maui, my second wife and I were leaving from a musical event held at the Arts and Cultural Center. She was a few paces ahead of me when, lo and behold, from the opposite direction and headed right for us, here comes part-time Maui resident Willie Nelson with a couple of his pals. Willie, lecherous old fart that he was, stopped himself short and followed Laurie's progress, an eager look on his face. With a wink—a "come fuck me" wink if ever there was—and a broad smile, he undressed her with his eyes as she strolled by. I was taking all of this in, coming along from behind. My reaction was to give him a Hawaiian *hand-shaka* and smile a "Hey, Willie!" at him, proud that he'd found my wife attractive.

Don't let anyone tell you we don't grow wiser with the years. Willie's since written a song titled "I've Outlived My Pecker," an anthem to age-related celibacy. He's probably not as libidinous as he once was, but I'll bet his smile is still just as wicked.

❧⸰❦

As a teen I was keenly interested in automotive technology and mechanics, and I attended the factory-sponsored schools and training sessions whenever offered by manufacturers. The mechanics who were Dad's employees were like uncles to me, treating me with respect and accepting me into their working world. I was especially close to Willie Davis, a hardworking mechanic and the shop foreman. He took me under wing early on, when I was just 14, and never treated me like the boss's son. If I screwed something up, he let me know about in no kindly manner, his expectations from me no different from the others under his domain. On Saturdays I would hold down the parts counter, perform minor emergency fixes on cars, and clean up the shop. I was equally at home with a torque wrench, a welding torch, or a grease gun.

Willie raced his '53 Oldsmobile Rocket 88 at the local drag strips, and his walls were lined with racing trophies. Sometimes I would go to the drag strip with him, where he was widely known by the other racers. He raced in a "stock" class governed by rules restricting what you could do to make your car go faster. Once bested by another fellow, Willie learned that he had "locked" his rear axles at the differential, an illegal modification that made him faster off the starting line. We went over to where a group of his friends was standing around, and Willie barked at them, "You tell that cheatin' bastard Pete Ryder if he shows up again with his rear end locked, I'll file a protest then kick his ass all the way to Georgia!"

I first got to know Max around this time as well. Dad had a satellite operation, "Howard's French Imports," where Max was a salesman, and where I first started working in the shop under Willie. Max always seemed to be smiling and happy, joking around with the other employees. As a marketing attraction, Max and Mom devised a Parisian sidewalk café out in front of the showroom. It had a small circular table with flowers in a vase, a wine glass, and a couple of chairs. One of the chairs was occupied by a store-window dummy dressed up to look like a Frenchman, a thin mustache, a beret, and a horizontally stripped T-shirt under his jacket. Max took it one step further and rigged up a microphone with a speaker hidden in the dummy. Sitting at his desk in the showroom, Max would engage passersby in conversation, inviting them to sit down and chat, usually with a humorous result. He always seemed to have fun with whatever he might be doing. Work was too hard not to be fun.

The detail specialist who kept all the cars shining was Roosevelt Williams, an especially kind, smiling, and soft-spoken black man from Louisiana. "Lot boy" was too demeaning a term for a man of Roosevelt's caliber and skills. But it fit me perfectly when Dad started bringing me in on Saturdays to wash the rows of used automobiles, teaching me the golden rules of used car marketing: #1 "you can't polish a turd," and #2 "no matter how nice the car, if the windows are dirty, it's still a turd."

Few knew how to bring out the luster in an automobile finish like Roosevelt. Most around Howard's called him "Rosie." If he ever objected to that nickname, he never let on. The racial division between blacks and whites was still a chasm, and many saw it as their duty to keep the black man down. Like all the black people of the era, Roosevelt, too, was subject to existing mores and conventions, but he never seemed bothered by this fact of life in the fifties and early sixties. He just worked harder and smiled broader and gave me the impression that he felt he was in the Promised Land. Roosevelt's warm personality and uncomplaining, dutiful work ethic made him as much family as any of Dad's employees. After Dad was gone, my mother made it her business to see that Roosevelt could buy his own home. She vouched for his work stability, put up some money, and cosigned the mortgage on his house.

At a time when my brother Robbin and our mutual pal Sheldon were rooming together in what can only be described as a "debauchery pad," they asked Roosevelt if he would come by in the company pickup and help them move some furniture. Roosevelt later confided to me, "You know that friend of yours they call 'Balls'? I went over there to help your brother an' him move some furniture an', Lord have mercy, he come outta the house buck naked!" Roosevelt, a quiet and respectful Christian Negro, was thoroughly scandalized by Sheldon's lack of modesty.

The Cuban missile crisis in October of 1962 gave me pause for reflection, but I had no idea of how close the world came to annihilation until years later, seeing history in retrospect. High-ranking generals were actually pushing hard for thermonuclear war. Buck Turgidson lives! Bless John Kennedy, also Nikita Khrushchev, for their resolve in not pushing buttons. Our son was then about nine months old and his sister was due at the end of the coming January.

A little over a year later, my American History class was dismissed in the middle of the day's lecture. New American history had just been created: John Kennedy was killed in Dallas. I remember walking to my car on the streets of Berkeley encountering people in tears, hiding their faces, unable to control their grief. I was still very much grieving the loss of my father a few months earlier and was further stunned by the loss of our president. I finished the current semester then left college half-completed in order to help my mother with the running of Dad's business.

❖

IN HIS LAST YEAR OF life, Dad added the Studebaker franchise (in addition to the French cars we sold), knowing that Studebaker would either sink or swim with its new Lark models and the secret-but-much-talked-about new model that would arrive in a few months, the Avanti. Dad was terribly disappointed when it did arrive, priced well above what the average working man could afford. It was nice looking and had a super-charged engine, but Dad instinctively knew what Ford seemed to know: the public wanted something stylish, but affordable. Instead of a Mustang, Studebaker brought out the Avanti, costing about twice what the Mustang would cost when it was released the following year.

Dad sent me and Jeanne to Las Vegas to represent him and take in all the fanfare around the Avanti introduction and dealer drive-away. Auto manufacturers of the era seemed to think that an introduction in Las Vegas was the best way to present their new models to the dealers. They probably still do. I would go again in following years to be wined and dined by auto manufacturers who trotted out their new models amid the glamor and gaudy extravagance that was then the forerunner to the ghastly overkill and excesses of today.

My fondest memories of Las Vegas come from 1957 when the family stopped over on our way to Missouri for the Christmas holiday, driving a southern route from California. There were then perhaps a half-dozen resort-casinos on the famous "strip," their classy elegance surrounded by desert. Mom and Dad chose the Sands and somehow got us a stage-side table for the dinner show featuring Frank Sinatra. Mom was thrilled at the opportunity to see and hear Sinatra. She also thought the brilliance in his shockingly blue eyes might have had something to do with drug use, habit many thought to be common among musicians of the day. Frank lit a cigarette during an instrumental interlude in the middle of a song and blew a stream of smoke that billowed like a brilliant white cloud when illuminated by the stage lighting. After just a drag or two, he stomped it out on the stage floor under the sole of his richly polished shoe and finished his song … "That's why the lady is a tramp."

Jeanne and I drove back to the Bay Area with Northern California's first Avanti. I chose the route up through the Nevada desert where I could open it up, stopping for a burger in a town called Tonopah. We weren't stopped by any curious cops on our way.

THE DISCOVERY CHANNEL

Nineteen sixty-four was a tumultuous year in America, the fabric of our society being stretched and torn from multiple directions. The war in Vietnam and the struggle for human redemption in the South had fast become the focus of social turmoil and division. One after another, college campuses around the country became hotbeds of rebellion. Marijuana and psychedelic drugs seemed a central part of the emerging youthful society. I was a family man, a father of two, a community businessman, and a member of the local Lion's Club. At first I paid little attention to the changing conventions of society around me, but I was attracted to the music of the Beatles and Bob Dylan. Then I found myself wondering if I might be the "Mr. Jones" Bob Dylan was singing about in his song, "Ballad of a Thin Man": "Something's happening here but you don't know what it is, do you, Mr. Jones?" That bastard Dylan was taunting me. Not wanting to be left behind, I consciously set out to find just what it was that was happening here.

> I received my working orders high on acid. The Lord came down and told me what to do and I have been doing it steady. I haven't received any other orders countermanding those.
>
> —Ken Kesey

Dad died by his own hand, victim of a freak and tragic hunting accident, just before the great explosion and turmoil that rocked our country. He never knew of Kennedy's assassination or got to consider the merits of the Vietnam War. He never heard the Beatles or learned of racial upheaval and triumph in the South. Dad never saw his 50th birthday, and I was shattered. My closest friend and confidant, the source of my own confidence and well-being was gone before I was twenty.

It wasn't long afterward that new and curious events began to happen nearby, getting my attention and interest. Dad's auto business, now run by Mom and me, was located in Albany, a conservative community bordered by Berkeley, where at the UC campus social and political upheaval was about to change the world as we knew it. The Free Speech Movement, skilled at raising hell on the Berkeley campus, was making headlines. I was moved to go take a look at these commies, often with my good pal Sheldon, whose parents owned a fashionable clothing store in Berkeley, where he often worked. Once or twice weekly, as schedule would allow, in my business attire—sport coat and tie—we'd have lunch on the Berkeley campus just to take in what was going on at Sproul Plaza. Tremendous crowds gathered and speakers with bullhorns would address the throngs. We heard Free Speech Movement leader Mario Savio speak one day, but couldn't make out much of what he had to say because of the general ruckus created by the milling crowds.

The Berkeley campus became what seemed to me the center of a new universe. It was nonetheless unthinkable to me at the time that people of my generation would oppose our government when it came to war. In my mind, war was represented by World War II, which I viewed as a righteous undertaking against an evil and formidable tyranny. I knew very little about the war in Korea, often referred to as a "police action" rather than a war; I knew even less about the difference. Now I had to learn to think about these things all over again, independently, while questioning my beliefs, many of which were then in lockstep with the average redneck.

In the community of Albany, anti-war protestors lined the railway tracks that went through town, holding signs and placards urging soldiers in the passing troop trains to revolt and to "make love, not war." This spawned the "Clear the Tracks Committee," Albany's answer to the protestors. It was headquartered right around the corner from our auto business at Vince's Barber Shop where I'd go to have Vince cut my hair. He was a cracker with a tough edge, but personable if you happened to be a white person. I had no idea what the Committee proposed, but assumed that it would probably include confrontation with the protestors, maybe armed with clubs and rakes and the like. I think it was mostly a fraternity of rednecks letting off steam and making sure the community at large knew on which side of the great divide they stood.

While having my hair cut at Vince's one day, a mixed-race guy came in and took a seat. I didn't pay much attention to him, and I don't remember which races he may have represented, only that he was brown rather than white. Pretty soon, Vince stopped cutting my hair and turned to address his new patron: "Hey, man ... are you a nigger?" The would-be patron just looked at him, put his magazine down, and left the shop.

"I don't do nigger hair," said Vince. I didn't tell him at the time, but I had just decided I would no longer do redneck barbers.

It was during this time of turmoil and protest when Sheldon explained to me that in order to get laid in Berkeley you had to be against war. That was a new concept. Sheldon, though, vouched for this doctrine and supported its conclusions. He readily admitted there were other reasons to oppose war, but this one made a good starting place. I was married and a faithful husband at the time, but Sheldon's belief that we had to change our way of thinking seemed reason enough to take a closer look at what I believed.

My one-time high school sweetheart, Arvalea, a very bright and progressive woman, returned to the Bay Area from Vassar. She and some of her very smart friends took up residence in an apartment on Green Street in San Francisco. At Vassar she would hang around with Ivy League people, including the famous Harvards, Timothy Leary and Richard Alpert, aka Ram Dass.

I would visit Arvalea now and then at the Green Street apartment, strictly non-romantic interludes, and listen closely as she and her friends and guests ventured intellectual opinion and anti-war dogma posed in confident and sometimes fascinating conversation over a backdrop of Miles Davis and marijuana smoke. I felt somewhat a rube among these bright and intellectual people, who on occasion wanted to know what I thought about something. I tried not to say much, afraid of exposing my naïveté and possibly red neck. Nonetheless, I slowly began to acquire new views and an understanding of much that was bantered about at Green Street and the Berkeley campus. Arvalea once took me to see the "Committee," a hip and early comedy troupe who would supply the abstract for *Saturday Night Live*. She was dating one of the Committee members, creating in me a mild and fleeting jealously.

Meanwhile, Sheldon and I, together with other friends, were discovering the fun and perception-bending properties of marijuana. Once or twice weekly, night would find us cruising Grizzly Peak Boulevard, high in the Berkeley Hills, surveying the incredible sea of lights that was the San Francisco Bay Area, and getting high while listening to Tom Donahue when he was still an AM disc jockey on radio station KYA. Then we might stroll Berkeley's Telegraph Avenue, teeming with exotic people, smells, and sounds. We visited Baskin-Robbins, dumbfounded at the confusion created when trying to choose a flavor, astonished to find how good ice cream could be when you were stoned.

One evening, strolling the Avenue again, we happened on some sort of Buddhist prayer meeting where we were invited to come in and learn how to chant "… Nahmiyohorengaykyo" in rapid succession while fondling sacred beads. The group leader tried hard to convince his audience that this practice would bring peace of mind and material wealth. Who's to say it was bullshit? I think today

I have a reasonable amount of each, even though I practiced very little and both took a few decades to arrive.

❧

FOLLOWING THIS PROCESS OF DISCOVERY, it was inevitable we would one day try LSD, even though we were aware that some viewed this drug among the most dangerous there was. Art Linkletter blamed it for his daughter's suicide. Others pointed to it as a key ingredient to negative personality change, while still others claimed it was a pathway to truth and enlightenment. Once made illegal, the feds looked on it with a great displeasure, which made trying it out all the more essential as far as we were concerned. Sheldon always seemed to have the good connections, and we chose San Francisco's Golden Gate Park as a setting for our initiation.

Some people are convinced they talked with God after taking LSD. I never thought that conversation took place, but maybe I was just too thunderstruck and speechless to form a reply. Imagine the discovery of a separate entity within yourself. I had somehow stumbled upon just that, an astounding revelation that has stayed in my consciousness ever since.

Under the influence of LSD, I found myself immersed in thought and contemplation when my attentions were somehow directed inward, into what I felt must be the very center of my soul and being. There I encountered another entity, occupying my mind and thoughts, sharing my existence with the self that was me. And that entity appeared to me in my mind, indistinct, as though stepping halfway from the shadows in a dark room. And it spoke to me in a calm, steady voice, audible in my mind, clear and matter of fact: "Don't worry. I've been here all the time."

I understood that to mean "had been and will be." Thus spoken, sensations as unbidden and miraculous as those created by my first kiss flowed through and engulfed me, an intoxicating, life-affirming warmth and knowledge that elevated my conscious mind to a reality I seemed to know was there all along, but heretofore hidden from view. I would always be the same and never be the same, for all time. Unlike my first kiss, this revelation didn't result in a boner.

For a long time I thought of this entity as my personal guardian angel. It wasn't until years later, hearing Ram Dass hold forth on spiritual matters, that I came to understand I had encountered my "spiritual" self. More recently, I heard Wayne Dyer talk about the two selves within each of us. He referred to the spiritual self as our "higher" self and the other more common self as our "ego" self, the one that fucks things up all the time. If I heard him right, Dyer was suggesting that it is our higher self that contains our Godliness, inherent in each of our souls, a spark and fragment of the Creator Almighty. Our ego self-imagines God a separate entity outside our being, the guy with the white beard who lives in the sky and hears everything we think. Beware the sky God.

Though I would look for it, almost expecting LSD to recreate it, I would never again experience this epiphany. Once it enters your consciousness it's there for all time, the only requirement, I think, is respect. I came to understand it's not the sort of thing you play at, trying to recall the entity like a genie from a bottle. Didn't you learn? It's been here all the time. It's here now. And now. And now again.

I have read of similar awakenings happening to other people and how the wisest of those people would praise this drug for its ability to expose an inner reality, at the same time warning against its use as a pathway of ease to gain enlightenment. I used to think of those who it was said to be enlightened as holy people who sat around in bliss, contemplating things like "the sound of one hand clapping" or "there is no teaching to teach ... *that* is the teaching" and other such paradoxes. I thought to be such a person would require a trust fund to exist because enlightenment's necessity, as I envisioned it, would require removal from the conflicts of the material world that surrounds us. But it could probably be a modest trust fund, because people such as these need only a little bit of rice every now and then.

Today I look upon people like the Dalai Lama, Ram Dass, Wayne Dyer, and others as spiritual teachers, enlightened souls who nonetheless are able to inhabit our crazy ego-driven world with a certain impunity, their desire to bring us their message of human strength, Godliness, and peace overriding anything else. And it's okay with me if they happen to make a buck in the process. There are plenty of phonies, too, who wrap themselves in the trappings of enlightenment in order to get laid, presenting themselves to the ladies as superior mates when compared to commoners such as myself. I hate those guys.

⟶⟵

THE OTHER TIMES I WOULD again experiment with LSD, it turned out to be strictly for the lark, a day off and an examination of other-worldly perceptions. I don't think I ever had a "bad trip," although on one occasion I can recall physical discomfort and anxiety that I thought were brought on by a badly manufactured drug, feeling as though spiked with amphetamine. A close friend once came to my door under the influence of LSD for the first time, lost and afraid, seeking sanctuary.

To escape the ravages of a particularly bad hay fever season, Sheldon and I did a road trip to Victoria on Vancouver Island in Canada. The whole trip was planned around a day off when we would again drop LSD. Sheldon's source claimed this dose as "pure Czechoslovakian laboratory" LSD, and miraculous visions and hallucinations occurred, full-color cartoons materializing on the underside of clouds and so forth. We just rode with it, dumbstruck and amazed. We enjoyed Victoria immensely, the quaint European-like setting, its parks and gardens brought to shimmering life under the influence of the Czechoslovakian pure.

Explorations into psychedelia were usually a joint venture with Sheldon, and Golden Gate Park was a favorite setting. Stoned on LSD, we once stood in a queue of thousands to see a collection of paintings by Vincent van Gogh, on tour and appearing at the de Young Museum. The paintings were electric and vibrant, the genius of his work stunning and undeniable. But I don't think you need to be stoned on LSD to see and appreciate these things in van Gogh's art. Fun though.

I once did a mild hit of LSD and visited my grandmother at a nursing home in Berkeley, taking her in her wheelchair for a springtime tour of the city when all the plum trees lining the avenues were in full bloom. The blossoms rushed past my peripheral vision in a mad spate of psychedelic, kaleidoscopic color. We had a great time together that day, at ease, carefree, and laughing. It was not an easy thing to achieve that state of kinship with my grandmother, and I am grateful for this day, one of the last I would see her.

Back in Golden Gate Park with the drug just coming on, Sheldon and I, on foot, crested a rise just in time to see, right in front of our eyes, a couple in their Sunday best flip their canoe in the lovely, tree-lined setting of Stow Lake. The water wasn't very deep and I can still recall the look of horror on the woman's face, standing waist deep and soaked, her bonnet drooping but still in place. She was no doubt wanting to throttle her date in this otherwise serene picture of gliding swans and leaning willows, perfectly framed by our state of mind. Sheldon and I seemed to attract such humorous and unexpected scenes, always when peaking on one drug or another. We had no desire to add to the unfortunate couple's embarrassment, and we did our best to suppress our laughter, but we couldn't hold it in. We had to go back over the rise and roll on the grass for several minutes, where we laughed until it hurt.

❧❦

THESE WERE YEARS OF EXPLORATION and personal growth, finding my way without Dad, trying to figure out which of the paths society was splitting into I would follow. I struggled with a restlessness that wouldn't go away. I understood I was traveling on a road that had been laid out for me by the expectations of the society and culture around me. But I could see other roads as well, distant and shining, with a promise beyond the structured walls that came with the daily life I was living. I imagined a life as individual as my fingerprints, and I began to strain against the harness that held me in place, fighting the thought that I was living in one of Malvina Reynolds' "little boxes on the hillsides," feeling like life for me was already indelibly cast before it really began. There were times I longed to be free of the stress and obligations of running a business that frequently struggled to make ends meet and the restrictions of a marriage that had found me at 17. Even so, such life was never bad, never wanting … just enclosed. Within that enclosure my existence was mostly happy and loving, the time spent with my family mostly joyous and mutually supporting.

I had at least made up my mind that I no longer belonged in the Lions Club, subject to tail twisters and lion tamers. My eyes were on another horizon. The meetings where the Lions plotted their good deeds to perform for the community were fueled by alcohol in smoke-filled rooms, attended by older white men in neckties, and couldn't compete with the other world I was exploring. I had no inkling of what lay in store for me, how dramatically life would change, or the choices I would make farther down the road.

I was still engaged in the search for the elusive happenings that eluded Bob Dylan's Mr. Jones, but I had formed some distinct opinions of where they were not.

FINAL COURSE

1

CAMP FED, "THE LAST RESORT"

"CAMP" WAS A GOOD NAME FOR IT, THOUGH IT LACKED ANY TENTS OR campfires. I was reminded of YMCA camp and Scout camp, and though I'd never experienced it, I suppose military camp might have a similar, rigid structure and all-male feel to it. Everything I had found menacing at Terminal Island was replaced by easier-going interactions and a sense of free, unconfined space. Robbin had already been there for about two years and had everything "dialed-in." The new sense of freedom and feeling of place was exhilarating, as though I had been living under a constant shadow that had somehow lifted. I knew I'd be there for years yet undetermined, but the movie had just shifted to Technicolor.

> Lawyer to his client being led from the courtroom by marshals: "... Look on the bright side. The right prison can take three strokes off your game."
>
> –Joe Martin, "Mr. Boffo"

I waltzed right into a private room with my brother and roommates

Artie and Lance. We were on the third floor of B-unit, overlooking the ball field and groves of pine and eucalyptus. Robbin, a consummate operator in any environment, had everything set up for me before I arrived. Artie had been posted to greet me at the front entrance. Robbin showed up in the middle of my check-in and started harassing the guard (aka "hack") in the good-natured manner at which he excels. Robbin and Artie showed me around and introduced me to so many people I could hardly catalog faces, let alone the names. The camp population was about five hundred inmates and growing all the time.

The difference in ambiance was immediately apparent. A lightness of being replaced an on-guard mindset, free from the constant containment of high walls, razor-wire, and the threat of possible retribution for some unintentional breach of etiquette among a population for whom violence was no stranger. There were no predators or thugs at the camp, although a few young-punk types here and there. The population was mostly an executive class of prisoner and even included a disgraced senator. Several of the Watergate scandal figures also did their time at the Lompoc camp. The majority, though, just about everybody in our social circle, had been convicted of nonviolent drug crimes, and most could point to informants as the source of their convictions. Some were high-level offenders whose operations involved shiploads of marijuana or truckloads of cocaine, but no one with a history of violence, weapons, or escape makes it to the camp. Like myself, many high-level offenders had served time in higher security institutions before graduating to the camp.

The social register was far more defined than that at Terminal Island. At the bottom of the ladder were the informants (aka "rats"), sometimes sent to camps for whatever reduced sentence they were to serve. The BOP (Bureau of Prisons) expended a lot of energy trying to keep the role of informants under wraps. Some inmates made it their business to expose informants, zealous in their efforts like Gestapo agents ferreting out suspected Jews in WWII Europe. East Coast informants were sometimes sent to western institutions where they were less likely to be known, and vice-versa. Informants were especially singled out for abuse by other inmates.

Most here were better educated and from more fortunate social circumstances than the majority at Terminal Island, though that in itself never makes anyone a better person. At Terminal Island, gay and transvestite inmates were largely left alone. If an inmate at the camp was thought to be gay, he became a victim of a nasty, machismo-fed discrimination from inmates who seemed to feel that sexual orientation other than their own was somehow a threat. There were no openly transvestite or transsexual inmates at the camp, ostensibly for good reason. Adjacent to the camp was the high security (level 5-6) Lompoc Penitentiary, where inmates were kept in cells like cages, all of them treated like the dangerous animals many were. Those at the camp were considered pussies and rats by the penitentiary population.

Also sharing the Santa Ynez Valley with the Lompoc prisons is the Vandenberg Air Force Base, a huge military facility that included some 40,000 acres of range land. In a federal partnership with the Air Force, the BOP used the range land to graze about 2,500 head of cattle, eventually processed at the camp slaughterhouse. There was also a dairy. The products of these livestock operations were used to feed federal prisoners throughout the western states. They were staffed by the camp inmates and supervised by professional farm and animal specialists who had the authority of a guard but, in general, were less cop-like and militaristic than the regular hacks.

The prison cops at the camp seemed to come in two categories. Some had no ax to grind with the population and simply did their job in a quiet manner, using force and position only when necessary. Others ranged from mean-spirited to psychotic bullies with chips on their shoulders looking for fights with anyone who couldn't fight back, cowards with deep psychological deficits. They considered any inmate a lesser human being, deserving of punishment, which they were happy to amplify. One such asshole cop was known among the camp population as "Make My Day," after the macho cop played by Clint Eastwood. He played the tough guy and singled out certain inmates for personal abuse and laid it on all the heavier to those who refused to be cowed. I never encountered anyone like that at Terminal Island, where similar behavior by a guard might have resulted in his becoming a target by inmates.

Being a member of the cattle crew was one of the most prestigious work assignments an inmate could aspire to. They left the prison environment each day to ride herd over the cattle on 40,000 acres, each with his own horse. There were about a dozen of them, my brother included, and they got to play cowboy all day long. They also seemed to control who might be allowed to join them when one of the members was replaced, keeping their little fraternity exclusive. The cattle crew supervisor was an especially decent man who respected the crew members and seemed to enjoy their company over that of prison administrators. With all that open space and relative freedom, it doesn't take much thought to imagine opportunity for supply lines of contraband. Staffed by a crew of professional smugglers, each a bright, high-level achiever, here indeed the fox was assigned duty in the hen house.

I once worked cattle as a favor to the owner of the 4-O, the big cattle ranch near Troy, branding, de-horning, inoculating, castrating, and so forth. I had no desire to work cattle ever again and declined invitation to join the cattle crew. The abject brutality of the task, poor dumb animals bellowing out in pain and fear, and the awful stench of burning hide from the branding iron remain anathemas to me. I'd never make it as a cowboy.

There were other off-grounds prison jobs as well. Dairy workers went to and from their work via a short drive in a van. There was an irrigation crew who kept pastures watered and a Vandenberg crew who worked at the Air Force Base doing landscape and maintenance. The cherry on top was the milk truck driver. He delivered dairy products to prisons around the western states, on the road and staying in motels for the longer runs. Everyone wanted his job.

My typing and clerical skills again landed me a clerk's position, first at the dairy and then for the B-unit manager and counselors. I was comfortable working in the office with the counselors, and I could usually accomplish all that was required of me in just a couple of hours; the rest of the day my own. There were lots of perks, too, including to some extent a protective oversight by the unit manager and counselors who wouldn't want some hack to lock up *their* clerk, whose job made their jobs easier. I had access to my own typewriter whenever I wanted it. When you qualified, furloughs were automatic if you kept your record clean.

❖

WITH LOTS OF FREE TIME at my disposal, I took up running on the dirt track that circled the baseball field, almost a mile around. What was once an inmate-built golf course and had been turned into a soccer field was also encircled by the track. It was open country as far as you could see, surrounded by trees and nature, and it felt like anything but a prison, at least to those who had experienced higher level institutions. Running three or four miles almost daily, I discovered that endorphins *do* make you high, providing elevated spirits and a sense of physical well-being.

Early one summer morning, before the 6:00 AM breakfast, I went for a run with then roommate "Booger" and scared up a bear on the track. We were running in opposite directions, Booger a faster miler than me, when I came on the bear in dim morning light. It turned at my approach and headed away from me on the track, my thought processes immediately derailed. My first take registered hyena. It was running with a stiff-legged canter on front legs that seemed longer than the rear, a sloping back. Hyena? ... Bear! I followed behind and ran him right into Booger who was coming from the other direction and couldn't believe his eyes. We stopped and exchanged our disbelief. Our story made us subjects of curiosity and celebrity around the camp for a few days. The assistant warden came to interview us.

❧─❧

THE INMATE GOLF COURSE WAS disassembled prior to my arrival. Prison authorities worked hard to dispel any appearance of being soft on crime, especially during the Reagan administration. Mean-bastard republican political ideology seemed to penetrate every bureaucratic arm of the government. In the Bureau of Prisons that meant any thought of rehabilitation was replaced by a doctrine solely of punishment. Some high-level BOP employees brought with them a disregard for inmate humanity that reeked of vengeance, a certain zeal in their efforts to extract what they viewed as society's revenge. Maybe it was especially meted out to campers because we had it so easy compared to a penitentiary population. A hack making twenty-five thousand a year held a dim view of the executive dope dealer who might make more money in a single year than he would in a lifetime. There were also those counselors and cops who nonetheless maintained a sense of human dignity, lacking the built-in hard-on for those in their charge, mostly democrats I suppose.

I sometimes used to imagine that prison administrators held a monthly committee meeting to decide how they could make life just a little more unpleasant for their wards. *What can we take away from them this month?* Whatever they took away, most recently the curtains and blinds in our rooms, it was usually secondary to the obtuse pettiness of the action, nearly always done in the name of "institutional security."

But I hasten to add, fellow conspirators ... listen well: By any standard our life is easy compared to the tens of thousands held in other institutions. We have it far too good, and we get over on them way too hard, to act like poor losers. For us to whine about our keepers' pettiness is to let them win.

In the good ol' days, when Jimmy Carter was in office and the "war on drugs" hadn't yet moved into major battle mode, first-time large-scale drug offenses brought offenders three-to-five, and inmates at the camp were housed two to a room and allowed such homey touches as keeping goldfish. Some even paid others to do their jobs and spent their days on the tennis court. By the time Reagan was done, the same offenses brought 15 to 25 and new parole guidelines required offenders to do about 90 percent of their sentence before becoming eligible for parole. Now only informants would be eligible for a sentencing break. A fitting legacy for Reagan, himself a documented FBI informant who turned over the names of his Hollywood associates to McCarthy's House Un-American Activities Committee.

A taste of the federal whip was plenty to encourage Robbin and me to find other lines of work. All of this enhanced punishment seems to have had little or no effect on the illicit drug trade and, in my view, simply turned incarceration into a growth industry. We knew we were fortunate to go down when we did, in the "middle ground" of the drug war. Those who followed were met with a stepped-up war on drugs, requiring sentences that all but removed any hope of reestablishing a workable life. Drugs weren't a capital offense, at least in our country, but it felt like things were moving in that direction.

Our room that once housed two—four when I arrived—would house six before I left. The industry spawned by the drug war kept growing all the time. Drug dealers are used as the bad guy examples, scapegoats politicians can point to, trophies upon whose carcass law enforcement officers could place their foot while smiling for the cameras. There was once a war on alcohol. It was called prohibition and it worked just about as well as our current war on drugs.

❖

THE CAMP GOLF COURSE MET its end when a local TV anchorman with a camera crew came to interview upper level prison administrators. Immediately following a segment with a high level prison administrator flatly denying the existence of a golf course, the producers cut to a scene of Robbin and Lance out on the camp links with golf bags over their shoulders, Hawkeye and Trapper getting in a few rounds on the three-hole inmate course. This sort of public embarrassment met with the usual BOP reaction: immediate removal.

Personal music players weren't allowed at Terminal Island. At the camp I was thrilled to have my own cassette player, able to listen to music of my own choosing while running on the track. Music can be empowering and to some extent take the effort and hard work out of personal training. My kids sent me cassettes of new music and taped my requests when I asked. But this privilege, too, was removed when a couple of wiseguys secretly recorded to cassette a conversation with the warden, catching him in some sort of embarrassing denial they then made public. Personal radios were still allowed and I tuned into the local country music station.

Running on the track early one Saturday morning, loud rock & roll blaring in my headphones, I was caught up in my own private world when prison cops called an unscheduled special count, wanting to make sure some fleet-footed inmate hadn't run into town for a quick beer. It was early enough that many were still in bed, few out and around at the time. I couldn't hear the announcement over the music and was oblivious to the count. My roommate, Boomer, was acutely aware I hadn't returned for the count, and the time to do so without penalty was drawing nigh. He went to the counselors' office and told them I might be out running with headphones on. The B-unit counselors, with whom I worked daily, Dave and Big Bill, were okay guys in my book. They got on the camp intercom and started calling me, but I couldn't hear anything over the music and remained unaware of the count. Rounding a bend, I looked back and saw Dave in his car, on the track, and traveling at a pretty good clip, coming up behind me ... what the hell? I looked around and registered the fact that I was alone. There wasn't another soul in sight. It finally dawned on me: a fucking special count! I beat it across the middle of the field, as fast as my feet could fly, the entire population on the south side of the three-story B-unit building aware of my plight, leaning out windows to cheer me on with applause and catcalls.

The dreaded cop we called "Cagney" (for his resemblance to the actor) was waiting for me at our room, a scowl on his face. But what could he do? There was no rule against headphones, and if they prevented me from hearing the count announcement, was that really a punishable offense? I think he wanted it to be, but I was protected by my innocence and, maybe to some extent, by virtue of being the unit clerk.

➥➢

CAGNEY WAS A COP OF legend, a worthy opponent for any inmate who thought he could get away with any shit on Cagney's watch. Rather than mean or psychotic, Cagney was astute and determined, an over-achiever who probably figured God was on his side. Getting away with shit was a contest, almost a sporting event, and Cagney was aware of this. He knew the inmate population was always engaged in perpetrating one scam or another, and for Cagney, it was a cerebral game. If you're going to match wits with Cagney, you'd best know what you were doing because consequences could be dire if you come up the loser. He took to his job with the zeal of a John Birch Society member hunting commies in 1960s Berkeley. It was said that Cagney spent his lunch hours searching for contraband and peeking around corners with his secret agent spy periscope, looking to catch a scam in action.

Prior to the implementation of the urine test for marijuana use, the cops had to catch inmates in possession of the substance to make a bust stick, even in the kangaroo prison court. Some inmates were in the habit of taking an after-dinner stroll on the running track to smoke a joint. Anyone coming your way could be seen from a distance. Then, one evening, without warning, an inmate was dropped upon from above, as though the prey of some primal hunting ape. It was, of course, Cagney who had become arboreal, hiding in a tree to await his quarry. On another well-re-membered night, Cagney hid himself in the popcorn machine at the GAC (General Activities Center) and popped out (hands up, motherfuckers!) just as the evening program had started, busting several guys who'd lit up their joints when the lights went down.

My first evening at the camp was a celebration of brothers reunited. We were feted with vodka martinis, followed by filet mignons pilfered from the slaughterhouse, and a slice of Marie Calendar cream pie, smuggled in by someone on the Vandenberg crew. This was by no means our common fare, but Robbin and the boys wanted to show off a little, letting me know that I had arrived at the last resort, Camp Fed.

A RESPITE FROM REALITY

If you ask me, "Tony, what's the best times of your life?" it's the two times I went to Lompoc. It was fantastic. If I'm lucky enough, I'll go back again. It's like locking a doctor who likes to practice medicine in a hospital.

–Tony Serra (on his two prison terms at Camp Fed)

NOTHING SO JOYFULLY REMINDS ME OF MY YOUTH AS TREE FORTS, FROG ponds, and baseball. I was elated to find that baseball was held in high regard at Camp Fed, anxious to see if I could get my baseball chops back. The competitive spirit exhibited by so many of the players invited participation, as a player or a spectator. Baseball would become a part of my regimen the whole time I was at the camp.

Baseball provided escape from any thought that I was actually imprisoned. We played slow-pitch softball rather than the purist form of hardball. It provided an engrossing focus and pastime for those who loved the game and the camaraderie of team sports. Non-players developed into an energetic fan base that often filled the stands. There was an adequate field with a backstop, bleacher sections alongside the first and third baselines, and lots of high-spirited competition between the teams.

During the years I was at the Camp, the league constantly refined itself, eventually ending up with a commissioner and a rules committee. Player statistics were kept and season-end trophies were handed out to players for the best batting average, the most home runs, the most runs batted in, and to the championship team. Statistics, always a vital part of baseball, were posted weekly for the top players in each category. A few inmates had taken it upon themselves to put many of these refinements in place and selflessly put in hours of spirited work to keep everything functioning at a high level. In addition to the intramural league, we also had a camp team made up of the best players. One of the dairy supervisors, a warm and decent fellow who knew the game, acted as coach. We even had uniforms, but we didn't get to travel. All our games were at home, mostly against Air Force teams from nearby Vandenberg AFB.

Ballgames were a fertile ground for heckling, teasing, challenging, and generally insulting your opponent, either on the field or from the stands. Here was the place where the boys of summer let their testosterone rule. Robbin has always been able to elevate harassment to an art form. He was one of the league's best pitchers, a position that allowed him plenty of opportunity to rain down his verbal torment on other players.

"Let that be a lesson, chump!" might be directed at someone who just hit into a double play. "Take that, you cheese-eating lop!" might follow a strike-out. A "cheese-eater" was camp slang for an informant, a natural morph from "rat." A "lop," if you don't know, is a combination of nerd and dork with an underlying foundation of wimp. Lance would chime in from first base, targeting the batter, "Lookit this lop ... he probably eats five blocks of cheese every day!" At other times, maybe following a weak or lucky base hit, "Hey, you dropped your purse on that one!" amongst other challenges to one's masculinity. The threat to "bitch-slap" someone was popular with many.

As insulting as it might seem, it was mostly harmless fun in an environment that never lacked for machismo. And, of course, there weren't any females around to be insulted by the overt man-starch. At bat I was heckled from the stands for my age, "Hey! This guy's older than Pop-eye!" The heckler referring to the nickname of another middle-aged inmate.

"Fuck you, Jack. Watch your mouth or I'll open a can of spinach on your ass."

If someone was found out to be an informant, they would likely be hounded off a team, as well as suffer social deprivation in general. Known informants didn't take part in the baseball league.

We were the "Lodestars," a team made up of friends and close acquaintances, all of us one-time drug merchants and smugglers. Named for a notorious pot-smuggling airplane, we weren't the best team in the league, but we probably had the most fun. One friend was a gifted graphic artist, and he made us a banner from a bed sheet showing bales of weed falling from a Lodestar in flight, one of them crushing a cartoon rat on the ground, his block of cheese nearby. The team slogan, "Go Up in 'Em—Deep!" was prominent. I was initially a utility player, filling in wherever needed, then moved to first base after Lance was released.

My rookie season came to a close with a playoff game against the Master Batters, a team made up of mostly black inmates. We were short two of our best players who were in the "hole" for getting caught at various mischiefs, and they beat us by six runs.

"At least they don't have any cheese-eaters on their team," said Artie, who would rather lose to a team of girl scouts than a team that included informants.

Our loss set up a consolation game with the "Barons." After three innings of play, they had a four-run lead and betting in the stands favored the Barons. The first baseman for the Barons had been the subject of camp rumors concerning possible homosexual behavior, setting him up for mean-spirited harassment. When he came to bat, Lance was merciless:

"Here comes the switch-hitter, boys. Look how he holds the bat—he thinks it's a dick!" The poor man never did get a hit.

Our shortstop was a tough and fearless player, a muscular little dynamo named Lou, and he slammed a vicious tag on a Japanese player from the Barons who was trying to stretch a base hit. Both players hit the ground and came up with dust flying, the Japanese player livid, crying foul, and claiming the shortstop illegally blocked the base path. Lou's reaction was predictable:

"Fuck you, Tojo. You didn't get boned down enough at Hiroshima? Want some more?" And the players squared off with their fists cocked.

Both benches emptied momentarily, and the players were held in check from one another, order eventually restored. Then we had a seven-run inning and went on to win 15 to 10. The win over the Barons set up yet another playoff game with the Master Batters. You'd think that we'd had enough, but we returned for one more spanking. The only memorable event was a home run by Robbin, who rounded the bases and, coming home, leaped into the air with a one hundred, eighty degree rotation while pulling his pants down, landing on home plate and presenting a vertical smile to the Master Batter cheering section.

⇥⇤

WHEN THE NEW SEASON ARRIVED, the Lodestar name was retired and we became the Cowboys, the team made up of cattle crew members and a few ringers like myself. I moved over to third base, thinking a left-handed third baseman a novel idea. My introduction was a searing one-hopper that came off the turf faster than I could follow, slamming me a crushing blow direct to the Adam's apple and cutting off my wind pipe for a few scary moments. This was the hard way to learn why they call this position the "hotbox." It was three days before I could comfortably talk again.

In our fifth game of the season, we again came up against last season's champions, the Master Batters. After four innings of play, we were behind 6 to 12 and things were looking bleak for the Cowboys. Though a good ball team, the Master Batters were a mouthy bunch, always eager to laud their prowess at the expense of their opponents. The game was peppered with sporadic outbursts. Robbin, never of a mind to let anyone climb a rung higher from where he stood on the insult ladder, threw it back at them at every opportunity. One of our guys smacked a double by the outstretched glove of their shortstop and into the alley. Robbin was immediately on his feet:

"You dropped your purse on that one, you lop. Pick up your skirts next time! Let that be a lesson to you chumps!"

The shortstop glared at Robbin, shouting back, "The scoreboard shows who the chumps are!"

"Yeah? Well here's your scoreboard, whiner-baby!" said Robbin, presenting his middle finger.

But they held us to just two runs in the inning, making some awesome catches in the outfield and scoring three more runs their next time at bat. Then we cut loose in the bottom of the sixth, scoring nine runs. Our hitting suddenly came to life, a dozen players coming to the plate in the inning. The stands along with our bench erupted in cheers and applause.

We were up 17 to 15 with one inning left to play. Betting in the stands reached a fever pitch. With no outs and runners on first and third, a Master Batter hit a towering fly ball into the right-center field gap, but our center fielder, the speedy "Marquis," had played the batter perfectly and made a spectacular over-the-shoulder catch, then threw to first to double off the runner who had made it halfway to third base before realizing the ball had been caught. But "Big Mike" was out of position to receive the throw at the base. All looked lost until Robbin was suddenly there from his backup position to make the catch and double off the runner by half a step. The runner on third tagged up and scored, making the score 16 to 17.

With two men out, the next batter walked and the following batter grounded to our shortstop, who went to second for the force, but it was declared a virtual tie and the runner was ruled safe. Our second baseman, Milton, heard someone in the stands call "out!" and started to jump around and celebrate victory, ignoring our shouts as the runner went to third.

"Get your head out of your brunser, Milton!" counseled Robbin. The next batter grounded to me at third, and I cut him down at first base with steps to spare, not even close. Our first win over the Master Batters! How sweet the victory!

YEAR AFTER YEAR, BASEBALL PROVIDED respite from the reality of my circumstance. There's a magic quality inherent in the game, the ability to turn men again into boys. In my final season, I captured the "Top RBI" trophy, engraved with my name and "FPC Lompoc Intramural League." I had developed my skill at hitting the ball to "where they ain't," especially when there was a runner in scoring position. I still display it proudly, a reminder that life is what you make it no matter where you are.

3

ROAD DOGS

Artie was Robbin's favorite "road dog," a close and trusted friend, respected and enjoyed, subservient to a degree where Robbin was concerned. Artie often served as a target for Robbin's devilish teasing and torment. He did his best to respond in these circumstances, but he usually fell a little short trying to match tricks with Robbin. Any pal could be considered a road dog, as long as both recognized the brotherhood in the relationship. Robbin gathered his road dogs around him as though in a kennel, a pal for every occasion. If I had a road dog in any sense of the term, then it was Robbin. We seldom engaged in mutual trickery. If Robbin would allow himself to be subservient to anyone at all, then it might be me or Ed Olson.

I arrived at our room for the 4:00 PM count, and there was Artie, standing at the door, locked out, stark naked, and drenched from his shower.

"C'mon, Robbin. Lemme in …"

"No way, Art. This is your payback."

"But I didn't lock you out of the room!"

"Paybacks always bite harder, Art. You know that."

"C'mon, Rob … I'll never take your towel again. I promise!" Artie had started this one, coming into the bathroom and stealing Robbin's towel while he was showering.

"Suffer, chump!" Robbin cupped his hands at his mouth and yelled through the door, "Hey, everybody—look at Artie!" Indeed, he was hard to miss.

Artie gave me a look of suffering indignation, oblivious to his lack of clothing and the passing crowds of inmates returning to their places for the afternoon count. Robbin finally slid the key under the door and I let us in, another trick-bag answered with a payback. Artie knew he had it coming, and the players recognized the lack of malice in the game. It was just road dogs at play.

❖

HEROIN SEEMED THE MAJOR CONTRABAND import at Terminal Island, at least where I was—in the drug unit. I was never once aware of any contraband alcohol at TI. The opposite was true at the camp. Reefer seemed readily available at both venues, although the recent introduction of urinalysis for marijuana use did its part to curtail use. Alcohol, though, was out of your system in hours. As long as you were careful and didn't overdo it, its use was reasonably safe.

The contraband supply lines were many and varied. Each social group had their own secret source and hiding places. There were clever, hidden stashes everywhere. Contraband in bulk was kept outside the camp perimeter and brought in on an as-needed basis by inmates working in the various enterprises outside the immediate area. On horseback with 40,000 acres at their disposal, the cattle crew had unlimited opportunity to smuggle almost anything they could imagine.

Vodka was the booze of choice, least likely to be detected on your breath and available at 100 proof for enhanced "liftoff." It was purchased by the case, usually by someone's wife, and left at a predetermined pick-up spot somewhere out on the range. We learned to have it packaged in small, individual juice cans (identical to those available at the camp commissary) that came with a gummed aluminum "pull-off" tab on the top. The juice was dumped, the can filled with 100-proof vodka, and the tab carefully replaced. Only very close examination might reveal that the can had been opened, but no one was looking for it. We called them "bears," so-called for the plastic honey bears that were once popular for concealing contraband before the juice cans became the perfect ticket. It worked so well that when Eddie the Kid was punished for some major infraction with a disciplinary transfer to a higher level prison across the country, he got all his bears delivered to him with the rest of his belongings. They arrived a week or two after he did, packed up and sent along by the prison cops. We kept our methodology under wraps from the general population. If the cops ever uncovered this scam, all of us would be at immediate risk. We kept an ear to the ground to learn of any bust involving a bear. The whole time I was at the camp the juice container scam was never compromised.

We participated in an almost nightly cocktail hour and we knew how to time it so that an unscheduled visit from some roaming hack was most unlikely. We opened the windows and sprinkled some body powder around the room to veil any smell of alcohol. We also understood that it was important to remain civil, not overdo things and be cool, stay in the room, and not go wandering around. We would be in our bunks by the 10:00 PM count and the count cops would just shine a flashlight through a window in the door to count heads.

Robbin and I had no problem maintaining our cool and neither did our roommates—after Artie and Lance. Those two had a habit of getting carried away. Lance overdid it one memorable night, standing on the table, singing and acting out, partying hard. Later in his bunk, he managed to let loose with a volcano-like spew of vomit just as the count-cops shined their light on him. After a brief examination, he was "rolled up" and taken to the hole. The cops didn't bother to check the other occupants of the room, all feigning sleep. One "roll-up" was enough for this night.

Artie was incorrigible and alcohol was not his ally. He was a social being who loved to get high and visit his pals, traipsing around the camp. He called on friends in the dormitories and dropped by the GAC, laughing and outgoing, wanting to share the happy feelings that had welled up inside him. On occasion, Artie would start drinking in the early afternoon. By dinnertime he could no doubt score two or three times any legal limit on a Breathalyzer. To keep him from self-destructing we actually strapped him to his bunk one night, like a madman in an asylum. The rest of us were forced into absolute sobriety whenever Artie went into his drinking mode, his drunkenness a danger to any around him who might also have consumed. He was once busted by a sharp-eyed cop who spied his stagger. The penalty was five or six days in the hole and loss of his 30-day halfway house assignment. Artie didn't give a shit about the halfway house, but time in the hole was a terrible bore.

⤞⤝

IT WAS ARTIE'S HABIT TO light a cigarette upon waking in the morning, still in his bunk, his pack and lighter at hand on a swivel tray attached alongside. Robbin ordered up some cigarette loads to be smuggled in, probably with Artie in mind. Artie's morning cigarettes started to explode when lit and we'd all start the day with a laugh. Artie was a good sport about it, getting some loads of his own from Robbin so he could trick-bag someone else.

Poor Artie, even this didn't work for him. Ray became suspicious of Artie's overly eager offer of a cigarette, an out of character moment for Artie. To ease Ray's suspicions, he pulled one from the pack and lit up ... he didn't know Robbin had loaded another cigarette in the pack and it would be the one he had chosen. It blew up in his face as an astonished Ray looked on, "Uh ... thanks, Artie. I'll get back to you on that, okay?"

Just before count one day we were lying back on our bunks, reading our books and waiting for Artie, when Robbin announced, "Watch this, you guys." With a small glass jar that had recently been used to smuggle some booze, Robbin deftly captured a fart in the jar, screwed on the lid, and set it on the table. Artie arrived for the count just prior to the warning bell.

"Art!" said Robbin in his sternest voice, "I thought you were going to wash that bottle out!"

"I did, Rob, honest!" pleaded Artie.

"Well just take a whiff of it, Artie. You could get us all thrown in the hole."

At this suggestion Artie picked up the bottle, removed the lid and stuck his nose in as though doing a "swirl and sniff" with a fine wine to capture a complex bouquet. His expression turned from curiosity to realization to outrage while the rest of us exploded with laughter. Robbin allowed few dull moments in B-3, Room 8.

>-<

WHEN LANCE WAS RELEASED, HE was replaced in our room by Bernie, who described himself as a "California" Jew. High strung, bright, and a smooth operator, Bernie was the camp "Yossarian," an ace businessman, smuggler, and wheeler-dealer whose nickname was "Be Havin' Things." Having things was Bernie's specialty. Just 24 years old, it was easy to imagine him with six-figure bank accounts and a stable of fancy cars. His vice wasn't alcohol or drugs. Instead, Bernie expended great amounts of energy acquiring food, mostly good, healthy food. He was generous with his roommates and didn't at all mind sharing his booty. He smuggled comforts, too, getting all of us fitted bed sheets for our bunks. He came up with things like a custom floor wax for inspections, vitamins, even a can of natural ingredients labeled "colon cleanser."

But mostly Bernie was interested in smuggling food and brought in things like fresh ground coffees and macadamia nuts, a supply of dried fruits and fresh vegetables, and cases of tuna fish. He had thieves on his payroll who worked in the kitchen. He himself worked on the Vandenberg crew. There were some advantages to this, like stores and restaurants, but perhaps the biggest was Bernie's boss, an Air Force sergeant who was gay and looked fondly on Bernie. He wasn't at all interested in policing what Bernie did.

"Maybe I'll let him give me some head," said Bernie. "That'd get us a case of wine for sure."

"Just a goddam minute!" interrupted Artie. "You pitch, you catch ... that's the way I see it and I ain't livin' with no goddam faggot!" Artie was one of those who felt threatened by a sexual orientation other than his own.

"Okay, Artie," said Robbin. "You're outta the car. I'll take your wine issue." "Out of the car" means that you don't get to participate in whatever it is the car delivers. In this instance, we were talking about a wine car.

"Relax, Art," I advised. "Bernie's only suggesting that he indulge the whims of his supervisor for everyone's benefit. For Queen and country, you know?"

"Yeah," said Artie, relenting, "I guess so. As long as he doesn't bone him down."

"Don't worry, Artie," says Bernie. "That never entered my mind. Anyway, he's not all that good looking."

→-←

WITH SINGLE-EDGE RAZOR BLADES, ARTIE and Bernie diced carrots, celery, bell pepper, lettuce, cucumber, avocado, and summer squash on the cutting board. Bernie's kitchen thieves came through with greens, an onion, hardboiled eggs, mayonnaise, and a bottle of vinegar. Robbin brought in a can of tuna from some hidden stash. Spices and an Italian dressing magically appeared from one of Bernie's hiding places. Dennis walked in and handed us four filets appropriated from the slaughterhouse, already cooked. We heat them up on the underside of a clothes iron that served as our stove. The room took on the busy hustle of a restaurant kitchen. The only thing missing was a bottle of wine, but Bernie was still working on that.

It was Thursday, a common night for a "food car." They were serving "liver fiesta" down at the chow hall, a weekly special usually served on Thursdays, and food cars were happening all over the camp. Camp residents took to liver fiesta the way adolescent children might indulge in hot beets for dessert. Earlier in my residence, I ignored the warnings and braved the dining hall one Thursday night, set on trying out a little liver fiesta. When I found the hall two-thirds empty it should have reinforced the warnings, but I can be a brave soul when it comes to food. It would be my introduction to this Camp Fed gourmet specialty.

I got my plate and took a seat at a table with about a dozen others. Right away a fellow just down and across the table from me screwed his face into a bitter grimace, "Jesus Christ!" he whined. "What makes this stuff taste so awful? It has the flavor of rusty iron that's been rubbed in dirt!"

I took a small bite and found myself more or less in agreement with his assessment. Then another fellow at the table, who works at the slaughterhouse, ran it down for us:

"Wull, ya' see, it's like this: when the steers get kilt, they hang 'em on a conveyor an' open 'em up, ya' know, an' inside the animal the piss-bag hangs right over the liver. An' these guys workin' at the slaughterhouse, they don't give a shit 'bout doing anythin' the way its s'posed to be done, an' most of 'em puncture the piss-bag with their dressin' knives, an' the piss runs down all over the liver an' makes it taste that way."

Okay, I thought, *I'm a vegetarian. At least on Thursdays.*

Back in our room, memories of liver fiesta etched in my mind, we finished off the night's food car with some figs and pears from Bernie's dried fruit stash. It felt like we should have some cognac, but some fresh-brewed mocha-java would have to do. Artie, shirtless, lay back on his bunk for an after-dinner cigarette that exploded in a shower of sparks, igniting the abundant hair on his chest, whoosh!

"Goddammit, Robbin, you trick-bag sonofabitch!" cried Artie, beating out the sparks. "When are you gonna run out of those goddam things?" The room smelled like burnt hair.

"That was the last one, Artie. Honest." Robbin's devilish grin guaranteed he had more.

Artie laughed along with everyone else. Our bellies were full and the mood was jubilant. We cleaned up the dinner mess and headed down to the GAC to take in a night of the summer Olympics. Tent Man was there, two rows in front of us, stuffing popcorn and candy into his over-burdened, 400-pound sack of a body. He was known to have a sharp temper and was said to be at the camp for assaulting someone on a federal reservation who had given him a hard time about his bulk. Robbin couldn't help himself and bounced a jellybean off Tent Man's shoulder. Tent Man turned around and confronted Devo, sort of a new wave weight lifter. The sign on his locker read, *"My name is Devo—Fuck you."*

"What're you lookin' at," said Devo.

"Somone's throwing candy at me—do you mind?" responded Tent Man.

"The only part I mind was when you picked it up and ate it!" growled Devo, and it looked for a moment that things might over-heat, but attentions finally turned back to the Olympics.

I suggested to Robbin that we not torment Tent Man anymore and he agreed. It must be torment enough for a man that size just getting out of bed. Artie found himself wondering how Tent Man goes to the toilet.

"Hush up, Art. Watch the wrestling."

"How would you like to wrestle, Tent Man?" asked Artie.

"Be quiet, Art. Gymnastics are coming up."

"Can you picture Tent Man doing a floor exercise or working out on the pommel horse?"

"C'mon, Artie. Give us a break."

"Wonder how he'd do in the pole vault ..."

"One more word, Artie, and we'll throw you at him."

"Okay. I'll be quiet ... think he could anchor the relay team?"

"Grrrrr ..."

On the way back to our room, we paused briefly in the hallway while Artie chatted with Palmquist, the on-duty hack. Palmquist couldn't take his eyes off the message on Robbin's T-shirt. It asked, *"What are YOU looking at, DICKNOSE?"* He lost track of the conversation with Artie and walked off to resume his duties, shaking his head. Twenty-five minutes before the 10:00 PM count, we opened a bear and had a nightcap before hitting our bunks for the night.

⤞⤝

ARTIE WAS GETTING READY TO go home, his time almost done. He was in the process of "cleaning up his act" in anticipation of being back on the street. Terms like "jeepers," "golly," and "gees" were replacing the four letter words in his usual vocabulary. "Bitch" and "Holmes" were tossed as well.

"That's a bad jacket to take to the street with you," said Artie. "Might as well wear a sign around your neck that says 'convict.'" Artie thought he could score more girls if his prison background was kept secret.

He'd also been on a rigid diet, along with lifting weights and sunbathing, getting his body ready for women and the beach. Bronzed, trim, and taut, he looked great. Artie would leave a void when he went, but that's prison for you. Robbin, especially, would miss him. A road dog of Artie's caliber was hard to replace. Initially, one wished his friends could stay, but you soon realized how flawed that thought was. We were all in there to get out, as soon as possible.

Artie and Bernie had been fasting for two days, drinking only water, herbal teas, and chicken broth. One of Bernie's connections brought him pure spring water, the only water he would drink there. Just before bed, they capped their fast with some of Bernie's colon cleanser. Bernie assured Artie that this was the way to ultimate health and a sparkling clean bowel. Several times during the night, Artie burst from beneath his covers and rushed to the bathroom.

"Is your colon keeping your up, Art?"

"'Fraid so, bud."

"It's turned renegade on you, huh?"

"Jeepers, I guess so."

"You weren't hiding another twenty-dollar bill up there, were you?"

"No, not this time." Artie once suffered the indignity and financial loss of forgetting about a twenty he had sequestered in that place of concealment popular in prisons, then emptied his bowel. Artie's twenty sleeps with the fishes.

>-<

"BLACK FRIDAY" FOR THE CATTLE crew unfolded at the end of a work week when it was decided that opportunity to party was upon them. The whole crew was toasted when they arrived back at the camp that day, the aftermath of a drunken bacchanalia out on the range. The cops were waiting for them.

The prison had just acquired some new cop equipment, state-of-the-art Breathalyzer devices. The equipment was so new they weren't yet certain how it worked. Always a focus of prison cop suspicions, the cattle crew would serve as their initial training session.

All of them were marched into cop headquarters, where they were searched and instructed to blow into a straw that inflated a small balloon. When prompted by the presence of alcohol, I think the balloon was supposed to change colors to indicate various levels of alcohol consumption. Just how they could fuck up so simple a test was unclear to most, but half the crew escaped unscathed, though the other half wasn't so lucky. Robbin's good fortune on this Black Friday was to pull a ham-handed hack to administer his sobriety test. I was on my bunk reading when he burst into the room:

"Holy Jesus, guys! We were ambushed! Here, hide these," and he tossed me two bears from his coat pocket. "The hacks were waiting for us when we came in and we were all shithouse drunk. I don't know if Boomer made it or not." Robbin was out of breath and running on adrenalin.

"Half of the cops didn't know how to work their new Breathalyzers ... I can't believe I got a pass! They pulled the bears out of my pocket, looked them over, then gave them back to me! Big Mike, Augie, and Milton all got busted."

The fear now was that the cops would discover some of the tests were bungled and might call some back to be retested, but it remained quiet. Pretty soon Boomer sauntered into the room and rolled his eyes at the ceiling, like Robbin, hardly able to believe his luck. Black Friday ended without further mishap, save a few hangovers.

➤◄

ROBBIN HAD A WEEKEND FURLOUGH coming up and we were getting the room ready for inspection. The unit manager, Harrison, would perform the inspection. He was a strange man and a stickler for cleanliness. Beds were made with tight hospital corners, sheets turned down, blankets stretched taut enough to bounce a coin on. Robbin was cleaning windows and Charlie mopped the floor while Boomer scoured the table and I dusted the lockers and wiped them down ... energy was flowing in room eight on the third floor of B-unit.

"Damn, Rob," I remarked, "those windows looked better before you started on them."

"Think you can do better? Have at them ..."

"Sure thing, bro..."

"See?" I said a little later. "All it takes is a little know-how."

"The know-how, chump, comes from knowing how to recruit a

new window-bitch," said Robbin, able to turn any circumstance to his advantage. "Window-bitch" would be my inspection day name and assignment until they sent me home.

"Heaven help us," says Boomer, "if our ol' ladies ever find out about our domestic skills."

The floor gets a coat of Bernie's custom floor wax. Clothes, towels, and blankets are folded and put away, lockers squared away, inside and out. A small bouquet of wild flowers is put on the table for effect. The furlough's a shoo-in.

→-←

PRISONS DON'T HAVE A LOT to accomplish other than security, so cleanliness becomes an item of supreme importance within the prison hierarchy. Each administrator knew he could expect a rash of shit from visiting superiors if their house wasn't shipshape. It worked that way from the top on down, ending up in the laps of the inmates, who had to perform the cleaning tasks and endure the fallout if it wasn't up to snuff. Charlie once opined that if you listened carefully, you could hear floor polishers starting up all over the western states the moment a BOP official from Washington crossed the Mississippi.

Harrison considered a floor polisher a thing of beauty, a treasure, like a vintage car. It took months for them to arrive, but the requisition order for two top-of-the-line maxi-torque, high rpm polishers finally came through, and Harrison was beside himself with pride. He gathered his orderlies around and handed out instructions for care and use, along with a stern warning of what awaited anyone who abused or mistreated the polishers. And all was well for a while.

Shining floors and a pristine environment seemed the single source of accomplishment available to Harrison's position. His was a world and mindset so far removed from those under his dominion that human interaction, other than purely superficial exchange, seldom took place. He was so transparent, inept, and bumbling that he often resembled a cartoon character. But he would hand out mean-spirited punishment with a certain relish for the most minor of infractions, and that made him a target for many. This was the man I worked for, and I was more or less exempt from his pettiness.

Heaping torment on Harrison was, for some, a sport, like getting one over on Cagney. Dangerous fun, as long as you didn't get caught or push too far. While he was with us, Lance excelled at pushing just the right buttons on Harrison's psyche, driving him right to the edge while he stayed just out of reach. Of particular anguish to Harrison was the "Phantom of the Turd," who smeared walls of the hallway near his office with human excrement. Others had gummed up the lock on his office door with superglue, but the Phantom packed the lock with shit to await the insertion of the key, which would then go into his pocket with its foul coating.

Then came a day when some tactless orderly started up one of the new floor polishers in a third-floor dormitory a little too early on a Saturday morning, when you were allowed to sleep in. A new arrival, a bad-ass with a lot of time under his belt from higher-level institutions, thought it a rude awakening. He climbed out of his bunk and followed the noise. Finding it, he jerked the polisher from the grasp of the unwitting orderly. Without a word, he walked to an open balcony at the end of the dormitory and flung the polisher into the parking lot, three stories below, where it shattered into pieces. Also shattered by the event was Harrison's state of well-being. No one would dare rat on the bad-ass.

꽃

TERMINAL ISLAND HAD BEEN LIKE living in the poorer, working-class neighborhoods of Fed City. Society there knew its place, most respectful of the other, and did their time quietly. Camp Fed was the high-rent, gated suburbs with an elite pecking order and a country club-like social hierarchy. Skid-row was represented by the county jails, while I thought of high-level penitentiaries as zoos and test laboratories where human beings were caged and subjected to conditions calculated to break the spirit, treated like dangerous animals from whom the guards needed to be kept safe.

In his fiercely funny film *Live On the Sunset Strip*, Richard Pryor tells of an interaction with a lifer convicted of multiple murders. "Why did you have to kill everyone in the house?" he asks. "Well," came the response, "they was all home." Pryor concluded that he was damn glad we have penitentiaries, I suppose his point well made.

4

HOW GRAND THY JURY

COURTROOMS AND JAILS TEND TO BE WINDOWLESS, DRAB, AND JOYLESS, not a hint of the natural world. They provide all the cheer of a bomb shelter. I had been at Camp Fed about two years when my routines and reasonably comfortable existence were suddenly jerked from under me and I was sent on a dark journey by subpoena from something called a grand jury.

❧❦

FOLLOWING MY INITIAL PAROLE HEARING, it was my aim to get my sentence modified to a level that at least approximated my comparative involvement, based on the role and sentences of the other participants. I started my quest for modification by writing to the judge, acknowledging my guilt and pleading my circumstance. I never perjured myself. I sat quietly and let the trial unfold as it would. I pointed to the now obvious disparities between my sentence and that of others whose involvement exceeded my own. It didn't hurt matters that the judge thought highly of my attorney, even hiring him for his own purposes. You'd think I was the beneficiary of a conflict of interest; I have no doubt that I was. Then we enlisted the support of Eric Swenson, the prosecutor, and I offered up a personal forfeiture of cash and tainted assets. All was moving in the right direction, when the FBI showed up at the camp to see me.

"We're concerned the 'Big Fish' got away," said the agent, well groomed and friendly. "We'd like to know if you can offer us any help."

"Who's the 'Big Fish'?" I asked.

"Brian Livingston. We understand that you were an acquaintance, maybe more than that."

BL. A Big Fish indeed. I knew him as an executive and nonviolent trafficker. His sense of fairness and refusal to accept any bullshit gave him a commanding presence. You simply knew that people didn't fuck with BL, not because he was scary, but because he was righteous. He was also a friend and a hell of a nice guy.

I pleaded my circumstance to the agent, "You know my history ... you can't possibly expect me to inform on someone."

"Worse things could happen to you," he said. "We are conducting an investigation. If you happen to be implicated in it, you could be facing new charges. Here's my card. I'll be back to see you in a week."

An anus-clenching encounter if ever there was. After my modification came through, as expected, I would have served more than half my time. I was headed downhill. The prospect of a new beef was particularly chilling. Then the US Attorney's office withdrew its support of my modification until such time as I could be cleared of the investigation.

When the agent returned, I told him I couldn't offer him any help. He seemed to expect this and remained friendly, shaking my hand and wishing me well. He also mentioned the possibility of a grand jury subpoena, the full meaning of which didn't sink in at the time. He had just been fishing. They had an ace up their sleeve.

The next couple of months were harrowing, but I somehow emerged from their investigation with a clean bill of health. The day before the hearing in front of Judge Schnacke, the US Attorney's office reinstated their support of my modification and my 15-year sentence was cut to six years and the $50,000 fine was reduced to $7,500. It was sweet relief, even though the actual time of incarceration was cut only by about a year. In addition to the fine, paid during my parole period with "clean" money, I returned a lot of "dirty" money to the government, part of the debt I owed them (I always loved that line in Merle Haggard's "Branded Man" where he moans, "I paid the debt I owed 'em," sounding like he was singing about the notorious gunslinger "Dead-eye Odom"). I felt good about it. Square with the feds, a fresh starting place on release. I was doubly relieved that I wouldn't be dragged into the mess that Brian was facing, though that particular relief was fleeting.

⇒-⇐

A GRAND JURY IS A secret proceeding where the grand jurors are led by their noses by prosecutors who outline a case and present evidence, including witnesses. Other than by the jurors themselves, there is no opportunity for cross-examination or calling evidence into question. The jurors are then asked to vote on whether or not an indictment should be issued. It is a given that grand juries are, for the most part, a rubber stamp for prosecutors. The grand jury also offers prosecutors a possible scapegoat should the result not turn out as planned. It is also used as an effective tool to make witnesses talk when they have no desire to do so. In many cases, including my own, immunity from prosecution is granted to uncooperative witnesses, effectively removing Fifth Amendment rights against self-incrimination and forcing testimony. Penalties for refusal to testify, as well as for false testimony, are in place for anyone not cooperating with the grand jury. In this manner, prosecutors use the grand jury to go "fishing" for evidence: "Let's put this guy on the stand and see what we can squeeze out of him." Faced with the prospect of unknown periods of incarceration in a jail cell, "dead time" during which the sentence you are already serving is suspended and gets no credit, many would give up their own grandmothers. I think I'd rather be waterboarded.

I had gone to the camp records office to see if official notice of my sentence modification had arrived. The records officer pulled my file and took a look.

"I don't see nothin' here for you, sonny, 'ceptin' this here federal writ."

"This here what?"

"Writ. I said writ. Someone wants you up in front of a grand jury."

He let me read it. A grand jury subpoena for a hearing into the activities of BL, to be held in the city of Eureka in Northern California. I guess it was my good fortune to at least know it was coming. They usually don't tell you what's going on; they just roll you up and head you out.

❖

TWO WEEKS LATER, I WAS deposited at the penitentiary next to the camp. They stripped me naked and put me through all of the indignities of a strip search. Then they dressed me in prison-issue khakis, shackled my hands at my waist, and put on leg irons.

"You can't take anything with you; cigarettes aren't allowed," said the prison cop. He told me I'd get a toothbrush where I was going. The whole vibe of the penitentiary was near-palpable, as though I was being squeezed by the air around me, every sensory activity on alert. It even smelled dangerous. By comparison, the camp was a springtime walk in the park, birdsong among the trees.

Taking baby steps in leg irons, I was marched to the bus with a dozen or so hard-ass looking cons from the penitentiary. When we reached the bus, they took the leg irons off. I was the only "camper" in the group, aware that I was in their eyes a pussy, probably a rat, too. We headed out to Vandenberg AFB to meet the federal Marshals' weekly airlift they used to move prisoners around the country. We were accompanied by four guards in bullet-proof vests, armed with shotguns, automatic rifles, and heavy-duty handguns. They took up positions around the bus before we were loaded and when we arrived at Vandenberg, I suppose so they could be ready for any Dillinger-like rescue attempts. I watched a couple of them swing out the cylinders of their handguns and give them a gunfighter spin. I felt like Dorothy, no longer in Kansas.

Delighting the hard cons, there were about a dozen females on the plane, all headed for FCI Pleasanton. Some of these guys hadn't been in female company for a lot of years and damn near came unglued at the sight of these young ladies as they sashayed their cute little butts up and down the aisle, talking among themselves like sorority girls, each aware of her allure.

The plane stopped in Sacramento, where I was handed over to two US Marshals in a souped-up Pontiac Firebird with out-of-state plates, booty, I supposed, from some drug bust. One of the Marshals, enthusiastic and friendly, remembered me from the trial. He had been Stephen Green's escort during the proceedings. He told me how well I looked and said some condescending stuff about Green and then wanted to know a bunch of stuff about Creedence (which he also remembered about me). I was seated in the back, handcuffed, with a tough-looking black convict named Tooley, "S'up, man?" We were on our way to the San Francisco County jail. The Marshals stopped and bought us burgers and a pack of cigarettes. Tooley and I split the pack of cigarettes and traded jokes. We knew that we shared a common circumstance, skin color unimportant.

San Francisco's county jail reminded me of an industrial boiler room with cages, a constant din of voices, shouts, and clanking cell doors. In my particular cage, there were 14 of us in a cell with 12 beds. Two had to sleep on a long, steel table in the "day" side of the cell. A shirtless, muscular black man named Jah-Jah gave me his bed, saying he was, "Tar'd a alla niggahs on dis side." His torso was tattooed with scars from stabbings. After the evening meal, an assemblage of black inmates would sometimes line up at the front of the cells, their arms through the bars, chanting and clapping, "Da freaks come out at night!"—clap, one-two!—"Da freaks come out at night!" It could go on for hours.

I sat in that cell for several days doing nothing, nine black men, two Mexicans, an oriental, a Pakistani with long, grotesque toenails, and me. I recognized one of the black men as a regular from Berkeley's Telegraph Avenue street vermin, one-eyed, unwashed, and Rasta dreadlocks. He spent his days crouched in a corner grabbing at imaginary flying things. The other black inmates refused to acknowledge his presence. One day Jah-Jah snatched one of the residents by his collar, jerking him to his feet, Jah-Jah cocking his fist, "Ah'm as serious as a heart attack, muthafucka! Now make yo' move!" This dispute was over ownership of an empty milk carton used by jail residents to insulate the coffee mugs they made from empty orange juice containers. I imagine men have been killed over less. Jailhouse manners and etiquette amounted to the courtesy of timing the flush of the open-air commode with the drop of your turd, the flushing action of the commode swallowing up the smell along with the turd.

A brief respite was provided by my pal Harry Jackson, a lawyer and member of the California Bar Association, whose credentials would allow him to visit. The jail provided us the privacy of a conference room. Good ol' Harry. He smuggled a cheeseburger in for me. I had lost enough weight for Harry to observe, "You look like a refugee from Dachau!"

Doron Weinberg, who I initially retained as a result of Harry's urging, finally showed up and filled me in on what he had discovered. The feds were after BL and thought him a major bad guy. The rat in this instance was "Cricket," a guy who'd worked for BL doing menial tasks and who I had met once. Cricket had been "reborn" and was now doing the Lord's work, informing on BL and throwing my name into the hopper as well. In many ways, I found that a relief. Cricket didn't know me at all. I'd never had any dealings with him. Anything he had to say about me was purely his own conjecture. Nonetheless, if I didn't reasonably answer questions from the grand jury, I could be facing a lot of "dead time," languishing in a county jail.

Stephen Green, too, was helping the feds in their effort to nail BL. He knew about BL, and he knew I had a relationship with him, but Green himself had had no direct dealings with BL. But he was apparently enthusiastic about his role as informant and told them all that he knew, and that was bothersome to me.

BL's attorneys had told Doron that BL had already been "buried" by prior witnesses. Doron, along with Tony Serra, belonged to a principled group of attorneys who would not represent informants, those who were shedding their own culpability by informing on others. Doron convinced me it wasn't my honor that was at stake here. I could likely offer testimony without consequence to me or BL. We went over some potential areas of testimony that I felt wouldn't do any more harm than had already been done. I hadn't had any dealings with BL for years. All I had to do was make sure whatever I said was credible. I was uneasy about saying anything at all, but came to terms with it, feeling only slightly cheesy.

❧❦

Now I would be escorted to the Humboldt County jail in Eureka to await my appearance on the grand jury docket. I was rousted from the cell at 4:30 AM and put in a holding cell to await my escort. There was another person already there, reclined on the cement bench with his feet up resting against the cell bars, a roll of toilet paper for a pillow. Probably a drunk I thought. Pretty soon one eye popped open and we looked at each other warily.

"Hi, bud ... what're you doin' here?" I asked. He was a nice-looking fellow, young and bearded, with a confident sparkle about him. Not a drunk.

"They brought me up from CMC (California Men's Colony, a

state prison near San Luis Obispo) last night. Got a court hearing in Oakland."

I noticed he had an orange band on his wrist, as did I, indicating he was a federal prisoner.

"There's no federal court in Oakland," I said (the federal court in Oakland was established some years later). "Who brought you up here?"

"Federal Marshals. I guess they were coming this way and picked me up as a favor."

"In a pig's eye, they did. What makes you think you're going to Oakland?"

"It can't be anything else. I just filed for this hearing three weeks ago."

"I never heard of a court system that responds that fast to a prisoner's request ... where are you from, anyway?"

"Santa Barbara ... Maui." He said "Maui" like an afterthought. This was going to get interesting. I asked if he knew my brother Robbin.

"Yeah, I've met him."

I asked if he knew BL and his expression changed, "Yeah, yeah, I know him real well."

"Do you have any idea of what's going on with him?"

"No, I haven't seen him in a couple of years."

"Guess what, my friend ... you're not going to any court hearing in Oakland. Your ass is coming with me to be dragged up in front of a federal grand jury that's after BL up in Eureka."

He sat up and looked dumbstruck, eyes wide in disbelief. "That can't be true. No one's said anything to me about a grand jury."

"Can't be, but it is. You've never had any experience with the feds, have you? These people don't tell you shit; they do as they please. I know what's going on because the records office at Lompoc let me read the writ. They probably weren't supposed to. Grand juries operate in secret, you know?"

His sparkle dimmed as he pondered what I had told him, not wanting to believe a word of it. "Are you sure?" he managed.

"Almost as sure as I am that the sun's going to come up in another hour or so."

I watched as all of this finally hit home for him, stimulating his bowel. He picked up his pillow and went to the grimy, seat-less commode that hung on a far wall of the holding cell and moved his bowels, timing the flush like a seasoned veteran. "S'cuse me," he said.

And so it was that I met Bob Goneau, a genuinely good bad guy and ne're-do-well outlaw with whom I would spend the following week in close quarters. He was serving a four-year sentence for growing marijuana and had so far served nine months. He had a bright mind and a striking sense of humor, and we made the best of it together, laughter the only refuge from our circumstance. We got our hands on some Louis L'Amour cowboy novels, and reading them, we each took on an Old West persona, acting out our daily activities as though we were Sacketts.

Three well-dressed FBI agents, each packing a big iron, escorted us through SFO to United's daily flight to Eureka. They took off all of our chains, surrounded us in step, and told us to just act natural, me in my scruffy federal khakis and Bob in his unkempt state blues. We made a strange-looking bunch.

At Eureka we were handed over to a lone female deputy sheriff with a big magnum holstered on her ham-like hip. She was a large, uncomely woman, built like a Buick. If that wasn't enough, she had a shrill, ear-shattering voice guaranteed to shrivel any would-be suitor into flaccid ineffectiveness. "Don't you give this woman no shit," I advised Bob. "She'd shoot the likes of us at the drop of a hat."

Taking over custody from the FBI, she put us in handcuffs chained at our waists and a single pair of leg irons, my right ankle chained to Bob's left. Beyond her initial barking of a few commands, she said little else. It was hell trying to nonchalantly walk through the Eureka airport to get to her cruiser. The airport lobby came to a standstill as people gawked at us desperadoes, hand-cuffed and stumbling along in our leg irons. We had the fluid movements of aging priests on a disco floor. I stopped in the middle of the lobby and told Bob, "Let's get it together, cowboy ... right, left, right, left ... when I say go, okay?" I forgot that my right leg was chained to his left, and when we took off, we damn near fell into a sprawling heap on the lobby floor, saved only by quick reflex. All we could do was laugh at ourselves, Bob wondering if I was an Arthur Murray graduate. We laughed hard enough to make all of the gawkers take a step back. ("Mommy, are those men on drugs?")

➤◄

I prefer rogues to imbeciles because sometimes rogues take a rest.

–Alexander Dumas

I WAS COMPLETELY UNPREPARED FOR the Humboldt County jail. It would make San Francisco's county jail seem an oasis of refined civilization. Bob and I shared a dark and dirty cell in a narrow corridor, packed with the dumbest, loudest, filthiest, most obnoxious redneck punks on the planet. It was as though anyone over 22 or with an IQ exceeding 2 digits was kept elsewhere. They spat through the bars, threw food all over the floors and walls, hurled their trays and utensils up and down the corridor after every meal, screamed, cursed, yelled, and rattled the cell doors, generally behaving like a tribe of rabid banshees. These punks would last about two seconds with the feds. Bob and I settled in for some hard hours while we pondered our moves with the grand jury and watched the cockroaches scurry over the walls and ceiling, ignoring gravity.

The first night was bad enough, the bellowing din going on past midnight. I had to calm Bob on a couple of occasions. The following night, with things still out of control at 2:00 AM, I lost my cool and committed a jailhouse no-no by requesting that our neighbors "shut the fuck up." Silence. Then came a snotty voice:

"Maybe you should have stayed home, huh?" And the chorus began to build.

"Hey, Augie ... these assholes in number six want us to be quiet ... whaddaya think, man?"

"Fuck 'em in their nigger-lovin' assholes. Anyone got a knife?"

"You mean them grand jury guys? They ain't nothin' but fuckin' rats anyway."

"Sorry, Bob," I whispered. "I forgot my own best advice."

We didn't say another word and let this sorry pack of unfortunates burn themselves out. Then, probably angered at not drawing us in further, they decided to burn us out. They crumpled newspaper and tossed it in front of our cell, then set it on fire. When I looked, there was a pretty good blaze going in the corridor and I wondered where the hell the cops were, but by now, it was obvious that the county jail cops didn't give a shit about anything that happened here. Bob and I exchanged glances of disbelief as if to say, relax, the worst is yet to come.

Twice weekly it was the practice of the jail to let all of the animals out of their cages for a couple of hours in the recreation room. You could play pool, watch TV, lift weights, or just walk around. We wondered if we were in for a hard time. Rather than worry about it, we decided to go on the offensive. We'd strut and flaunt our status as federal prisoners, "We're feds, man—we're bad!" All of those tough voices that came out of the dark were reduced to daylight reality, that of whiny, witless losers, stunted punks who hadn't the sense to pour piss out of a boot. They looked at us with cautious glances and gave us a wide berth. Not a soul said a word to us.

"Yeah, man. We're bad. We're feds. Don't fuck with the feds."

→-←

I WAS ESCORTED TO THE grand jury by a young FBI agent who packed a long-barreled .44 magnum, a strange piece to hide beneath a three-piece suit. He fit the profile of the other agents I'd met, clean-cut, ivy-league, calm, and pleasant. He was apologetic about the hassle and accommodations. We walked the block or two to the courthouse, side by side, no handcuffs required. I was deposited just outside the grand jury room.

The Assistant US Attorney running the grand jury was Peter Robinson (who later switched sides, becoming a criminal defense attorney). He seemed a little nervous and stumbled over his introductions. He was a short man who looked at me through coke-bottle glasses resting on a pudgy face crowned with a shock of wooly hair. He had an animated look about him and approached me like a submissive cur, wondering if I would accept his overture or bite his head off. He was probably feeling some remorse for having hauled me out of my comfy camp to this shithole of a county jail on a fishing expedition.

The first thing he wanted to establish was my background as a drug dealer, which I testified to openly. Some of the grand jurors, each a hardworking, God-fearing, flag-waving taxpayer, looked at me like I was the lowest form of earthly life.

My plan was to not add to the damage BL had already incurred and to not implicate anyone else. I had given matters a lot of thought and studied hard. I was prepared to handle a lot of tricky questions with evasive logic, memory loss, or if necessary, feigned lack of knowledge. If needed, I even had a dead person (R.I.P. Tonto) in mind I could point to. Everything they wanted to know was covered in less than 15 minutes. Most of the questions were answered with a simple "no" as I hadn't seen BL in several years and I knew none of the other players. I alluded to some nonspecific transactions in the distant past and was then amazed I was never questioned on dates, weights, others involved, or any other details. These were the sort of particulars Stephen Green testified to at my trial and I had expected this line of questioning here.

The grand jurors listened with passive interest but became more attentive when Robinson asked me about my relationship with Creedence, a fact that came out when he wanted to know if I had any knowledge about a money laundering scheme BL apparently had going with some recording studio. I fucked up once, mentioning some exotic car BL had when I hadn't been asked about it. Robinson jumped right on it, but I didn't let the subject get any further. I was never asked about the things I feared most. It seemed solely a "fishing" expedition to see what might come out of me.

It was all over and I wondered at all the needless stress and worry I'd expended over nothing. It felt a little cheesy to me, having to say anything at all, but I knew my admissions about BL were nothing that amounted to hard evidence. I was perplexed that Robinson seemed pleased with my testimony, and I later figured that it was just my friendly manner and feigned cooperation that made him think I would be a willing witness for him at BL's trial. On that point, he missed my intentions by a mile.

Anyone who knew BL liked him, save perhaps a jilted lover or the newly reborn. He had a lot of personal mana, a strong character, and sense of fair play. On Maui he had been a highly regarded surfer. When his trial date came around, it became clear to Peter Robinson that he had no knowledgeable cooperative witnesses against BL, not me or Robbin (who probably escaped the grand jury call because he had already been released), no intimate snitch on the inside who would paint a clear picture for a jury. The whole thing was settled in a plea bargain that included very little time for BL. The witnesses who had previously "buried" him, including Cricket, turned out to have very little credibility or knowledge. BL's life ended before I had opportunity to see him again, a victim of pancreatic cancer.

Happiness for Bob and me that day was the Humboldt County jail in the rearview mirror. We parted company back at the San Francisco County jail, where they lodged me for one more night on my way back to Lompoc. My room back at the camp felt like a Plaza suite.

MEANWHILE, FOLLOWING MY LEAD, MY codefendant at trial, Bump, ponied up less than half of what I did and got his 12-year sentence reduced to three and a half years, the disparity in our sentences based solely on what Stephen Green had to say about us. The word of Green served as gospel for the feds. I guess if they actually knew the half of it, Robbin and I would have been sentenced to twice what we were.

Bump served his time but failed to heed the all-important doctrine he should have become familiar with during his stay. Only months following his release, he was caught up in a new conspiracy involving a large quantity of cocaine and, this time, an undercover fed. He quickly pleaded to 20 years under new guidelines.

Robbin and I had long since had our fill of the dope trade and the feds. Instead of bad guys, we would become valued taxpayers, a status achieved thanks to a work ethic learned from our parents and the counsel of our friend and benefactor Ed Olson, who taught us that clean money is the only kind worth having. We would also abide by that simple doctrine that lets life roll easy in America: "Don't fuck with the feds."

THE LAST FURLOUGH (COMING HOME)

As I NEAR THE END OF THIS STORY, I FIND MYSELF WONDERING IF SOME of my friends and conspirators (if you've read this far, you're one of them) might now look at prison as an entertaining experience. If I have presented it in that light, at least in part, it's been largely to balance the negative. The truth is our penal systems mirror the political climates that spawn them. Loathsome blow-hards and obscene and nauseous party-line politics do their part to shape the microcosm of prisons, insuring that penal institutions retain a mean-spirited edge, the decent individuals incarcerated or employed therein notwithstanding. Thirty years ago I was aware of a subtle and ongoing tightening of the noose, and I don't think any slack's since been cut. Stray dogs have a better chance of encountering kindness than most in our prisons and jails.

> **If you know where home is, you know everything.**
>
> **–Billy, Navaho Shaman**

It was bright and balmy, a diamond of a day somewhere in the mid-seventies, not a cloud in the sky. The ball field was covered with a soft green carpet of new grass and all the trees seemed full and about to bud. Out on the soccer field, a crew of inmates made ready to drag industrial-grade mowers behind an antique-looking tractor, the old equipment shined up and working well. Looking beyond a line of trees to the south, mountain peaks cut the horizon like a big-city skyline, doing their part to form the bowl that is the Santa Ynez Valley, in which sits Lompoc, the flower seed capital of the world. Acre upon acre of blooming flowers cover the valley floor in an astonishing patchwork quilt of brilliant color, nature's finest. We only get to see it when we come and go, but the mind's eye can see it daily. Even the vultures that live in the trees around the prison slaughterhouse seem in place, gliding overhead, feathered fingers at wingtips making delicate adjustments as they soar and wheel above farm and field where plow and disc have recently turned the rich, dark soil. Sweeter air and brighter surroundings are remembered only on Maui. The scent of springtimes recalled from childhood was in the air. No way this could be January 17th.

But it was, and my last year of incarceration was just getting underway.

Robbin was already well on his way to starting life over again. Anyone betting against his ability to thrive and make his fortune in the legal business world would prove a huge loser. All of the unknowns about my final resolution with the feds were now known. All of the hard stuff—parole hearings, sentence modification, fines, investigations, grand juries, possible new charges—was behind me. I could begin to look to the future and a new go at living a productive life. Somewhere up ahead, just over distant mountains, lay crystal pools of promise and a future without any feds in my face. I could feel the excitement building almost daily. Now, within a year of transfer to a halfway house, I was also eligible to participate in the prison furlough program.

A prison furlough is technically an "unsupervised release" of a prisoner for a specific period of time. My first furlough was a period of 10 hours to allow me to travel from Terminal Island to the Lompoc camp. They reasoned that I had turned myself in and followed the rules, and I wouldn't now turn fugitive. Once your release date and prison record qualified you, furloughs would become available every three months, starting with just a day, expanding to an overnight, then up to nearly a week as you approached release. They represented a brass ring held out by prison authorities, a reward for toeing the line.

The withholding of a furlough could also be used as an effective threat by unit managers, whose approval was mandatory. My brother and I badly wanted those excursions into the outer world, and we kept our quarters sparkling clean and maintained the good graces of our unit manager. We were very careful, and no doubt very lucky, when it came to all the harmless-but-unthinkable bad shit we would pull off over the years. Just prior to my release, an episode involving a prisoner furloughed to travel to the Lompoc camp resulted in headlines that caught my interest.

FCI PLEASANTON, ABOUT 40 MILES east of San Francisco, was a medium security federal prison that was also coed. I always wondered how that could work. Though living quarters were of course separate, common areas were not. How do you lock up males and females together for years at a time and expect them to behave in a saintly manner? It seemed to me almost cruel. I'd heard rumor of rampant disciplinary transfers from Pleasanton for "inappropriate contact" with a member of the opposite sex. When I thought about it, I was thankful I didn't have to deal with that particular temptation. I thought about this, too: I never heard of a disciplinary action for inappropriate contact with a member of the same sex.

At Pleasanton a prison drama and love story worthy of Shakespeare played itself out in the headlines during the final month or so before my release. Samantha Lopez was serving a 50-year sentence for her role in a string of bank robberies, and Ronald McIntosh was a journeyman con artist who was getting "short," near release. While incarcerated at Pleasanton, they fell in love and forged a powerful bond, then planned a daring escape, which they viewed instead as a "rescue" for Ms. Lopez.

McIntosh had a spotless record and had served enough time to be rewarded with a furlough transfer to the camp at Lompoc. He never arrived at his appointed destination. A former helicopter pilot in Vietnam, he spent his first day or two on the lam honing his helicopter chops. Then, posing as a real estate executive, he commandeered a helicopter at gunpoint and set it down at a prearranged time and place at the Pleasanton prison. Ms. Lopez climbed aboard and off they went, the first stage of her rescue a complete success.

Federal authorities, of course, viewed events as anything but a rescue. Realization that it was McIntosh who had engineered the removal of Ms. Lopez, using his furlough as opportunity to execute the plan, no doubt resulted in soiled federal britches around Pleasanton and at western BOP headquarters in nearby Burlingame. Similar to air travel following 9/11, the entire furlough program came to a crashing halt. Response to fuck-ups by the feds seem to share a common thread.

Reading about these events, caught up in the romance and daring, I was pulling for the fugitives. I hoped they wouldn't be caught. I also knew that if they were, they would literally be crushed by the enormous weight of the vengeful machinery wielded by our federal government. Unfortunately for them, 10 days of blissful freedom would have to last a lifetime. They were caught near Sacramento, the feds tipped off by a jeweler from whom they had purchased wedding rings.

Their defense at trial centered on the "rescue" aspect of Ms. Lopez's removal from her captors, claiming she had suffered sexual abuse, assault, extortion, and torment at the hands of prison guards. Separating fact from fantasy in claims by prisoners is never an easy matter, nor is it a particularly level playing field. Getting information out of the BOP is a hard go, no matter who's asking.

"Institutional security" is the blanket excuse used to deny requests and withhold information. Just how far a subpoena penetrates that blanket is a tricky business in itself. "No one can out-lie a cop on the stand" also holds true for prison guards, especially if they are engaged in denying their own culpability. And through it all, the federal bureaucracies can drive you to the brink of madness with special rules and one-way streets, all the while drowning you in a sea of paper. This, of course, is not to say that all claims by prisoners are gospel.

Whatever the truths may have been, the result was an additional 25-year term for each of them. Even if all of Ms. Lopez's allegations were proven, there was little chance it would have prevailed as a valid defense for escape, let alone the armed theft of a helicopter. That they would be returned to Pleasanton together was as likely as postponing tomorrow's sunrise.

Sometime following this conviction, McIntosh was further convicted as complicit in a murder conspiracy occurring years earlier and was sentenced to Leavenworth for the rest of his life without the possibility of parole, voiding all his other sentences.

Reminder: Don't fuck with the feds—don't piss these people off. They can hurt you.

⋙⋘

LIFE AND DUTIES AT THE camp had long since settled into routine. Roommates and others who had become close friends were released and replaced by new recruits, the revolving prison doors in constant motion. Lance, then Artie and Bernie, and more than a year before my own release, Robbin, were replaced by Boomer, Charlie, Booger, Pat, and Bruce. All were drug merchants in one form or another, and each became a close and trusted friend.

Bruce was a smiling and joyous Japanese fellow christened the "Harbor Bomber" by taunting friends who wouldn't let events of

1941 die a quiet death. His marijuana imports were measured in tonnage. Boomer was an Air Force officer, an academy graduate, who piloted C-5 cargo jets and later turned his flying skills to loads of contraband. He was a member of the cattle crew, unpretentious, very bright, and a tremendous athlete. Boomer and I played a lot of basketball together, read a lot of the same books, and generally enjoyed each other's company. Booger, so named by a colorful local character known as "Tommy the Hoob," moved in when Robbin went home. His given name was Brock and he thoroughly hated his nickname, but just couldn't shake it. He was a warm and bright individual and had owned a laboratory that manufactured various pharmaceutical products. He had been sweet-talked into manufacturing a batch of amphetamine by a "friend" who then set him up for the feds. I first met Charlie at Terminal Island. He once imported heroin from Thailand into Hawaii. Charlie today lives in Thailand, clean and sober, with his Thai wife and two lovely daughters. Charlie preached the gospel of the "bag": When your days are few and pain is your daily reality, "get in the bag" and ease your way out. Pat lifted weights and was tougher than bent nails in hard oak. About his bulging biceps, Pat said, "It's not for the women ... when I get some motherfucker in a headlock, I want him to understand he's in serious trouble."

➤-◄

IT WAS DURING THIS FINAL year when, out of the blue, I got a letter from a woman who I had known only fleetingly on the outside. We began to correspond, trading thoughts and laughs, eventually reaching out to one another. She made for happier, more interesting furloughs, and provided me with further reason to once again and forever give up smoking, a habit she abhorred. When she would visit, two or three times monthly, we would engage in another sport that provided intimate and dangerous fun, inappropriate, but thrilling. We became expert in having it our way, unobserved, even under the watchful eye of Cagney. A lot of the guys would dress "commando" (no undies) when loved ones would visit, making some things easier to get at.

The camp visiting area was generous in its layout, with trees and picnic tables. It was within the rules for your visitor to bring a meal in a picnic basket and a table cloth, items that could be arranged on the table to provide a small framework of privacy while seated. If you were to engage in "inappropriate contact," no matter how brief, care, caution, and an eagle eye were always a necessary part of it. One memorable summer day, on an especially difficult afternoon to find opportunity, we had all but given up on any thought of intimacy when there came a terrific crash from colliding vehicles on the highway just outside the visiting area. Cops and visitors alike all ran to the scene, attentions directed to the calamity in which some were seriously injured. We just looked at one another, words unnecessary, and headed off in the opposite direction. Even in prison, good fortune would hunt me down and force its will on me.

❧◆❧

AN ATLAS G ROCKET SHATTERED the sky at Vandenberg, an occasional local spectacle provided by our military. Its mighty engines shook the ground and rattled our windows there at the camp. The roar was deafening, ending in a primal shriek as it tore the wind and ripped holes in the heavens, freeing itself from Earth's gravity. It was too much for me, this adult version of fireworks. Is this what comes of our boyhood bottle-rockets?

❧◆❧

The day dawned cold and gray. Low clouds and a heavy fog covered the landscape, obscuring treetops and hillsides with a soggy drizzle … another slice of January in Lompoc. The night before the boys all gathered in Room 8 on the third floor of B-unit to say goodbye and wish me well, my turn to exit through the revolving prison doors. The next morning Big Bill drove me to the bus shelter on the highway, shook my hand warmly, and smiled his farewell, "Don't suppose I'll be seeing you here again," he said.

No, Bill, you won't. Not a chance. A 1987 report on recidivism—prisoners who were rearrested or whose parole was later revoked—found 41% returned to prison. Some categories reached 70% (those dependent on heroin), while poor, urban people of color made up higher percentages as a group. Older people living with a spouse returned the least, apparently finding a wife preferable to prison. The possibility of coming back for more, ever, existed nowhere in my mind.

I sat in the bus shelter alone with my thoughts, bittersweet, the pit-pat of falling raindrops a hypnotic backdrop as memories of my time with the feds rolled through my mind. I wondered, were the years well-spent? Then answered myself: absolutely they were. I had no doubts I was a wiser, healthier, and happier man than had started out all those years ago. If I owe thanks to anyone for my personal salvation, then I'll choose the informant, Stephen Green, a thought repugnant to many of my fellow prisoners: *"All hail the cheese-eater for forcing the issue!"* I shudder to think of how my life may have otherwise turned out had I not been forced to deal with my reality.

We never know what might be waiting for us, but of this much I am certain: responsibility for the choices I have made lies at my doorstep. I set the table for this particular banquet, just now coming to its end. I didn't know what might lie ahead, but I couldn't wait to find out.

Before long, there was the white Honda, Laurie at the wheel. We were about to seat ourselves at a brand new banquet, a banquet of life. A kiss and a smile. Outta here.

AFTERWORD

FOLLOWING RELEASE, I SPENT SEVERAL MONTHS AT AN OAKLAND halfway house, a god-awful, boring place where you were half-incarcerated. I had a bed there and little else. A friend who is an attorney with his own office employed me right away, making the actual time I spent at the halfway house as minimal as it gets. Amazingly, I stayed working at his Oakland law office for a decade, until the call of Maui and my wife's insistence that we move on could no longer be ignored.

After graduation from the halfway house, I had opportunity to show the feds how unnecessary five years of parole would be. True to their nature, they made me serve every day of it. But I didn't really care. Parole is easy when you don't have anything to hide, unless maybe you have a "Make My Day" for a parole officer. After three years of astutely toeing their line, I offered to pay my fine in full if they'd cut me loose, just so I could travel without first getting permission. But there was no interest on their part. So I continued with my toes on the line, filed my monthly reports with my fine payment, and continued to request permission to travel, which was never denied.

Laurie and I spent the last furlough, five days, on Maui. We were married about a year later, a festive celebration in Mom's backyard with Hawaiian music and hula. A wedding cruise aboard *White Bird* followed our honeymoon night at the Pioneer Inn in Lahaina. Max, of course, was at the helm, recently returned from the voyage that took him around the world. Many friends and conspirators were on deck.

THANKS AND ACKNOWLEDGMENTS

L OVING ACKNOWLEDGMENT TO MY SON, DAN, AND DAUGHTER, TRACY, for their unwavering love and standing by their dad through all of it, and to their mother, Jeanne, for her considerable part in raising such fine, caring human beings; and to my wife, Laurie, for invaluable editorial assistance and helping me to bring it all back home. Thanks to Bruce Anderson for his encouragement and support, and to Alexander Cockburn and literary coach Jasmyne Boswell, and to Holly Tri, editor, and Masha Shubin, designer, whose combined skills have made these pages far more readable and presentable than they might have been. Love and appreciation to my sister, Mary Goodrich, who's always been there for me with and without her cameras; to my brother Peter; my old pal Sheldon "Balls" Bialkin; to Evelyn Billington and to Ed Olson; to all the boys, from El Cerrito and elsewhere; and of course to Robbin, for the good times, for the hard times, for the love of a brother. A salute to the memory of Dannie "Red Hog" Martin (1939–2013), a reliable friend and a courageous writer. A final salute to the loving memories of Howard and Louise Rohrer and our brother in arms, Max Halsey.

EDITORIAL

Don't forget: drug policy in the U.S. is about social control. That's the name of the game.

−Alexander Cockburn

I F YOU WANT TO BE WELL CONNECTED IN THE WORLD OF ILLEGAL DRUGS, Camp Fed is the place to be. Here reside experienced specialists in every facet of the field. Current trends and market reports are often a topic of conversation. Expert smugglers discuss scams and methodology, old and new, while growers trade agricultural techniques and executive merchants carefully share ideas, sources and outlets. I thought it a curious way to fight the drug war. What would happen if you locked up all the Wall Street criminals together to form personal bonds and trade ideas on how to further fill their pockets at public expense? No wonder they don't arrest these guys. There is no war on Wall Street.

The drug war enriches an industry built on legislated crime and punishment. It has otherwise succeeded only in jailing millions of Americans, our shameful incarceration rates by far leading the developed countries of the world, while supply and consumption remain largely unaffected. Some states spend more on prisons than on education. Powerful lobbies represent corporate owned prisons and prison guard unions, opposing change and pushing for stricter drug laws with longer terms of imprisonment. Appointed task forces and various commissions, staffed with wise and intelligent

297

individuals, have done detailed studies and extensive examinations of our war on drugs. Conclusions all seem to agree that it does more harm than good, wastes incredible amounts of money, and in the end, cannot be won. Archaic marijuana laws appear responsible for a great deal of this waste and present the obvious starting place for reform. Response from Drug Czars, politicians, prisoncrats, cops, prison guard unions and others hasn't varied and remains cloaked in a monied self-interest: "... These findings are unfounded."

The opening volleys were fired by Richard Nixon and the war on drugs has grown ever since. Viewed in the larger picture, what other groups might also be included as criminal? How thin is the line between the drug merchants and the so-called "legitimate" element who profit from it? Which is the bigger thief of one's humanity, drugs or a lengthy, mind-breaking term of imprisonment? Where is the honor in a for-profit prison industry that lobbies out of self-interest, their currency counted in human souls? What would be the result if we instead spent our [drug] war chest on education and rehabilitation?

Apologies for my participation in the drug trade are heartfelt, but extend only to here.

CPSIA information can be obtained
at www.ICGtesting.com
Printed in the USA
FSOW01n0806081014
3208FS

9 781629 011387